IMAGES
of America

DANVERS
FROM 1850 TO 1899

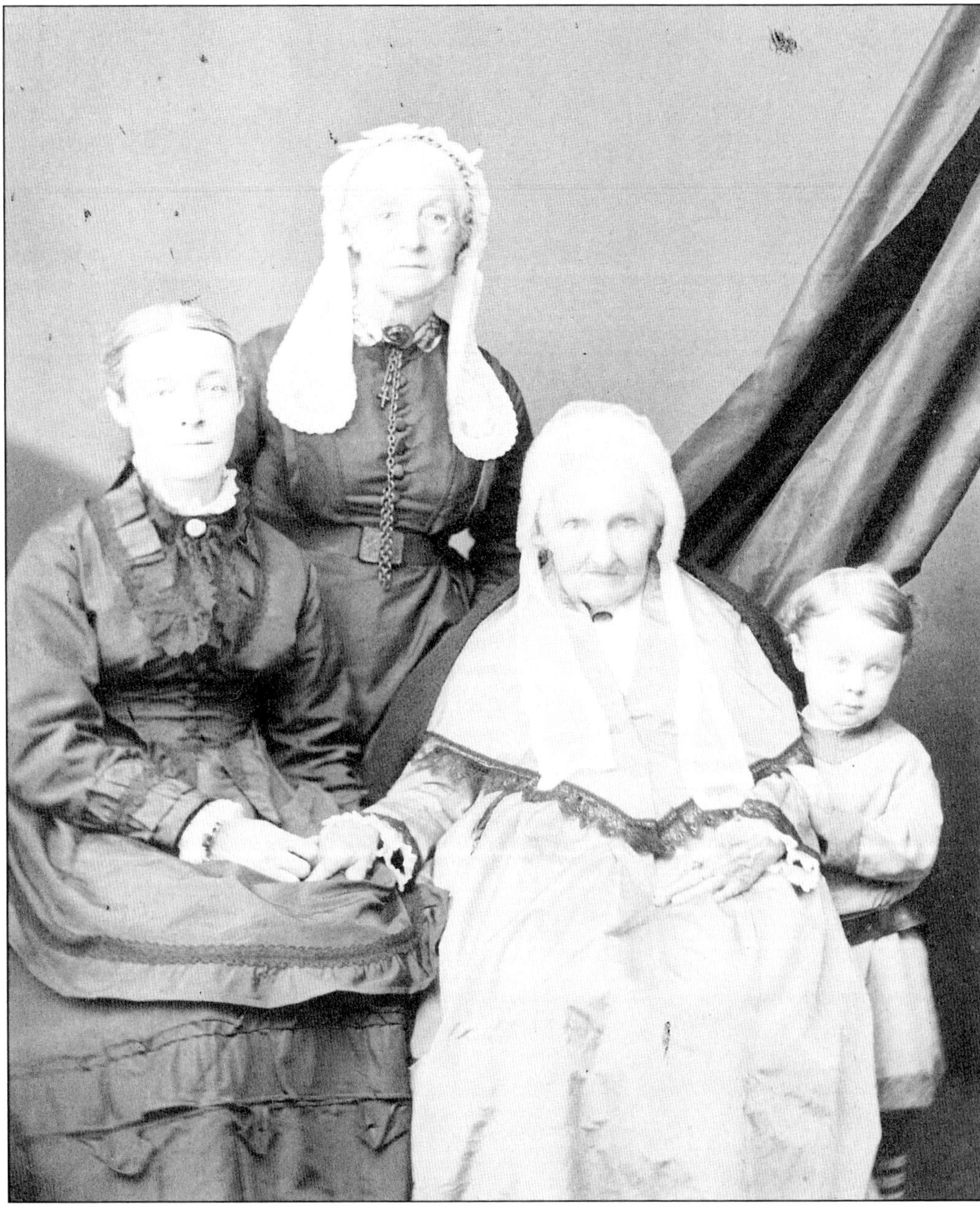

This special portrait was taken in 1874 of four generations. Mary Fowler Page (1787–1876) was the wife of Danvers brickmaker John Page. She sits next to her four-year-old great-grandson, George H. Goodell. Standing at the rear is Mary Page Hunt (b. 1806), daughter of Mary Page; while Martha Page Putnam Goodell (b. 1834), holds hands with her grandmother Page. Portraits like this were an important visual keepsake remembrance of earlier generations and family ties.

Cover photograph: Famed poet John Greenleaf Whittier, the Johnson sisters (his cousins), and little Phoebe Woodman relax on the east veranda of Oak Knoll on Summer Street in the 1880s.

IMAGES
of America

DANVERS
FROM 1850 TO 1899

Richard B. Trask

ARCADIA
PUBLISHING

ISBN 978-0-7385-8849-0

Published by Arcadia Publishing
Charleston, South Carolina

Printed in the United States of America

For all general information contact Arcadia Publishing at:
Telephone 843-853-2070
Fax 843-853-0044
E-mail sales@arcadiapublishing.com
For customer service and orders:
Toll-Free 1-888-313-2665

Visit us on the Internet at www.arcadiapublishing.com

With appreciation to Ethel Trask for her assistance and support.

Photographs are from the collection of the Danvers Archival Center of the Peabody Institute Library of Danvers, and from archive deposit collections including those of the Danvers Historical Society and the Rebecca Nurse Homestead, as well as from the author's personal collection.

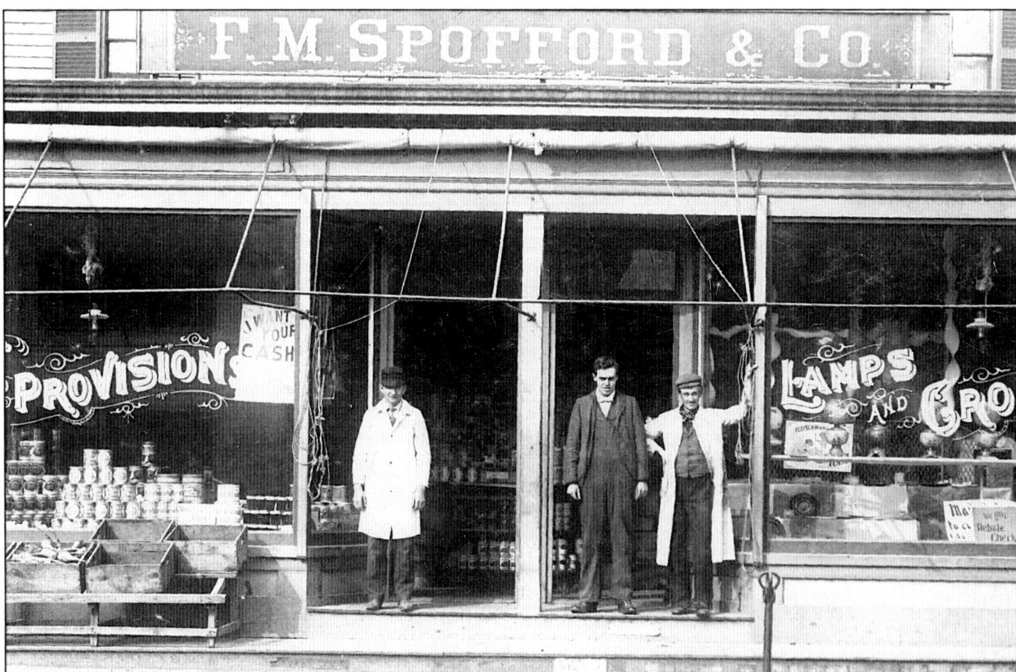

Frank M. Spofford (left) and two clerks stand for an 1890s photograph in front of his store on Maple Street.

Contents

Dedication

This book is dedicated to the memory of Thurl Dryden Brown (1908–1995), veteran, poet, historian, and mensch. And also to that relatively small but dedicated group of people who attempt to preserve the original structures and objects of Danvers' history, so that the citizens of the future will have more than just pictures in books with which to remember their heritage.

Introduction

This volume is a visual sampling of a relatively short period of fifty years in the history of Danvers, Massachusetts. Today we live in an extremely visually oriented world. Magazines, picture books, free and cable television, videos, theatrical films, CD-ROMs, and personal still and video cameras make available to us an avalanche of images relating to our own personal life and that of the world in which we live. Yet photography, the first medium which allowed man to preserve actual fragments of visual reality, is a relatively recent invention. The Daguerreotype, the first generally accepted photographic system, was developed in 1839 by Louis Daguerre.

We begin our visual discovery of Danvers at the mid-point of the nineteenth century. The decade of the 1850s was a milestone in Danvers' history. In 1852 the town celebrated one hundred years of independence from its mother town of Salem. Three years later, in 1855, Danvers split itself into two separate communities. South Danvers, the larger of the two in population and commercial development, would change its name in 1868 to Peabody, while the north section would retain its 1752 name. In 1856 both towns jointly celebrated the homecoming of millionaire George Peabody. After 1856, however, the histories of Danvers and South Danvers would take on their own identities.

The nine chapters in this book will reveal the earliest preserved visual images of Danvers. In the first chapter we shall examine the connections of George Peabody with Danvers. Next we will gaze into the young faces of Danvers shoemakers and farmers dressed in uniform and prepared to fight in a bloody civil war. Then follow six chapters illustrating the architecture, commerce, and population of the major pocket villages of nineteenth-century Danvers. The final chapter will spotlight the grand country houses which dotted rural Danvers in the last years of the 1800s.

Prior to photography, visual images of small towns like Danvers were rare. There were few local artists, and they would seldom spend time creating out-of-door or pedestrian scenes, pursuing their talents with the more salable art of portraiture. Though the newly developed photographic portraiture came into full swing during the 1850s and '60s, exterior views were still quite rare. Thus the 1852 Danvers centennial and the 1856 George Peabody visit are only visually recalled through the work of artists, rather than through the lens of a camera. By the 1870s, however, with the common use of multi-image-producing photographic systems, the many professional photographers were shooting outdoor scenes. Numerous amateur photographers also began recording what they believed to be important. Many of the older homes, particularly those from the time when Danvers was known as Salem Village and had been involved with the 1692 witchcraft hysteria, became popular subjects for photography. Though we may bemoan the frequent use of photography in creating static images of buildings rather than the candid interplay of people, these images do reveal to us facets of life in the last half of the nineteenth century for which we have no duplicate for earlier times. We see Danvers as its inhabitants then perceived it to be, focusing on what they believed to be the most important aspects of the town in their own time. This window into the past, no matter how small or limiting the view, is still a precious and revealing glimpse of people and places now forever lost, save for the slice of reality preserved in the images themselves.

Richard B. Trask

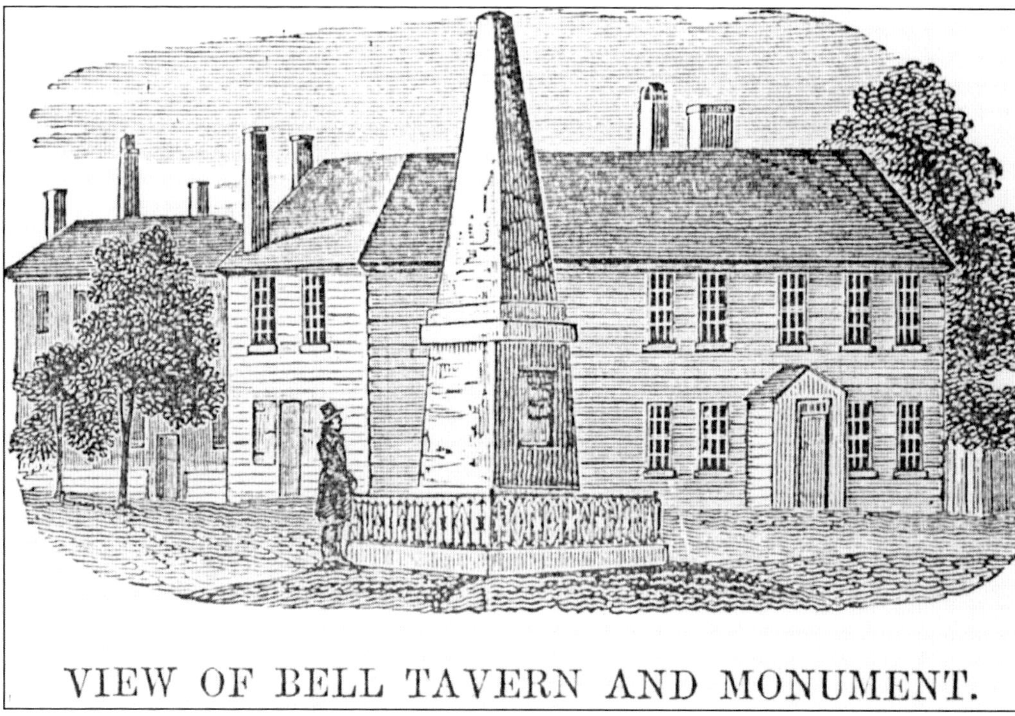

VIEW OF BELL TAVERN AND MONUMENT.

This granite obelisk was constructed in 1835 in the South Parish of Danvers (now Peabody) to commemorate the sacrifice of seven Danvers men in the Lexington Alarm of April 19, 1775. In one of his earliest public donations, George Peabody gave $300 of the $1,000 cost of this monument.

One

George Peabody

Born of humble beginnings in 1795 in the South Parish of Danvers, George Peabody went on to become the most famous local boy of the last half of the nineteenth century. He left Danvers at the age of sixteen, beginning as a clerk in a dry goods store. With hard work, tenacity, good business sense, and luck, he bettered himself through business moves first to Baltimore, Maryland, and eventually to London, England. A simple and frugal bachelor, Peabody eventually amassed a personal fortune of many millions of dollars, and became one of the most important merchant businessmen of the century.

Though always a charitable man to family and good causes, Peabody initiated his first major public act of philanthropy with the 1852 gift to his native town of $20,000 for the establishment of a public library and lyceum. From then on until his death in 1869, Peabody made gifts to American and English educational, charitable, and civic causes amounting to over $9 million. His several visits back to Danvers became major celebrations.

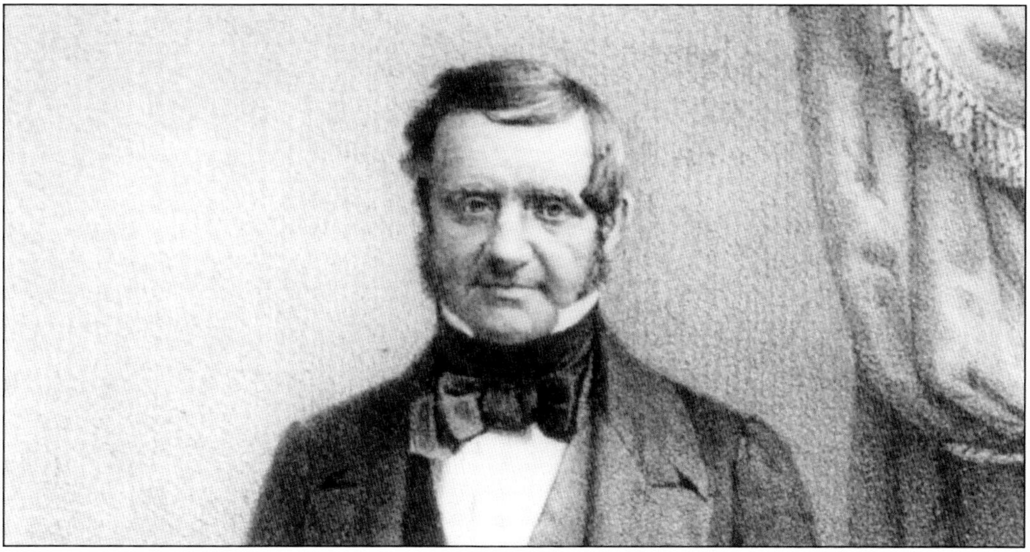

George Peabody.

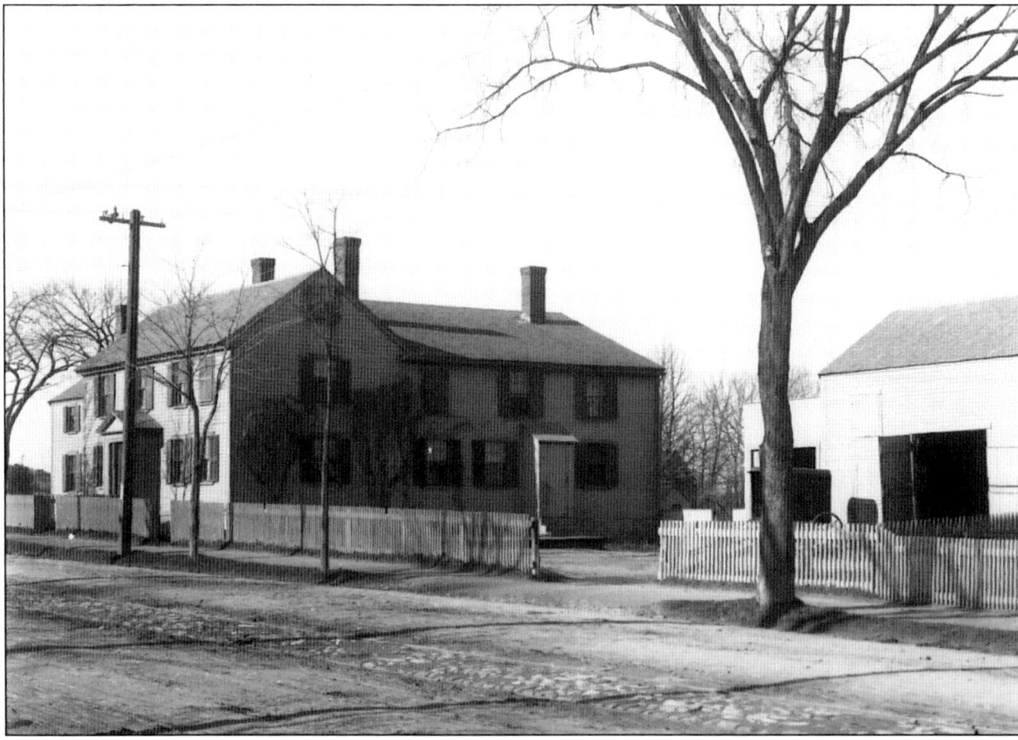

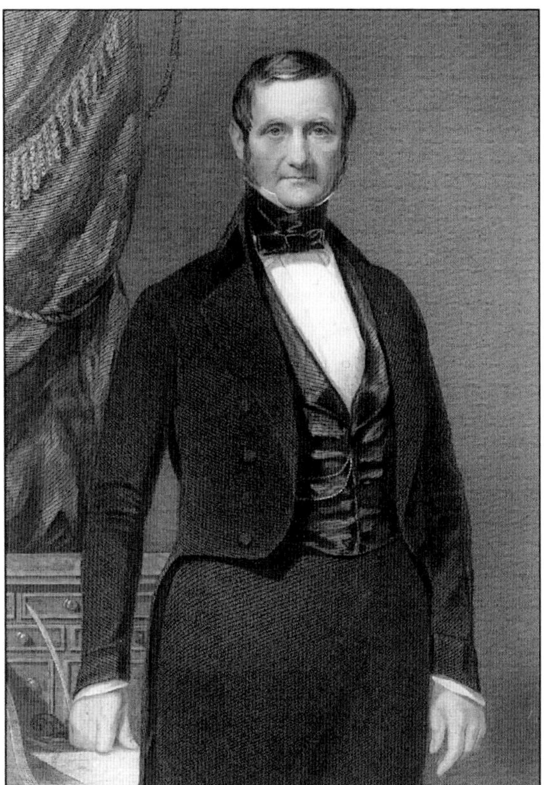

Peabody was born on February 18, 1795, to Thomas and Judith Dodge Peabody in this house on Washington Street in the South Parish. In 1855 the parish became the independent town of South Danvers, later renamed Peabody.

An engraving from a Daguerreotype of the energetic middle-aged George Peabody, who had taken up residence in London in 1837. In 1843 Peabody had begun the highly successful commercial and banking firm, George Peabody & Co.

This broadside heading touts the centennial of Danvers' separation from Salem in 1752. By 1852 George Peabody had become well known for his donations to various causes. He was invited to his hometown celebration; unable to attend, he instead sent an envelope to be opened at the banquet.

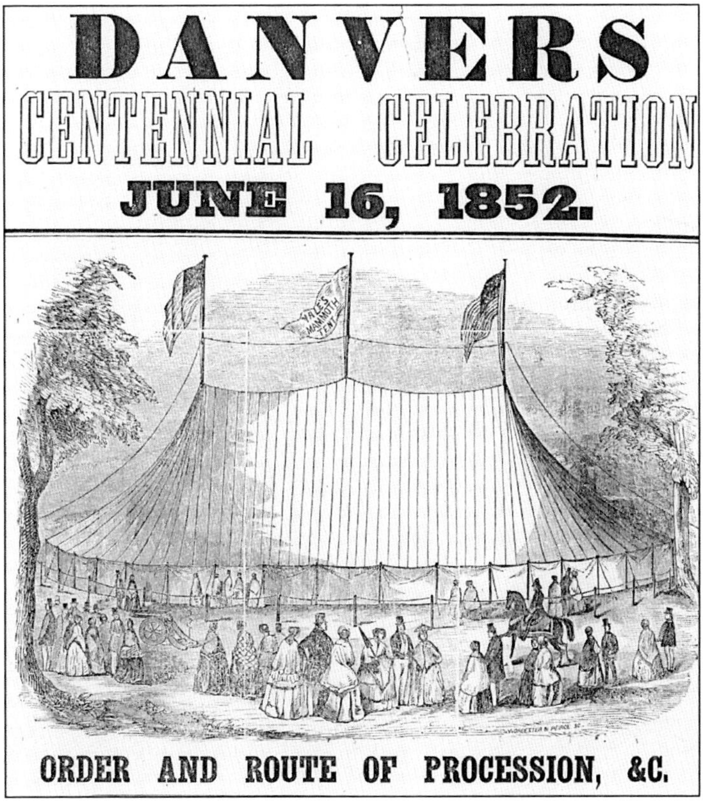

DANVERS
CENTENNIAL CELEBRATION
JUNE 16, 1852.

ORDER AND ROUTE OF PROCESSION, &C.

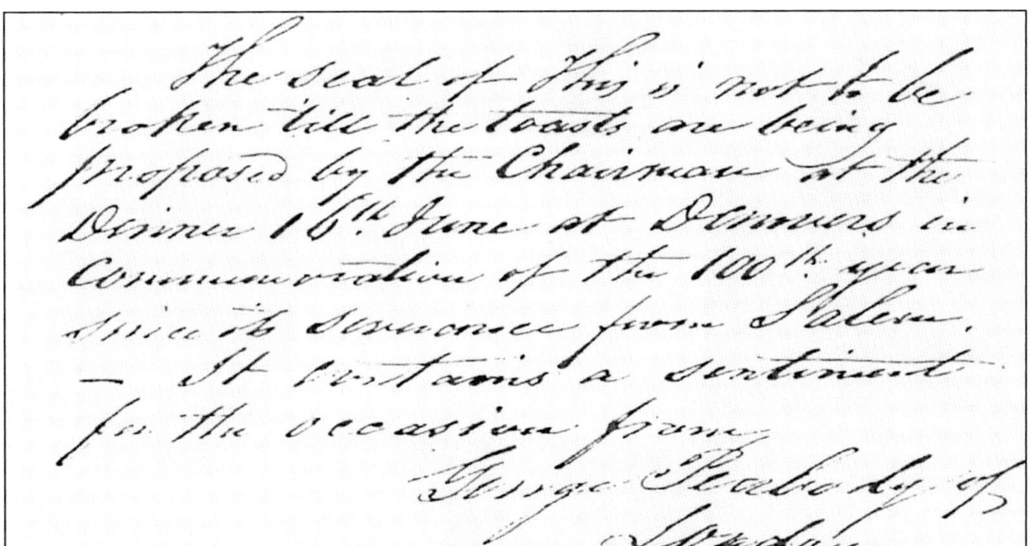

The seal of this is not to be broken till the toasts are being proposed by the Chairman at the Dinner 16th June at Danvers in Commemoration of the 100th year since its severance from Salem. — It contains a sentiment for the occasion from George Peabody of London.

The inscription written by George Peabody on the envelope containing his donation letter to Danvers. Inside was his sentiment, "Education, a debt due from present to future generations," together with a gift of $20,000 for the establishment of a town library.

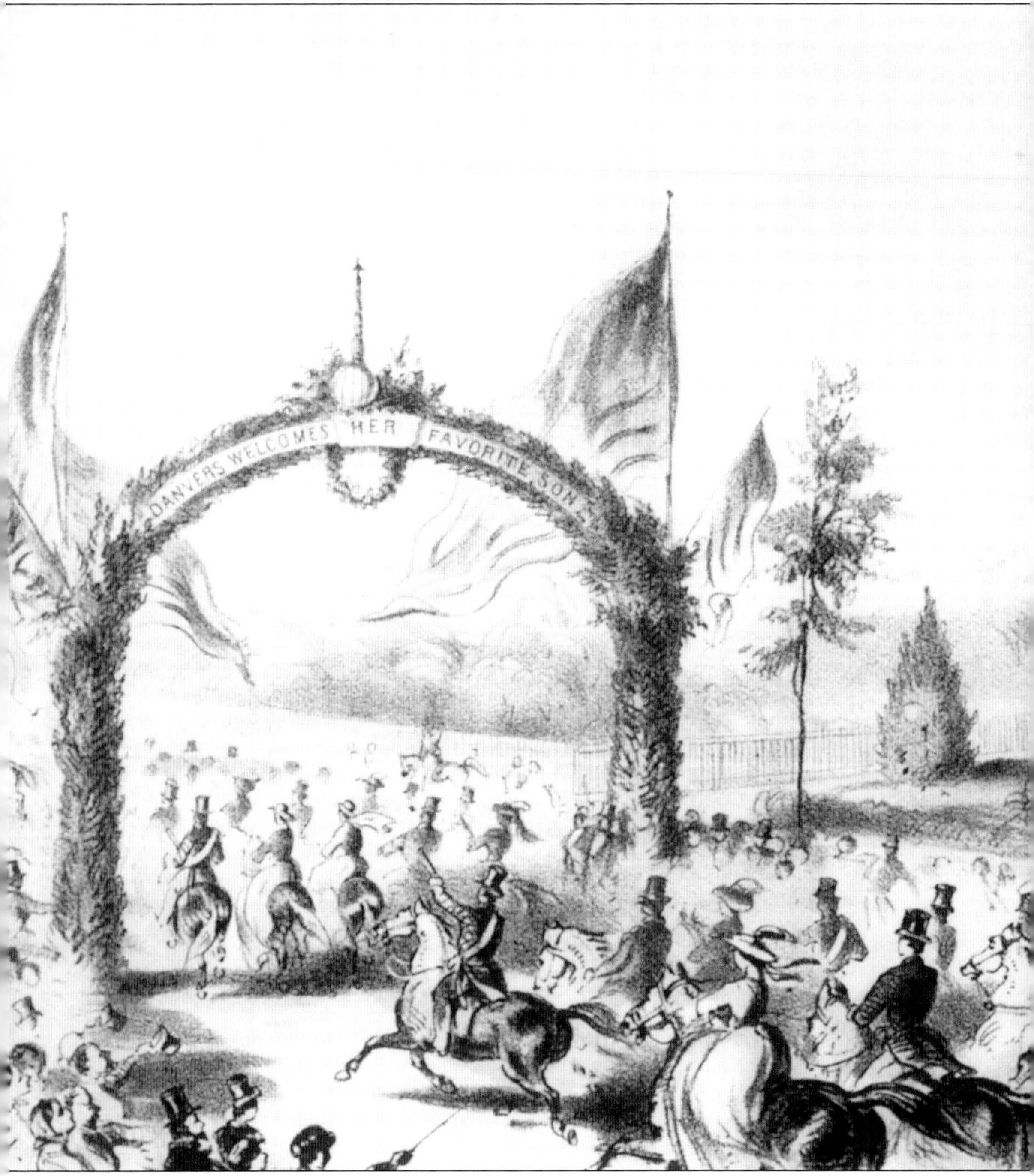

In 1856 Peabody decided to visit his native country. Though he was offered grandiose receptions in many cities, Peabody chose to first visit his home town. A combined reception committee of Danvers and the newly created town of South Danvers united for a spectacular welcome including a large parade. Peabody arrived in Danvers Plains on October 9, 1856, to a one hundred-gun salute. He boarded a six-horse barouche which traveled through both communities amid flags, bunting, and arches of flowers and greens. The parade included dignitaries, bands,

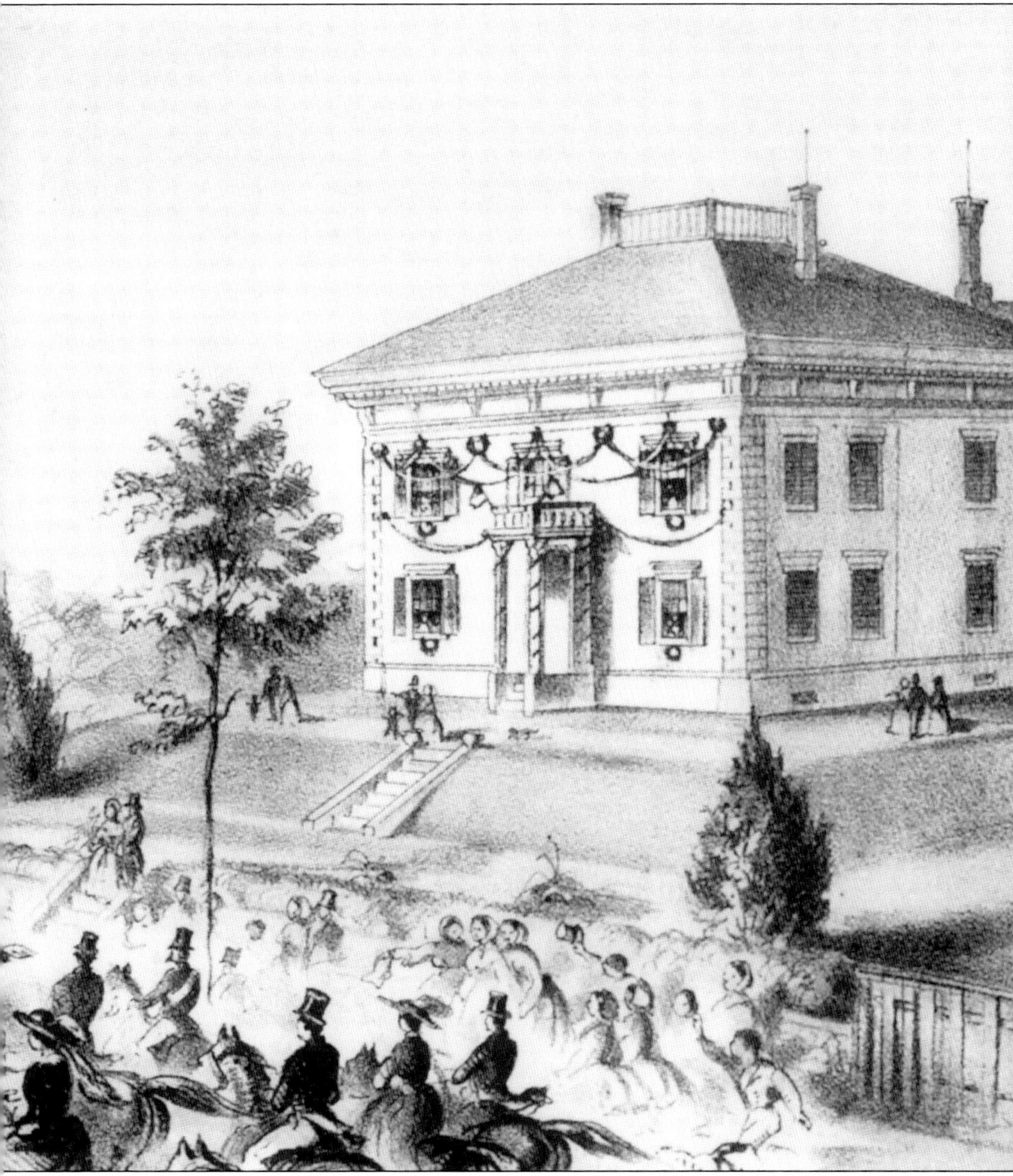

fire engines, military units, and the schoolchildren of the towns. The above view illustrates the mounted ladies and gentlemen riding down High Street past the Italianate 1855 home of James Black. In 1927 this house was converted into the Hunt Memorial Hospital. This 1856 engraving was drawn by famed American artist Winslow Homer.

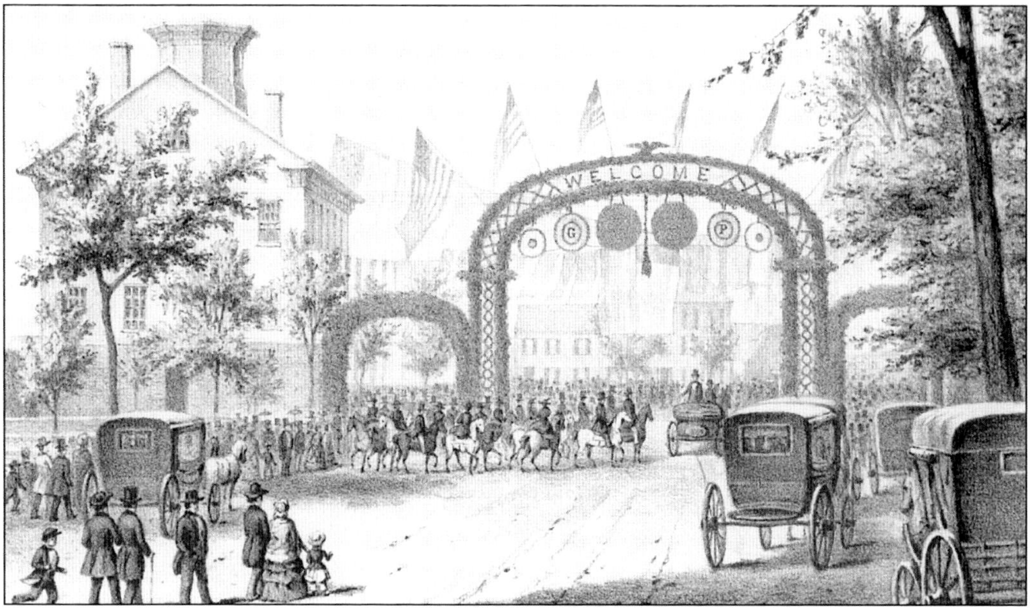

Mr. Peabody being greeted at the threefold arch on Maple Street in Danvers Plains. The Village Bank building is at left.

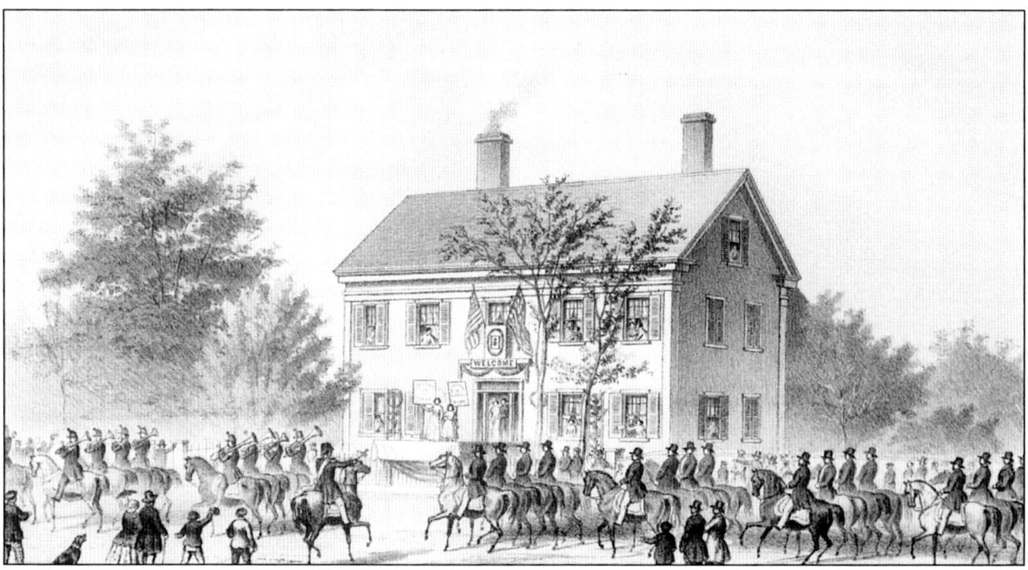

A mounted brass band and gentlemen's cavalcade ride past the William L. Weston house at 35 High Street.

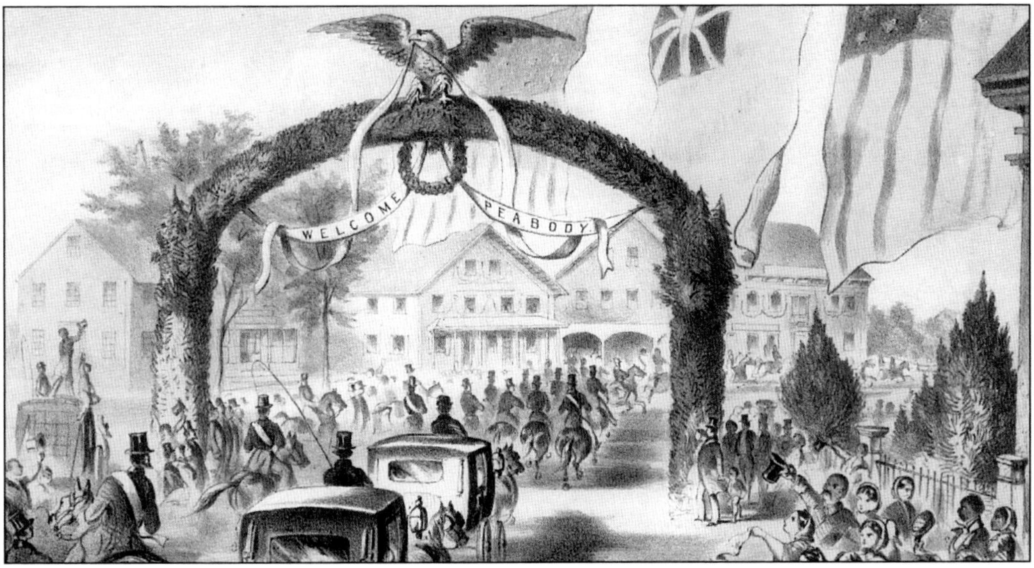

Another Winslow Homer engraving showing the procession turning from High Street onto Water Street in Danversport. The corner of the Baptist church is at right.

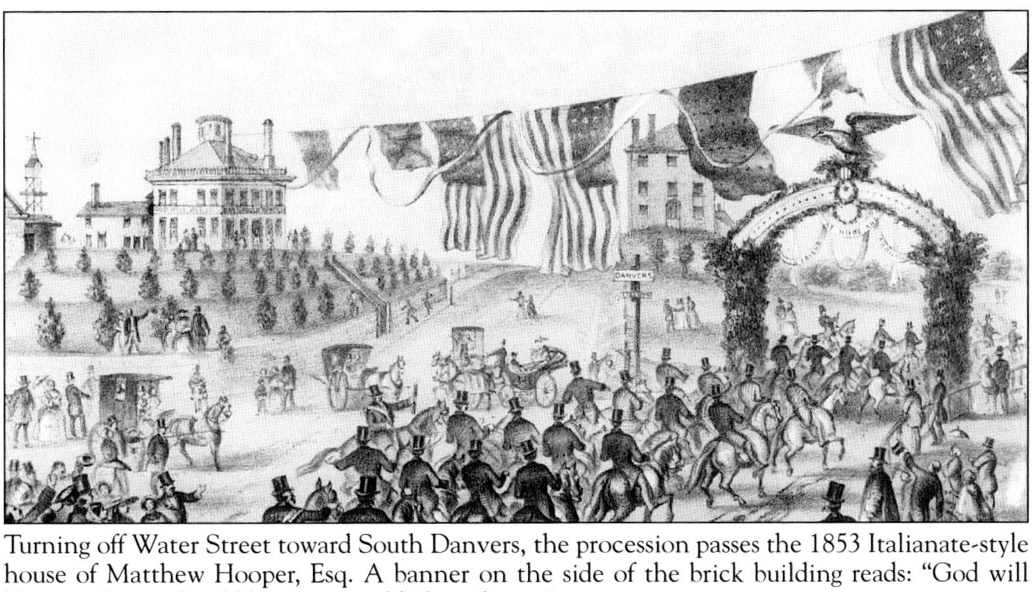

Turning off Water Street toward South Danvers, the procession passes the 1853 Italianate-style house of Matthew Hooper, Esq. A banner on the side of the brick building reads: "God will bless, and man should honor, a world's benefactor."

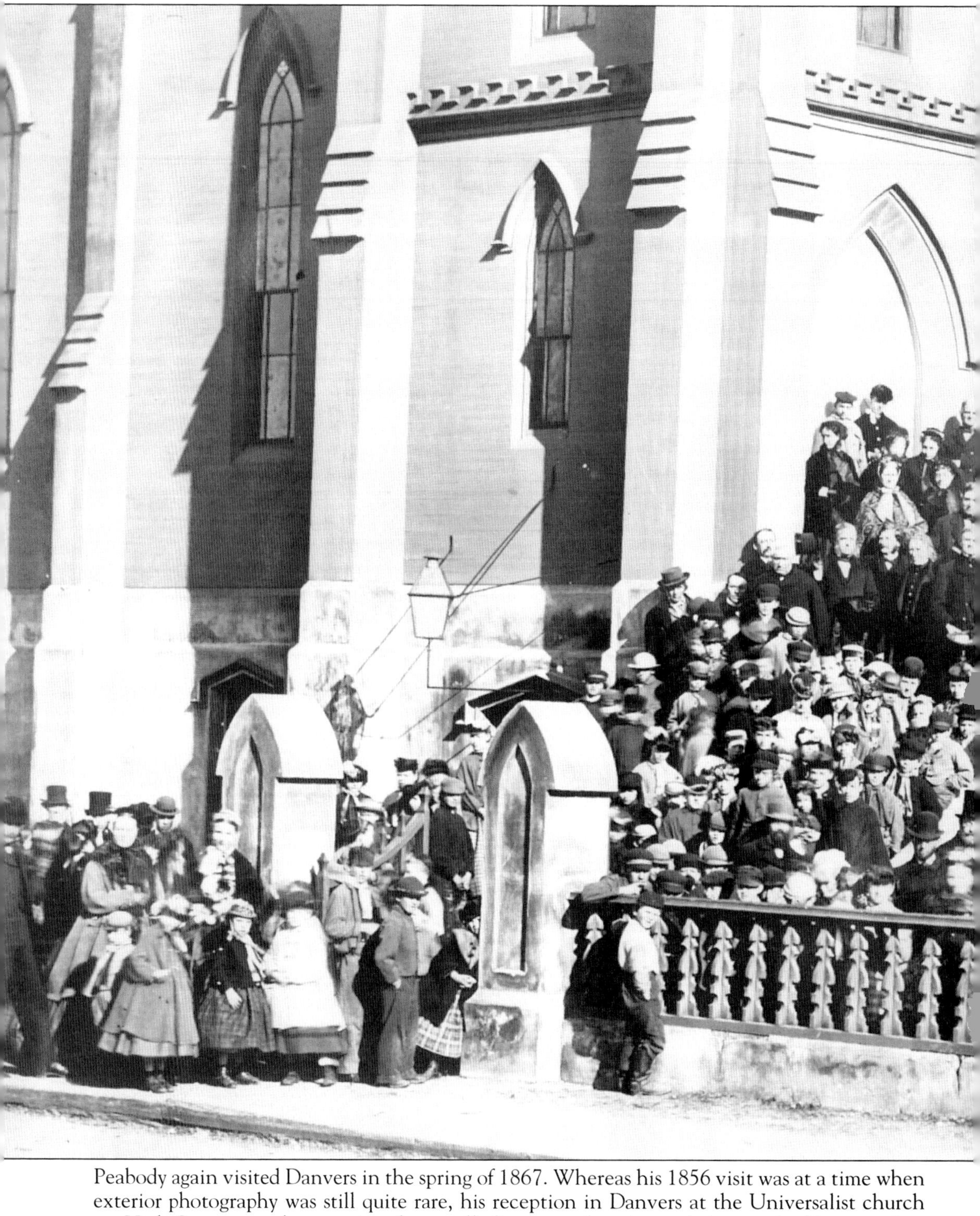

Peabody again visited Danvers in the spring of 1867. Whereas his 1856 visit was at a time when exterior photography was still quite rare, his reception in Danvers at the Universalist church on High Street was the occasion for a collodion wet-plate image being made. Photographer Charles W. Stiff captured a grand view of Peabody (near center, with stovepipe hat in hand and

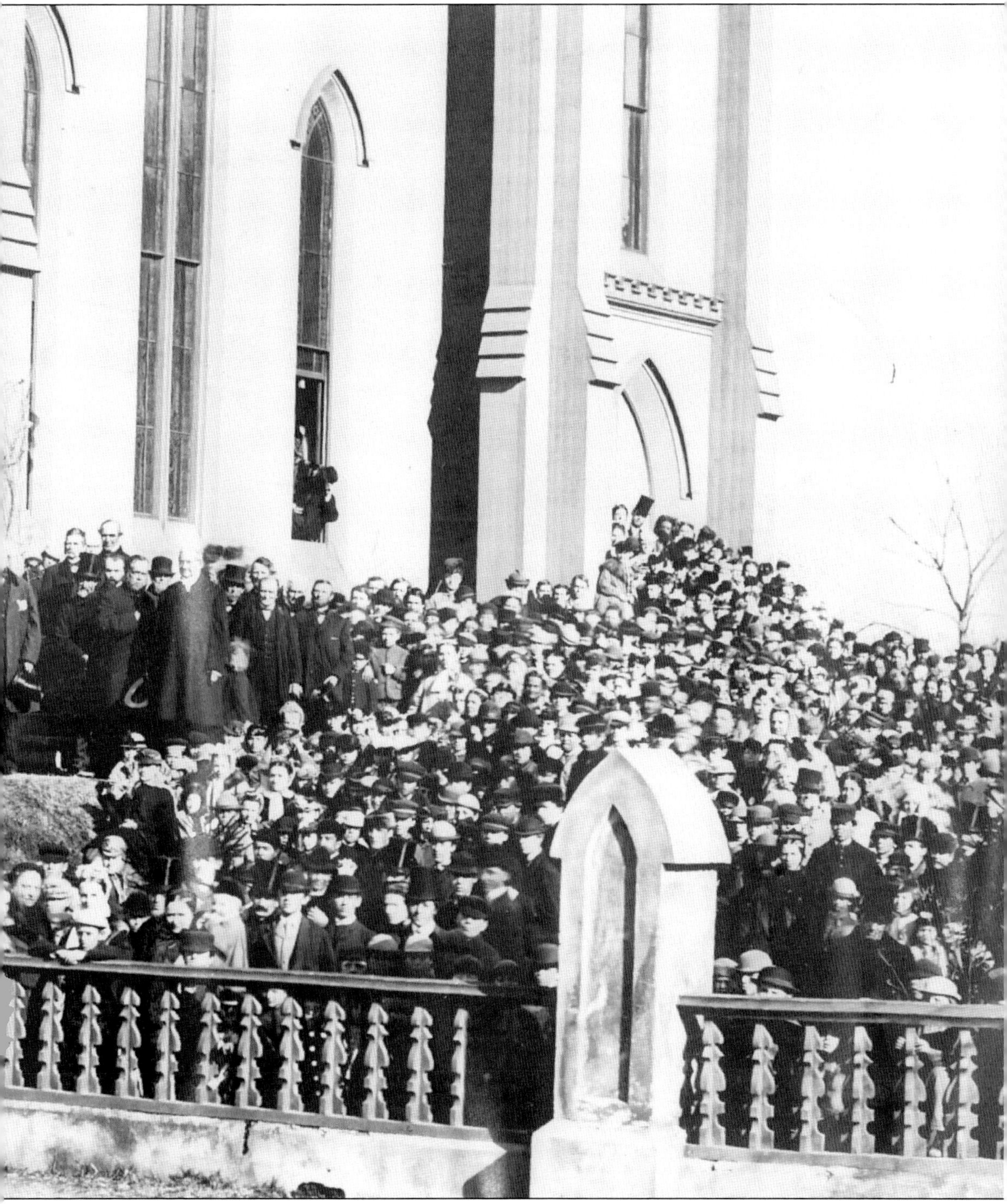

white handkerchief in coat pocket) with other local notables looking over a crowd of citizens and schoolchildren. Peabody is reported to have remarked that this photograph was "the best work of the kind he has seen."

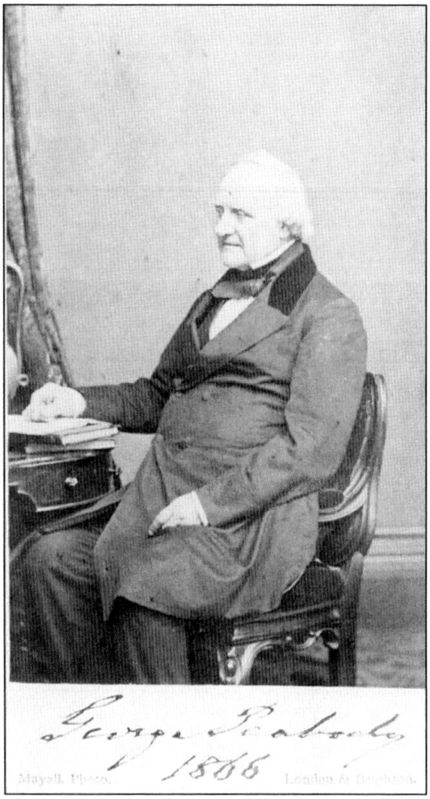

Peabody retired at age seventy, handing the firm over to partner Junius S. Morgan and devoting his full efforts towards philanthropies. Among his contributions were $2.5 million to the Peabody Donation Fund for housing London's poor and $2 million to the Peabody Education Fund for southern education. This carte-de-visite photograph was signed by Peabody in 1866.

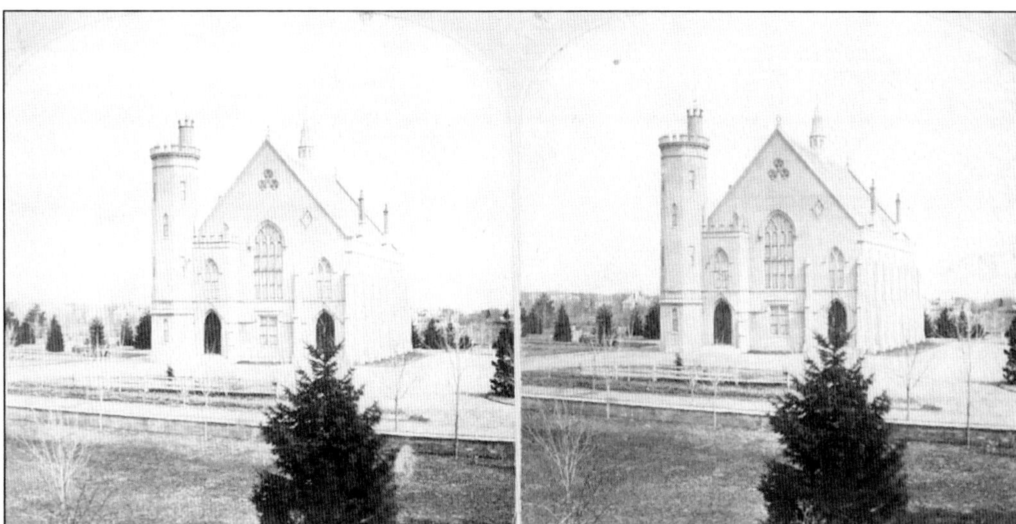

One final trip to America was made by Peabody in 1869. He participated in the dedication of the Peabody Institute Library of Danvers on July 14, 1869. This stereograph view shows the rear of the Gothic-style library from Peabody Avenue.

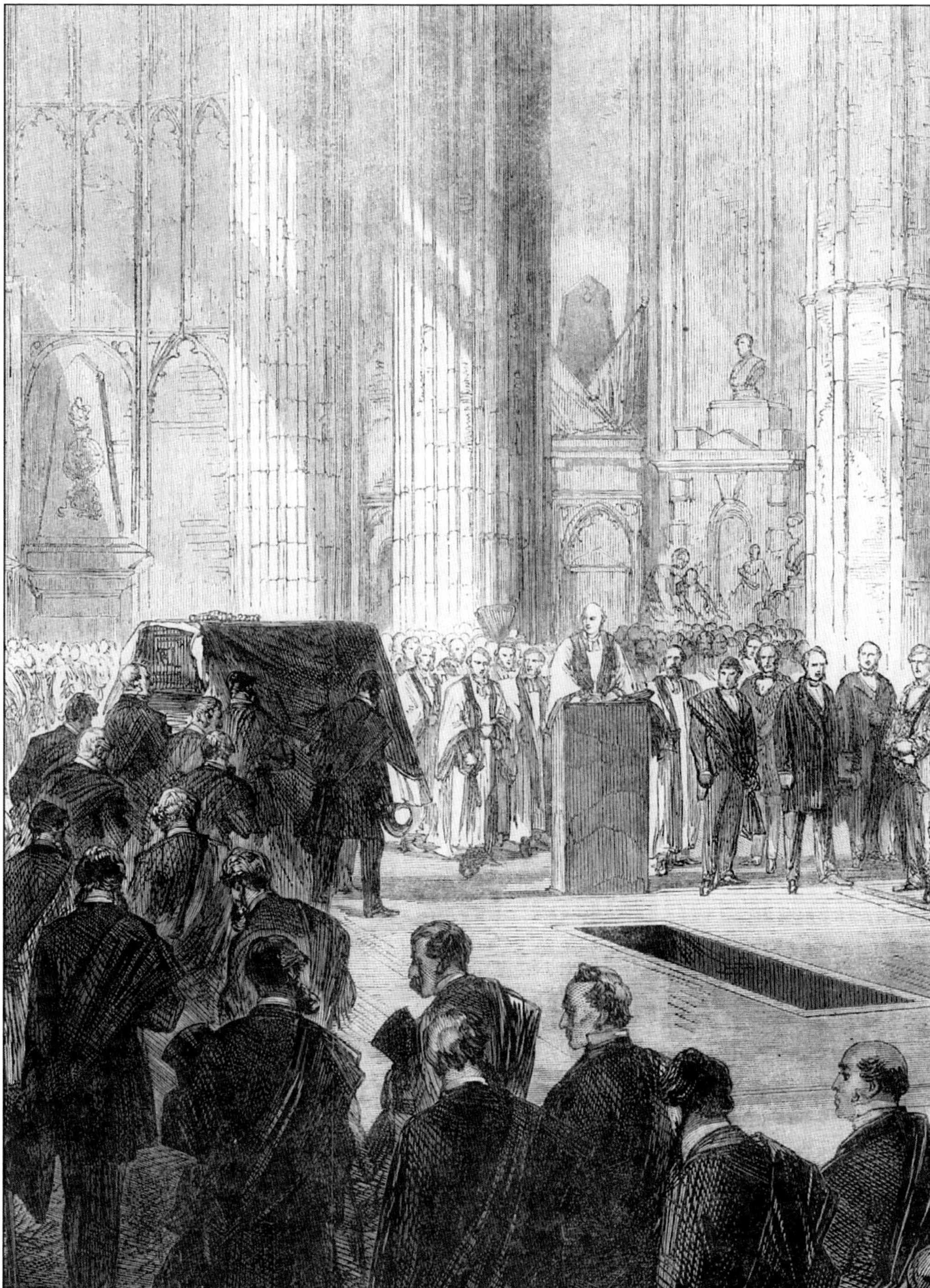

Peabody died in London on November 4, 1869. The English showed great respect for him by conducting a funeral at Westminster Abbey, where his remains lay for a month. This detail from an engraving depicts the service.

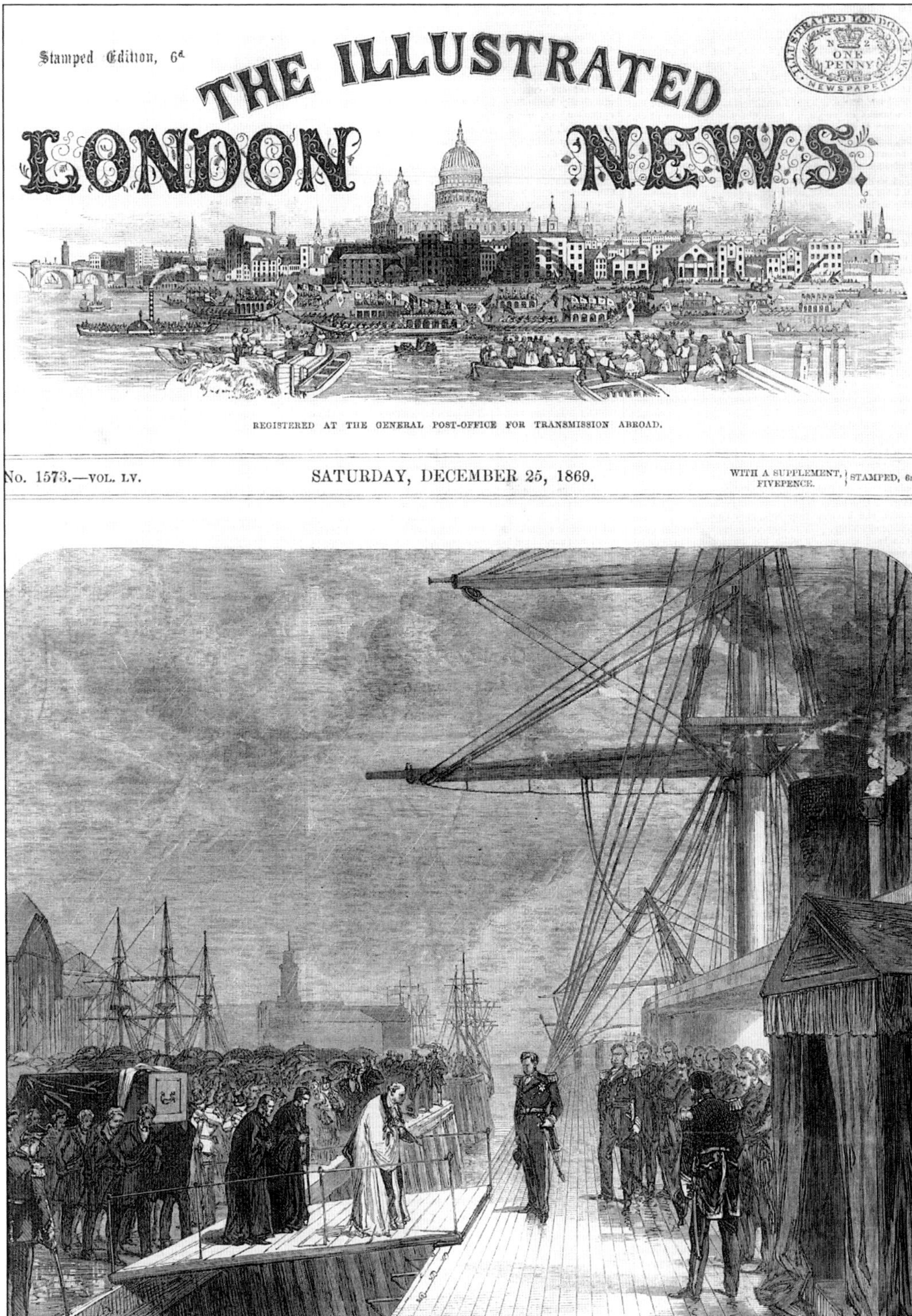

Stamped Edition, 6d

THE ILLUSTRATED LONDON NEWS

REGISTERED AT THE GENERAL POST-OFFICE FOR TRANSMISSION ABROAD.

No. 1573.—VOL. LV. SATURDAY, DECEMBER 25, 1869. WITH A SUPPLEMENT, FIVEPENCE. } STAMPED, 6D.

Peabody's remains were brought back to the United States aboard the new British warship, the HMS *Monarch*.

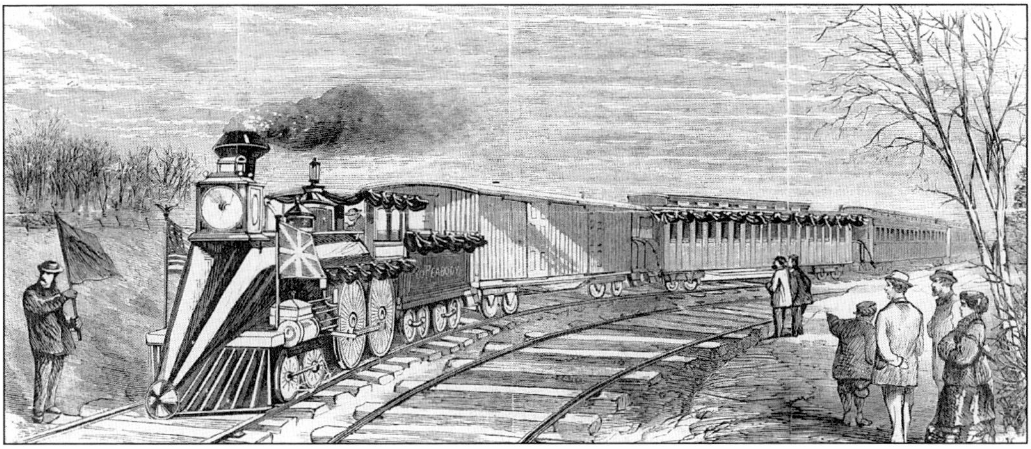

Arriving at Portland, Maine, Peabody's coffin was escorted by funeral train to Peabody, Massachusetts.

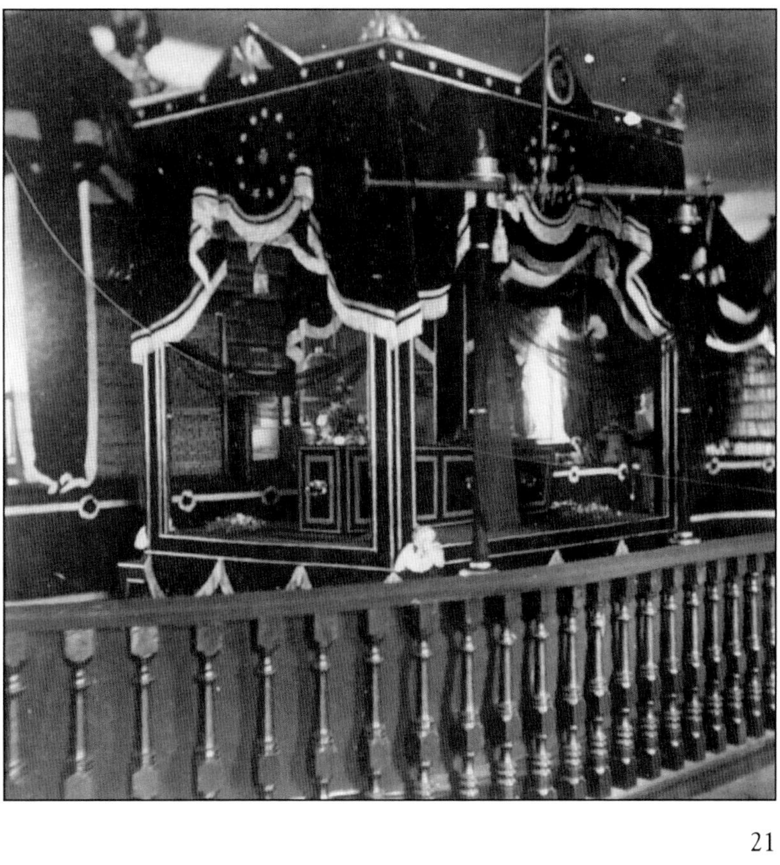

A stereograph view of the coffin lying in state at the Peabody Institute. The great benefactor's American funeral was held on February 8, 1870.

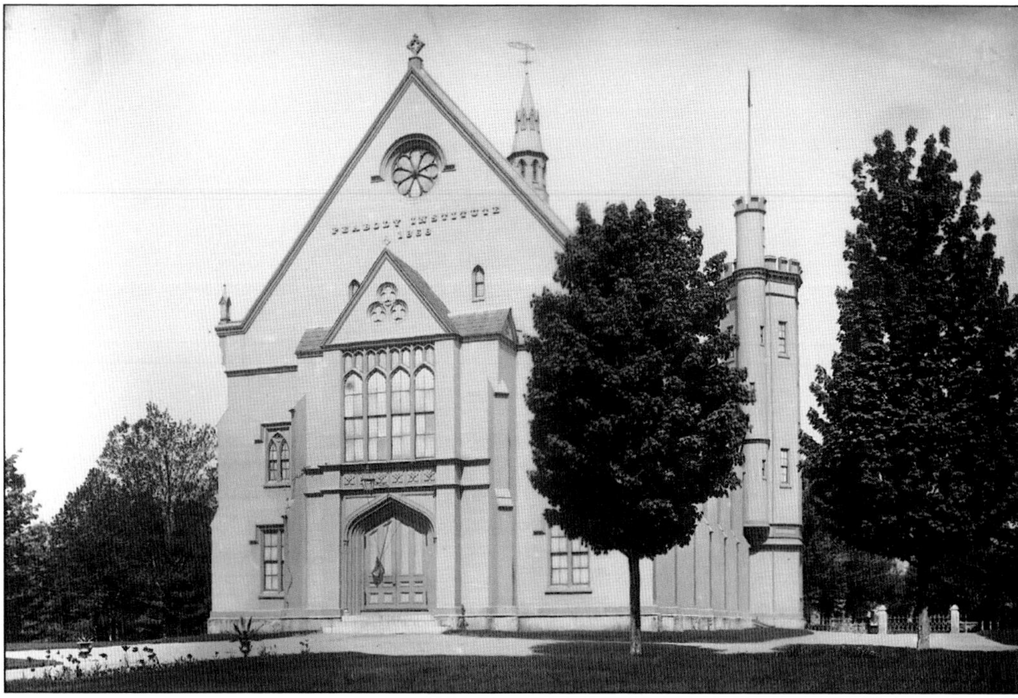

Peabody's various donations to the Peabody Institute in Danvers amounted to over $100,000. The 1869 library was designed by Gridley Bryant. This glass-plate photograph was taken of the Sylvan Street main entrance in the 1880s.

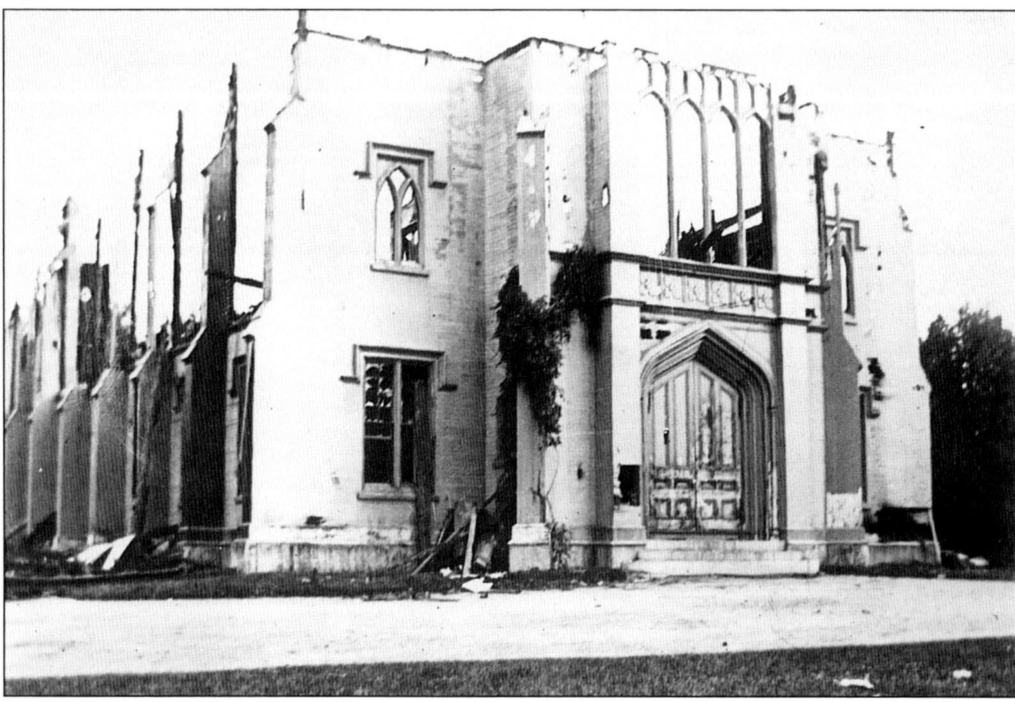

A July 1890 fire gutted the building, though through the efforts of volunteers at the scene most of the 11,000-volume collection was saved.

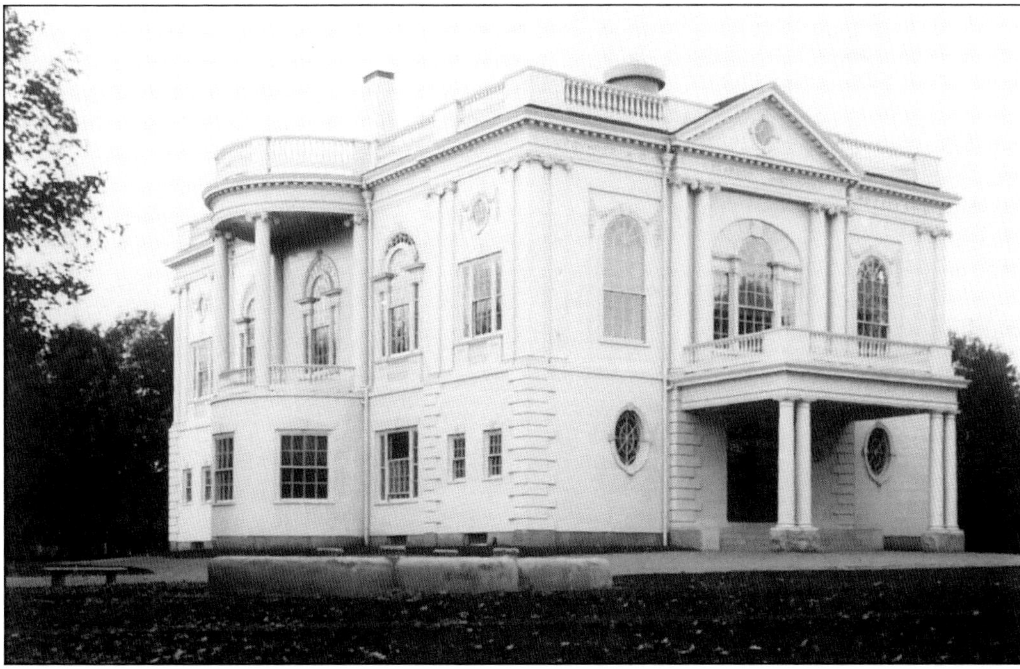

A beautiful new Colonial Revival-style library was designed by Lester Couch and dedicated in October 1892.

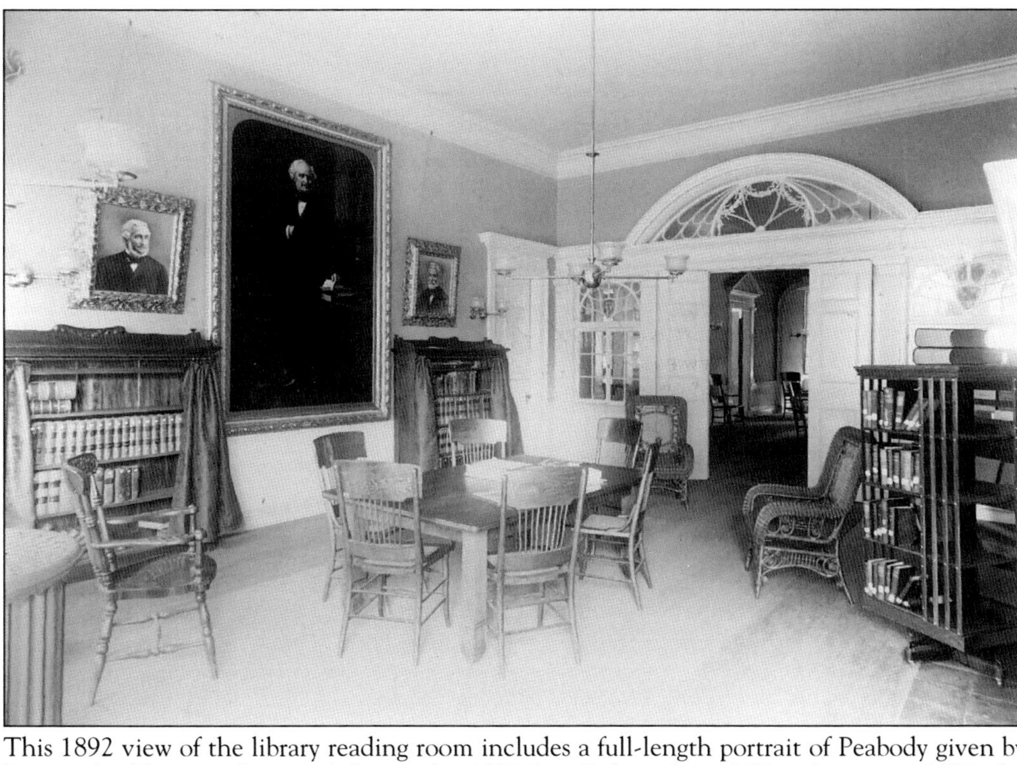

This 1892 view of the library reading room includes a full-length portrait of Peabody given by him to the library and rescued during the 1890 fire. Enlarged in 1962 and again in 1981, the library continues to serve the community.

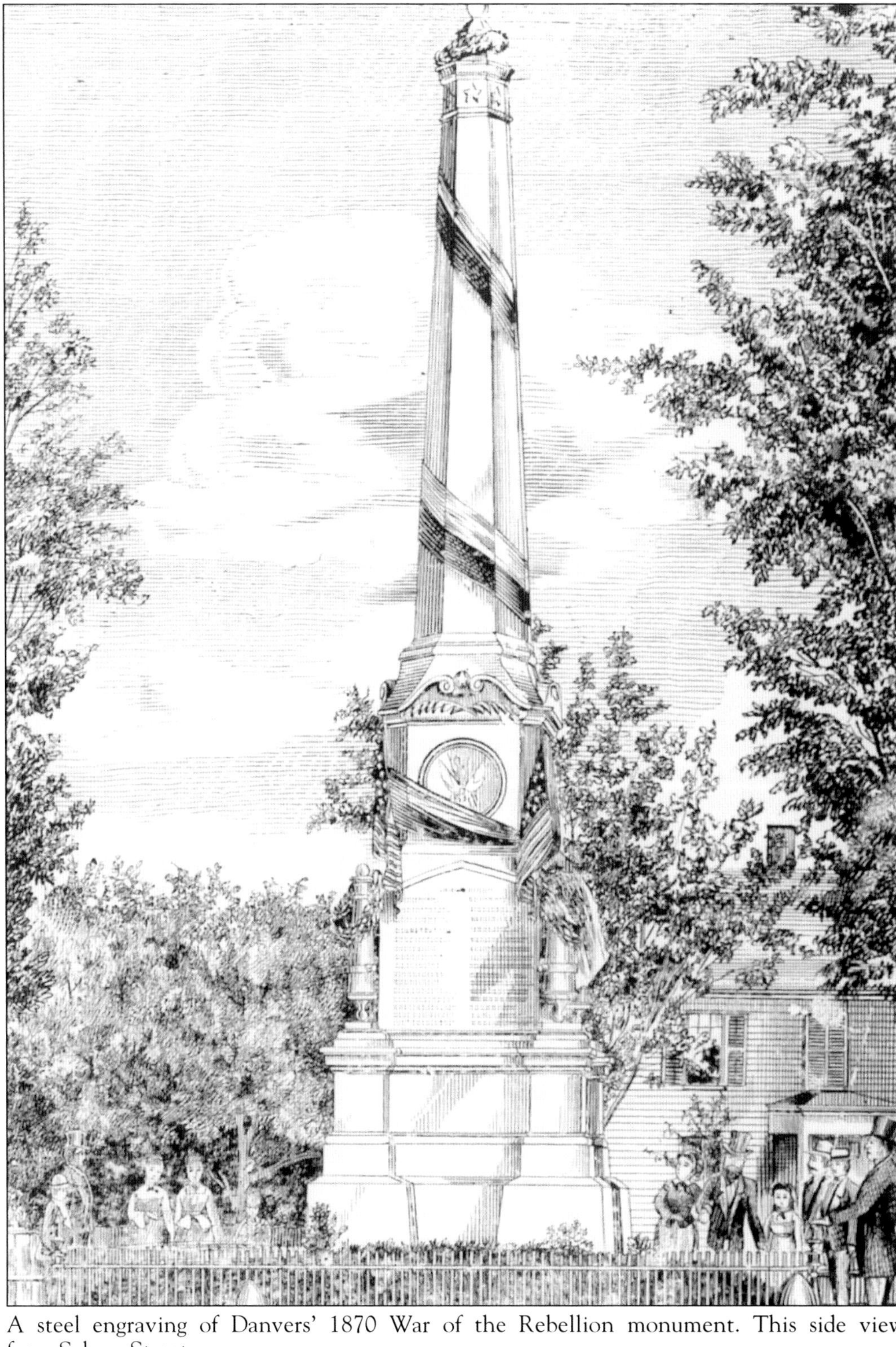

A steel engraving of Danvers' 1870 War of the Rebellion monument. This side view faces Sylvan Street.

Two

The Civil War

Many citizens of Danvers struggled over the moral dilemma of the slave question during the several decades before the outbreak of the Civil War. Both the Danvers Plains and Danversport sections of town were hotbeds of anti-slavery activity. Known as "come-outers," many of the most volatile abolitionist supporters practiced civil disobedience and condemned those who did not totally commit to the eradication of slavery. Others, however, found the antics of these extremists abhorrent. Much of the economy of the town was linked to selling shoes to the slave market in the south.

Shortly after Fort Sumpter was fired upon by the secessionist southerners, Danvers rallied to the call to preserve the Union. At a War Town Meeting on April 16, 1861, men committed to volunteer for military service. Soon two volunteer units, the Danvers Light Infantry and the Putnam Guards, were at company strength, and within months were taken into Massachusetts regiments.

The effect of the war upon the people of Danvers was tremendous. Approximately seven hundred men joined the army and navy and were represented in all major engagements. Ninety-five men, 2 percent of the entire town's population and 13 percent of those who served, were killed in action or died from disease during the four years of war.

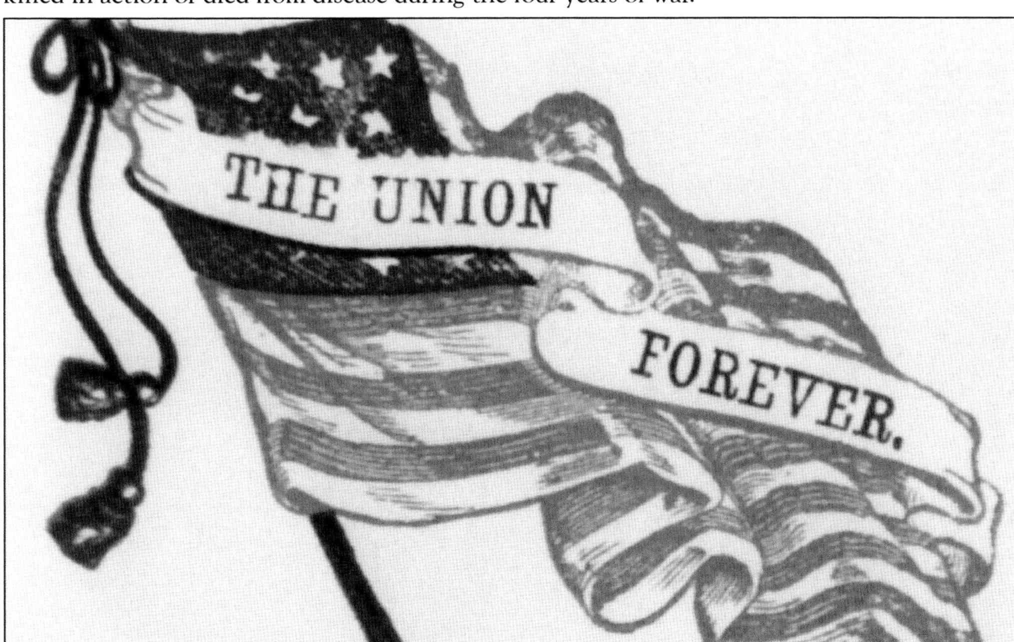

The Union banner.

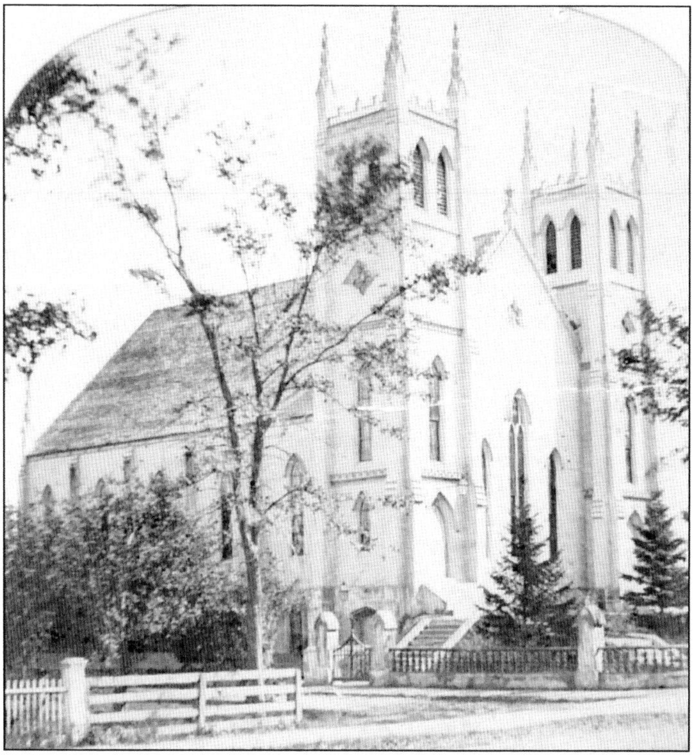

In 1861 at the Universalist church on High Street, women of Danvers prepared uniforms for the town's volunteer soldiers. Light blue jackets and trousers with red trimming were created for the Putnam Guard, while dark blue jackets and trousers with red trimming were created for the Danvers Light Infantry. Both fully uniformed companies attended services here prior to active duty.

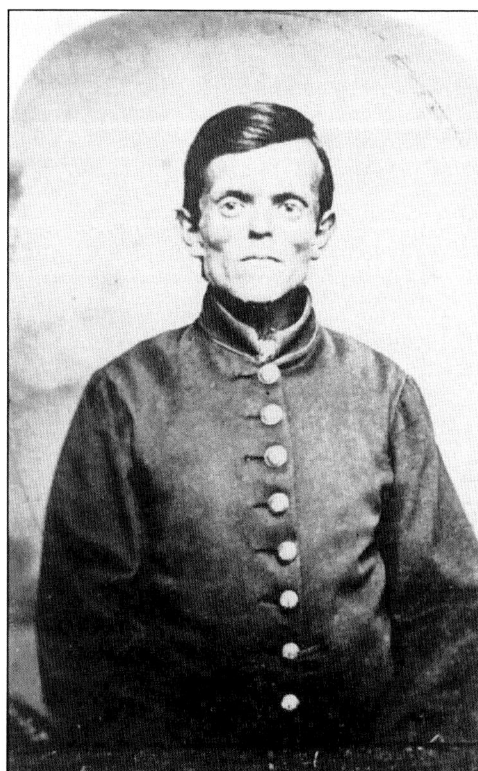

The ravages of rebel prison camps are reflected in the face of Nehemiah Putnam Fish. As a nineteen-year-old, Fish had joined the Putnam Guard in 1861. Captured twice, Fish once made a daring escape with fellow soldier John Wescott. In August 1864, Fish died from the effects of his captivity.

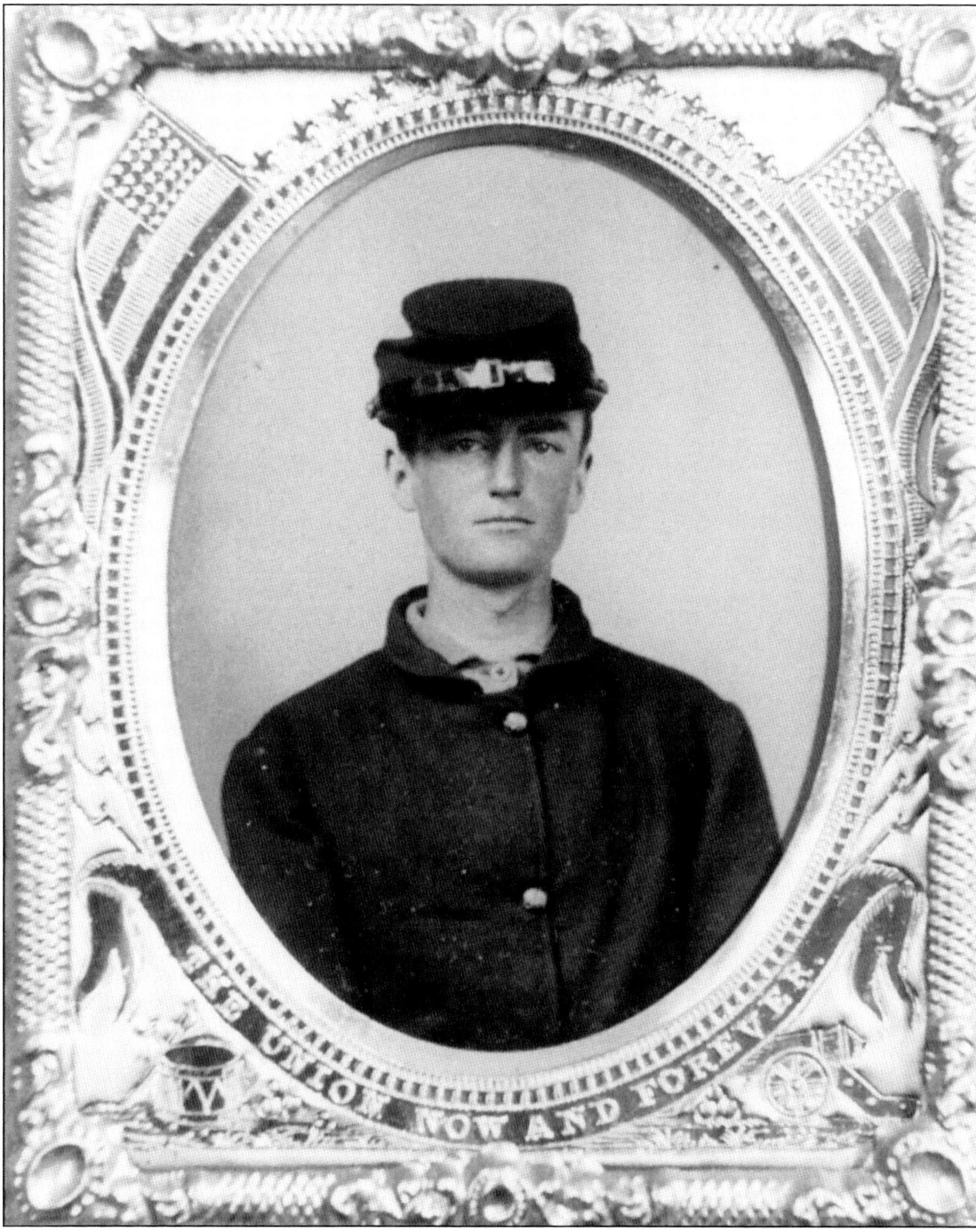

Robert Winthrop Putnam was born in the same room as his illustrious ancestor, Revolutionary War General Israel Putnam. A child just turned sixteen, Robert joined the army in 1861. In a letter home Putnam declared, "If I am to die, I shall be happy to die in the service of my country." In June 1862 Putnam was wounded in the breast at Malvern Hill, Virginia, and was taken prisoner. His family agonized over his fate for months. They finally learned that he had died in Libby Prison at Richmond, Virginia, in July, the day after paperwork had gone through allowing for his exchange.

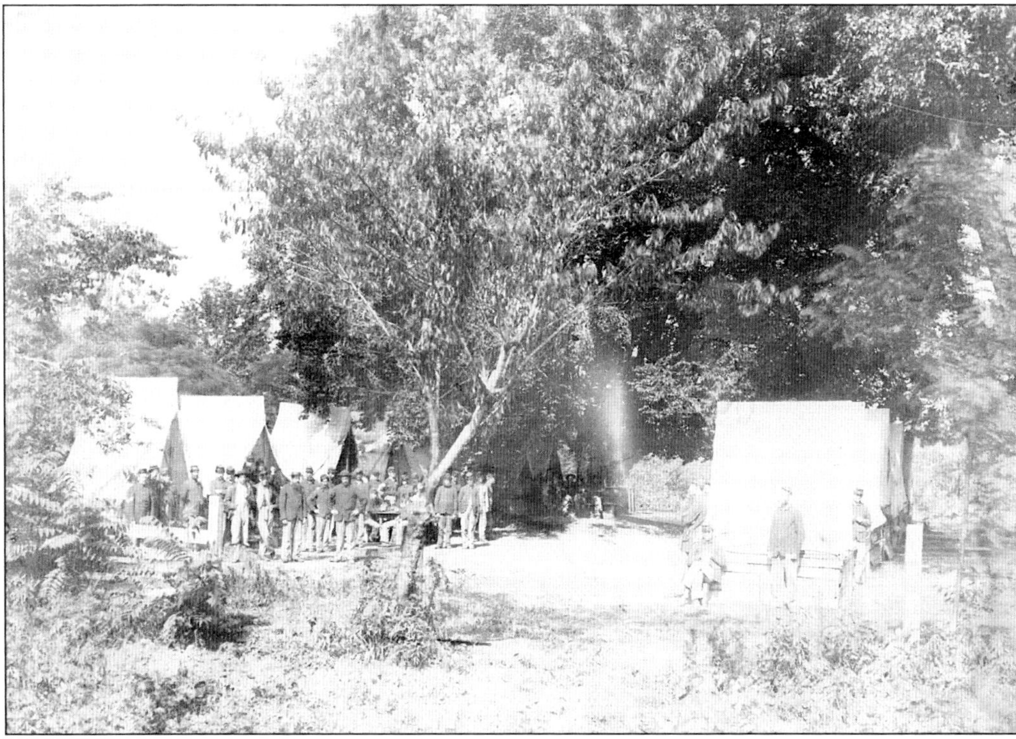

The soldiers in this rare view of a Union camp with wedge tents built over a wood base have been identified as being from Danvers. Whether this photograph was taken at a Massachusetts camp or one further south is unknown.

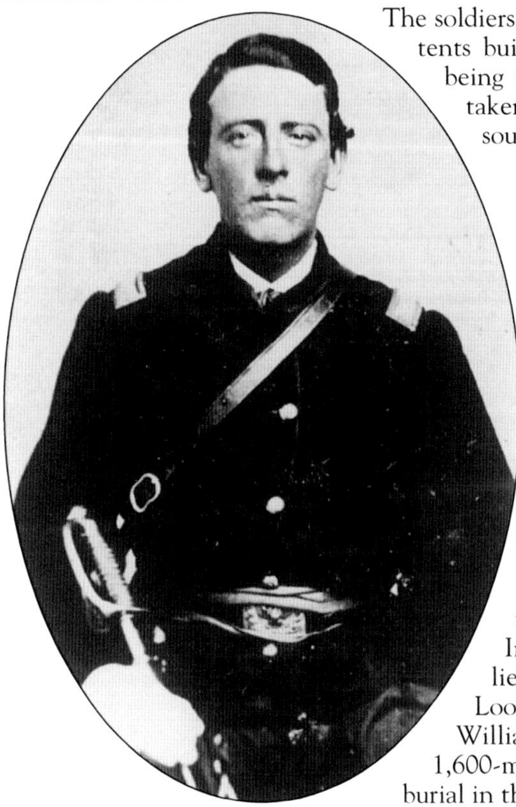

James Hill's family had moved to Tapleyville from England to work at the carpet factory. In 1861 Hill enlisted in the army. As a second lieutenant, he was killed in an assault on Lookout Mountain, Tennessee, in October 1863. William Green, Hill's uncle, made a treacherous 1,600-mile trip to bring back his nephew's body for burial in the Holten Cemetery, next to Hill's home.

Wallace Ahira Putnam rose to the rank of brevet major in the 56th Regiment. While commanding his men, Putnam took fire from rebel sharpshooters at North Anna, Virginia, on May 24, 1864. Wounded in the head, he was sent back home to recuperate. His wound proved fatal and he died in Massachusetts on June 20, 1864, while visiting his fiancee.

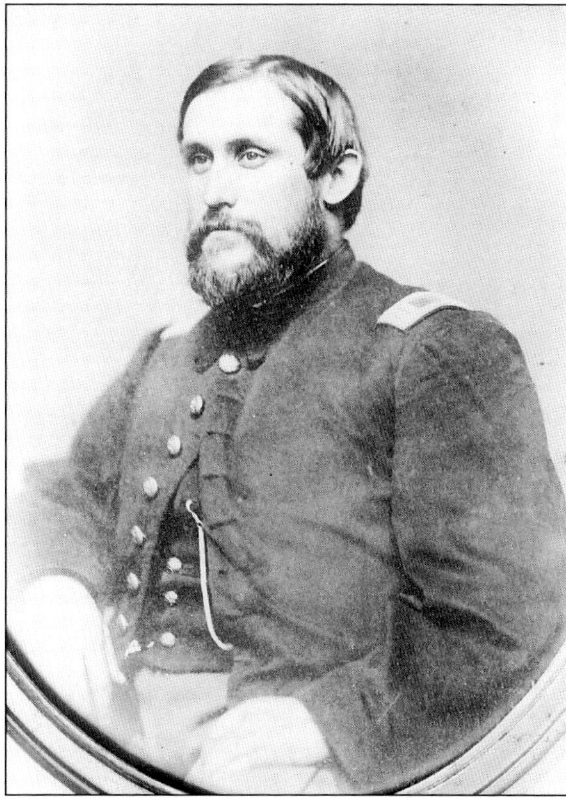

This structure was built in 1862 as one-half of an army barracks. Originally located at Camp Lander in Hamilton, Massachusetts, it was used to house newly mustered troops including men from Danvers. In 1865 the barracks were sold. This one was eventually moved in 1873 to 20 St. Hilaire Avenue and renovated into a residence.

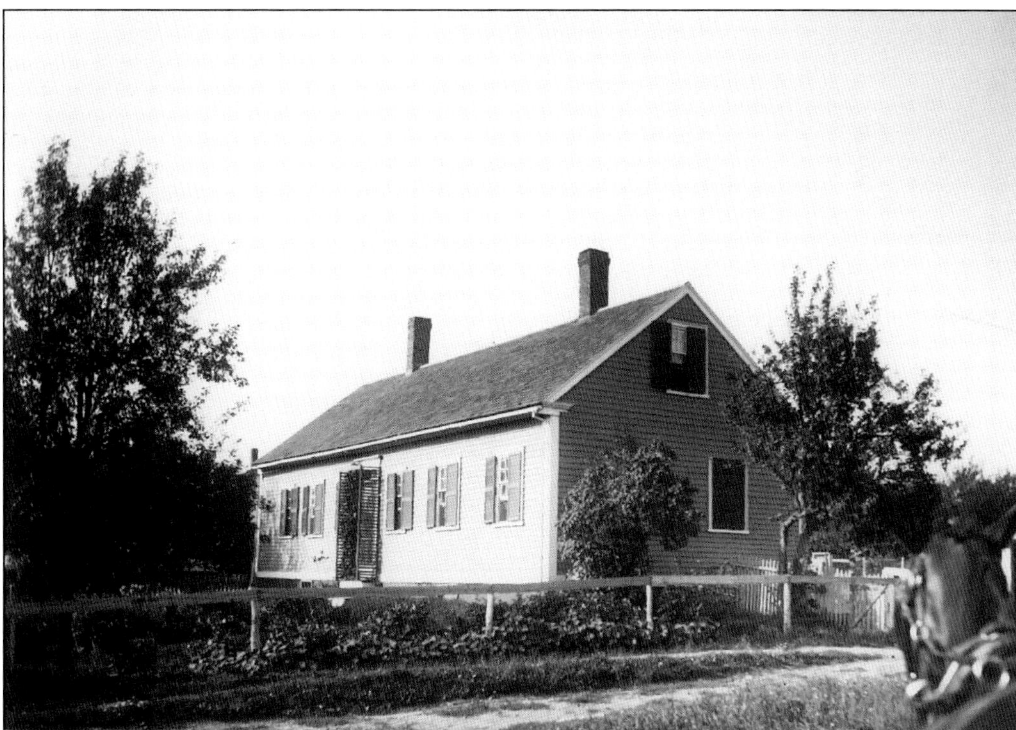

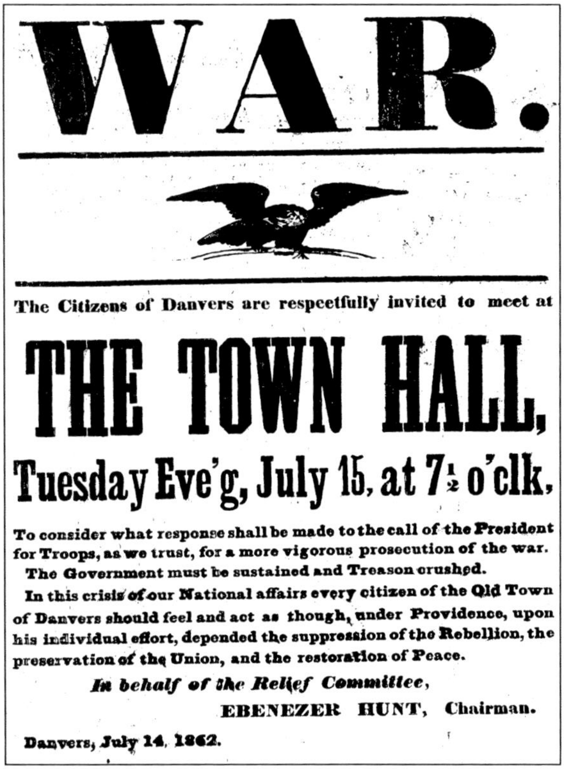

WAR.

The Citizens of Danvers are respectfully invited to meet at

THE TOWN HALL,

Tuesday Eve'g, July 15, at 7½ o'clk,

To consider what response shall be made to the call of the President for Troops, as we trust, for a more vigorous prosecution of the war. The Government must be sustained and Treason crushed.

In this crisis of our National affairs every citizen of the Old Town of Danvers should feel and act as though, under Providence, upon his individual effort, depended the suppression of the Rebellion, the preservation of the Union, and the restoration of Peace.

In behalf of the Relief Committee,

EBENEZER HUNT, Chairman.

Danvers, July 14, 1862.

A broadside notice of an 1862 Danvers meeting to encourage enlistment.

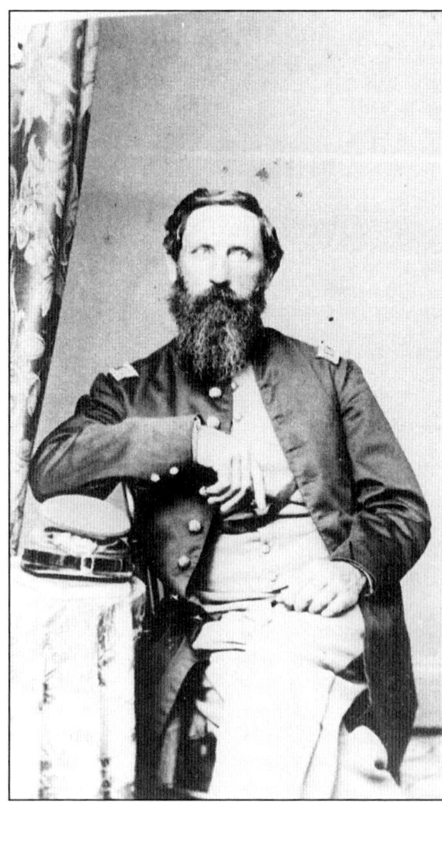

Daniel J. Preston, a forty-five-year-old Danvers shoe cutter, had become a captain in the 35th Infantry by 1862. In 1863 he was offered and accepted a major's commission to serve as a white officer with the 36th United States Colored Troops.

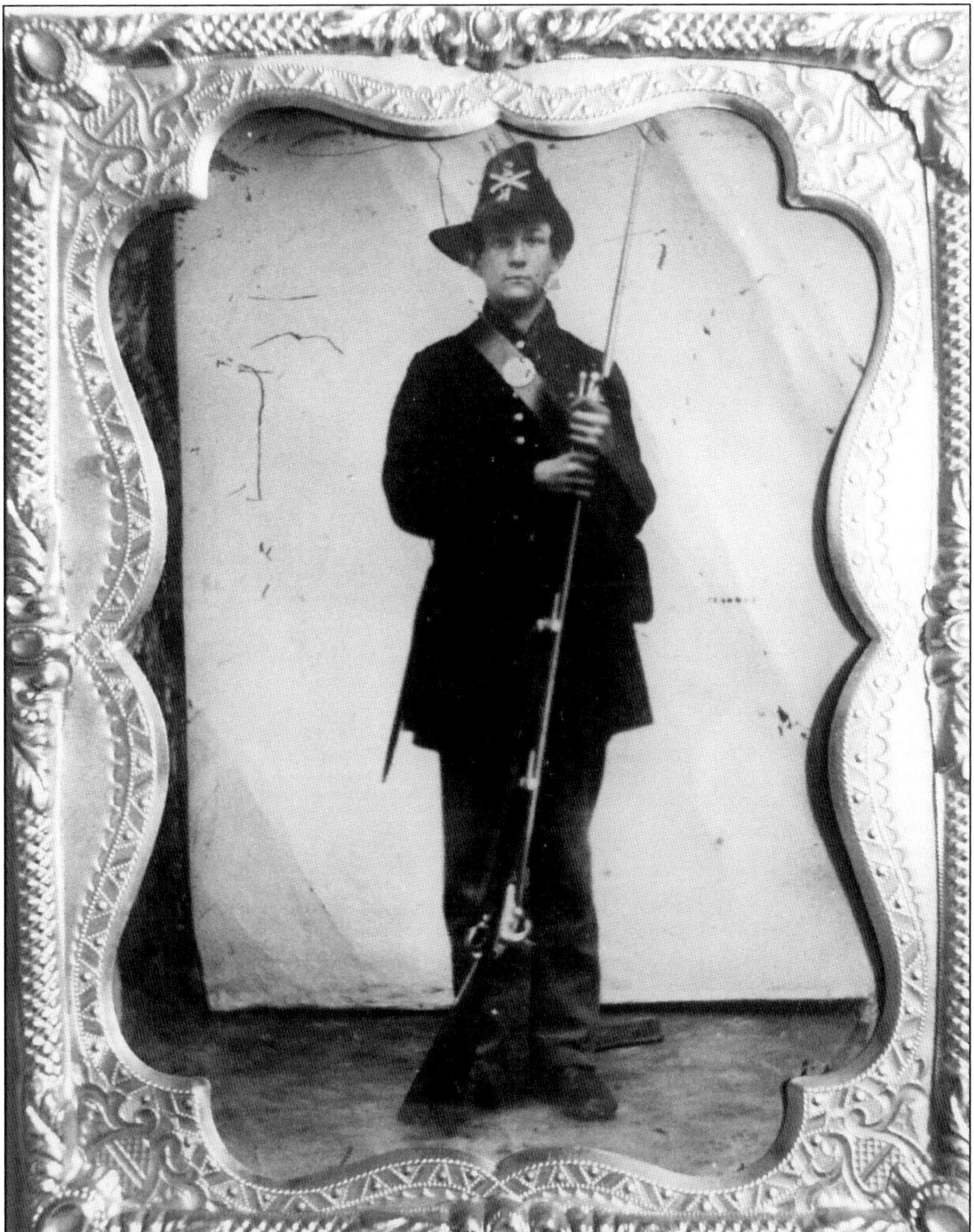

Alonzo A. Rackliff had this Ferrotype portrait made of himself following his mustering into Company K of the Second Heavy Artillery in December 1863. The negative image of these "tintype" plates is evidenced by the backward lock on his rifle and in the reversal of the number and letter on the front of his "Jeff Davis"-style hat. Rackliff lived until 1937, being the last commander of the Danvers Ward Post, Grand Army of the Republic.

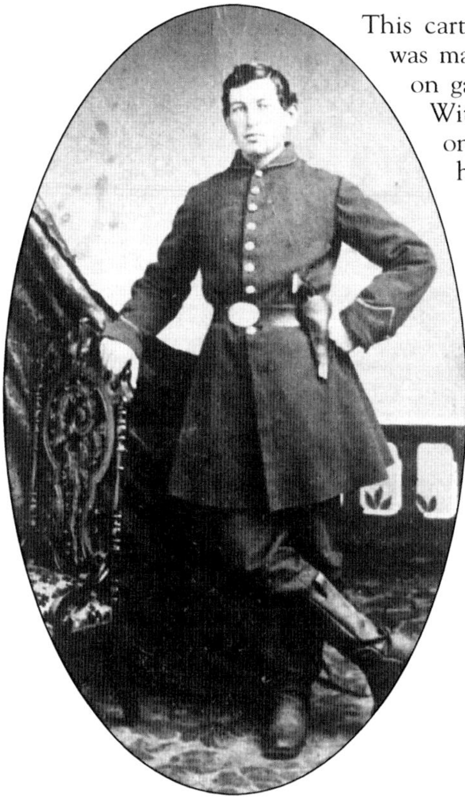

This carte-de-visite photograph of John Pickering Withey was made in Washington, D.C., where he was stationed on garrison duty in 1861 and 1862. In 1864 Sergeant Withey was wounded at Spottsylvania, Virginia, one of 312 casualties during that engagement in his regiment alone.

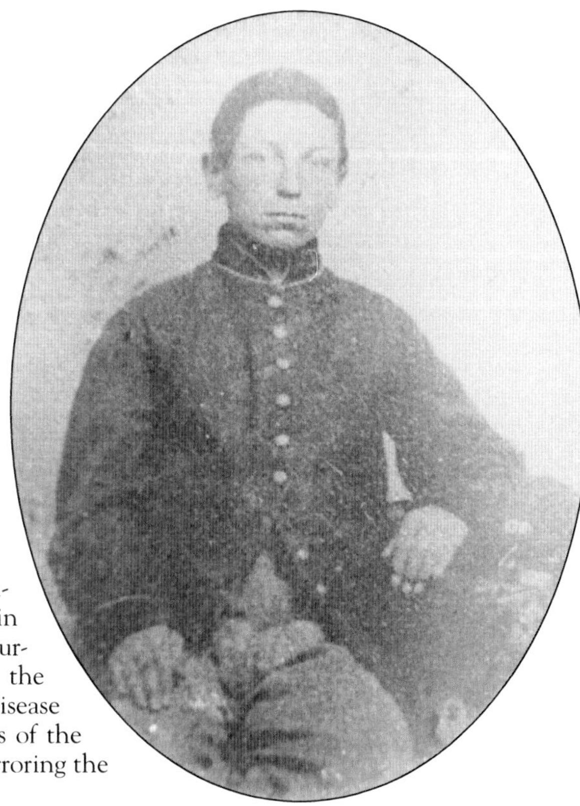

Samuel Pratt Withey was a sixteen-year-old shoemaker when he enlisted in 1862 as a musician. Samuel's forty-four-year-old father, John Withey, joined the 40th Regiment with his son, but died of disease while in service in 1864. Four members of the Withey family fought for the Union, mirroring the sacrifice made by many other families.

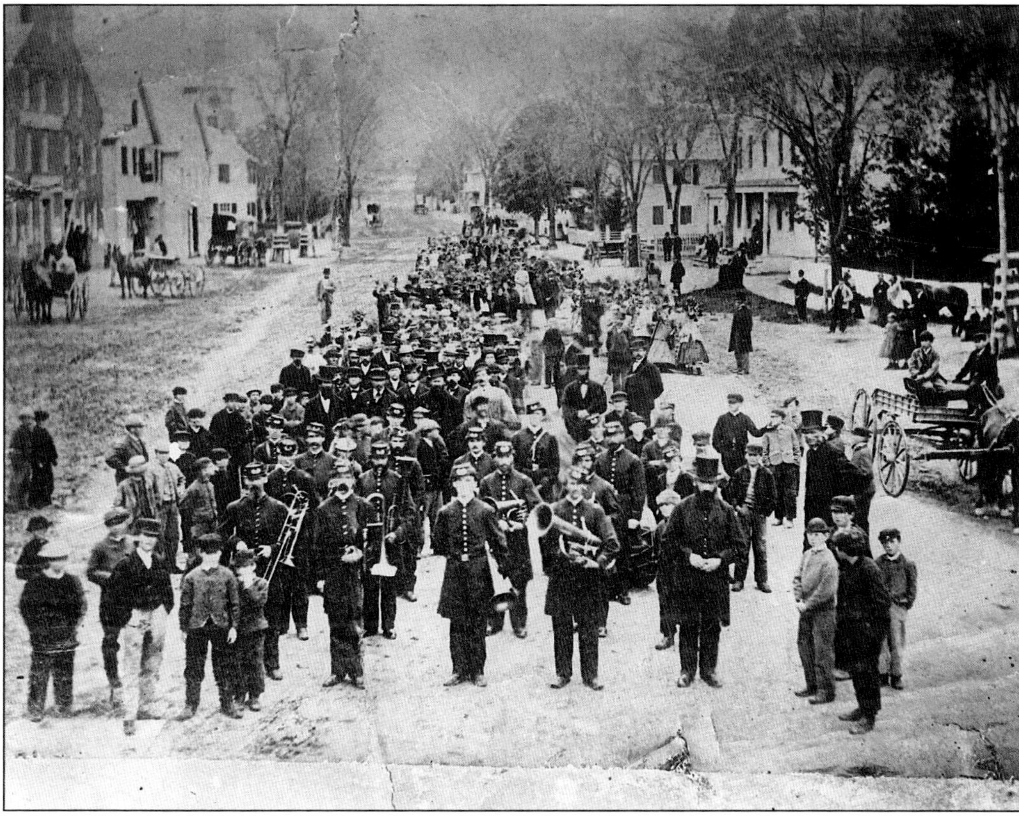

An 1866 view of Danvers Square looking up Maple Street toward Locust. The occasion pictured was Danvers' first Decoration Day observance. A procession composed of the Danvers Brass Band, the board of selectmen, Civil War veterans, a slew of young boys, and women and girls with flower bouquets prepares to march to the Walnut Grove Cemetery to decorate the graves of fallen soldiers.

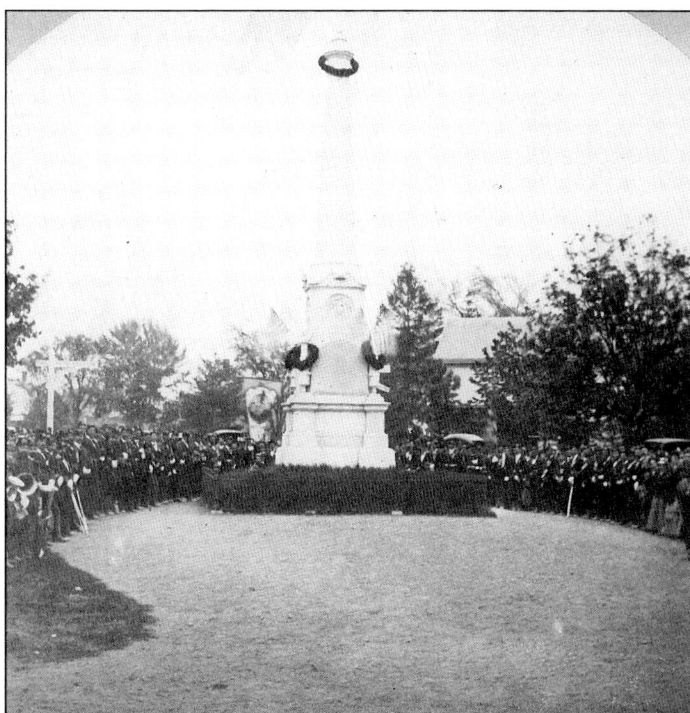

Civil War veterans and others honor their fallen comrades at the monument in front of Danvers Town Hall in this c. 1872 stereograph view.

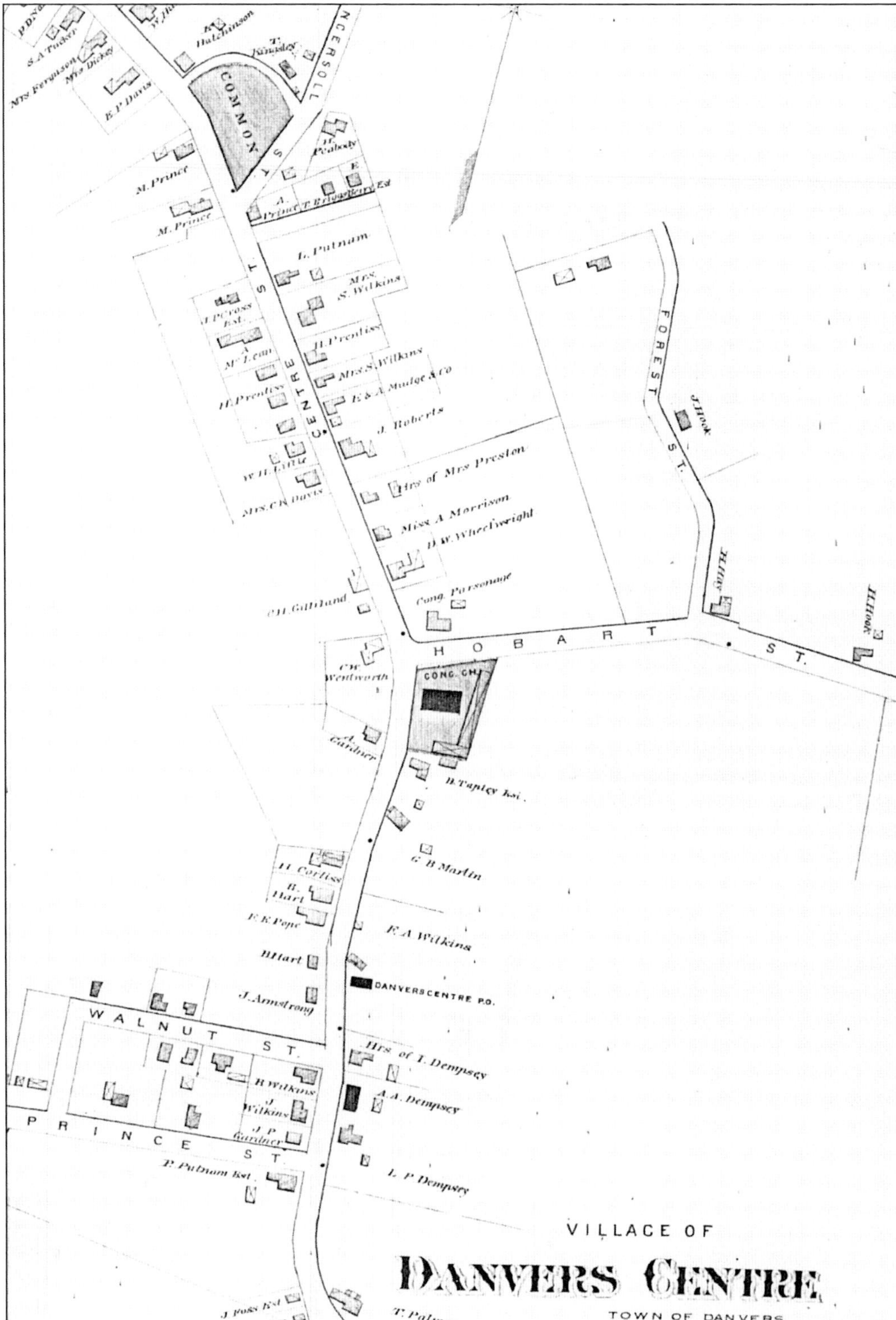

A portion of Danvers Centre (Salem Village) from an 1884 map.

Three

Salem Village

The first territory settled within the environs of present-day Danvers was that area now in and around Centre Street. Occupied by yeoman farmers beginning in the late 1630s, this area was called Salem Village to distinguish it from the Salem Town settlement 5 miles to the east. The first village meetinghouse was built here in 1672, and in March 1692 it was here that the infamous Salem Village witchcraft delusion began. The eight months of accusations and arrests commenced at Reverend Samuel Parris' house, and resulted in the eventual imprisonment of over 150 people and the death by hanging of nineteen.

Danversites of the later half of the nineteenth century were very much aware of the history of the earlier "witch times," and continued to live among the structures and sites associated with this tragic era. Farming and shoe manufacturing were the principal occupations of residents of the area. The old village name "Salem Village" was eventually superseded by the title "Danvers Centre" to differentiate this neighborhood from other town villages. By the 1890s many began calling this area "Danvers Highlands" to distinguish it from the then current commercial "center" of town, which had shifted to Danvers Plains.

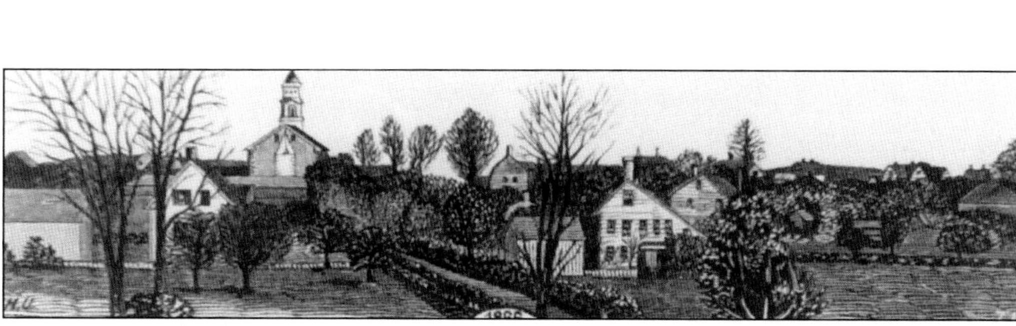

An 1866 view of Hobart Street with the First Church in the background.

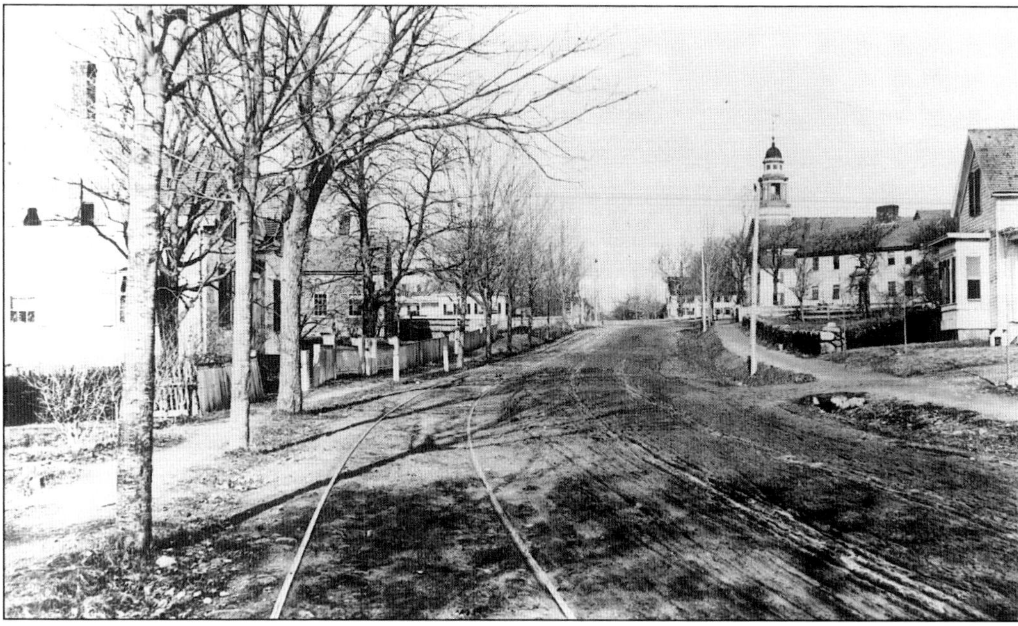

Looking up Centre Street in this 1888 view, one can see the *c.* 1681 Thomas Haines house on the right with its center chimney, and the steeple of the First Church jutting toward the sky.

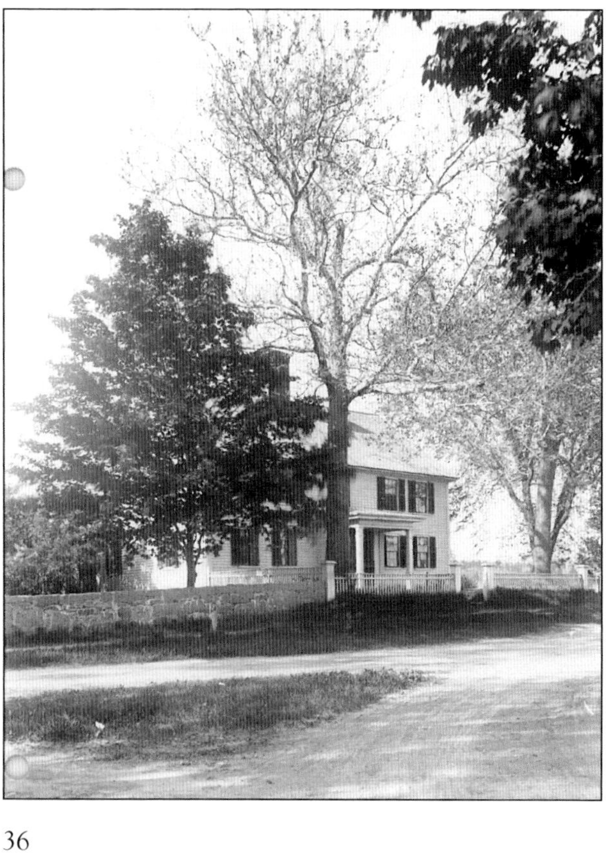

Originally part of the Nathaniel Ingersoll ordinary where 1692 witch examinations were conducted, this house at 199 Hobart Street was renovated and enlarged in about 1753. During the nineteenth century it served as the minister's parsonage to the First Church.

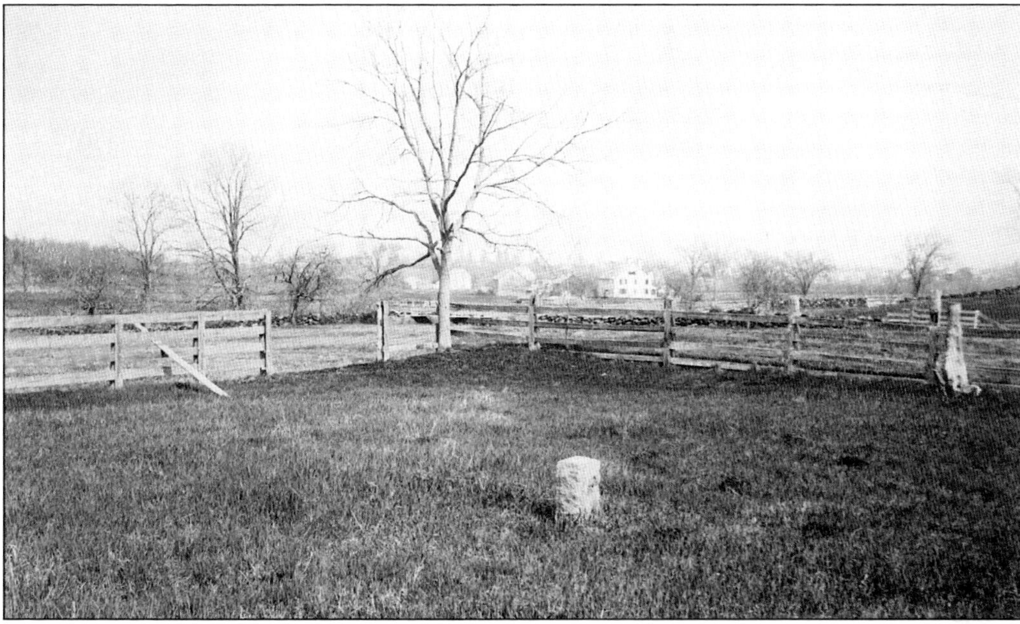

The granite post in this 1890s photograph marks the site of the 1681–1784 First Church parsonage. Here in 1692 began the infamous Salem Village witchcraft delusion in Reverend Samuel Parris' house. This site behind 67 Centre Street was excavated in 1970, and is now a town park.

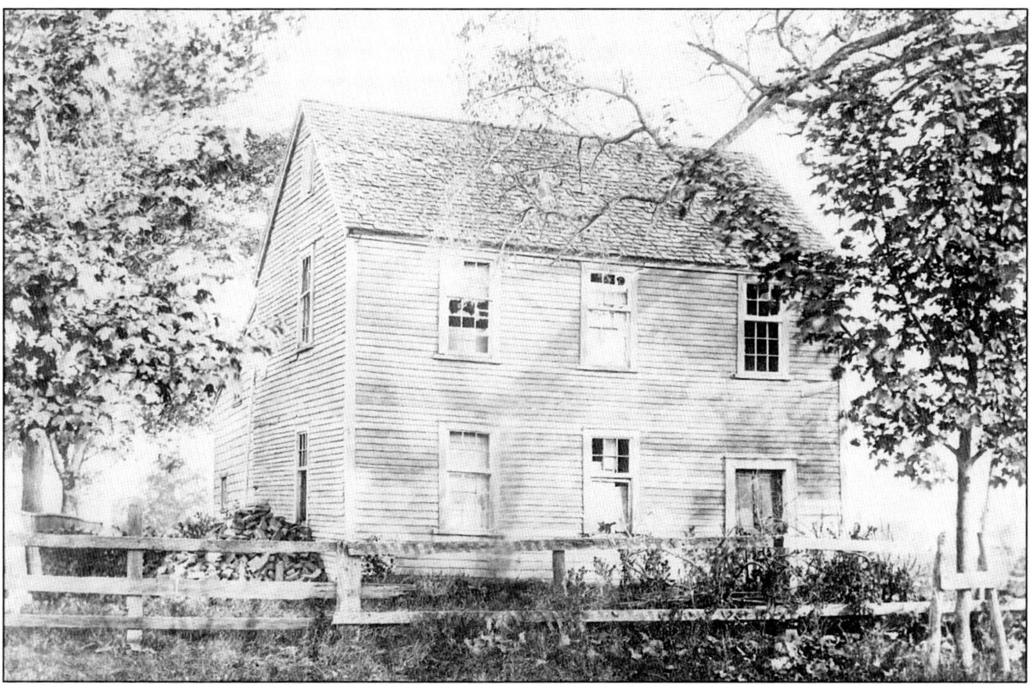

In 1734 an addition was built onto the 1681 parsonage for use as a minister's study. When the main house was torn down in 1784, this addition was eventually moved to another site. It was popularly known as the "witch house" even though it was built after the witch times. The structure is no longer standing.

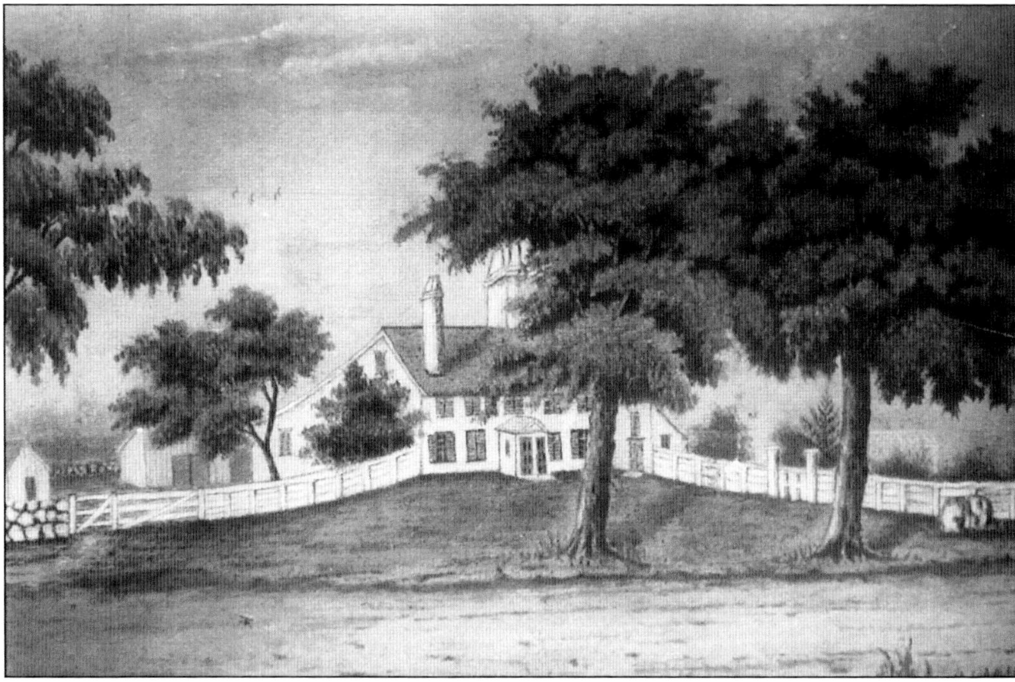

An 1866 painting of the Holten house at 177 Holten Street. Originally built in 1670, this was the 1692 home of Sarah Holten, who gave testimony against witch suspect Rebecca Nurse.

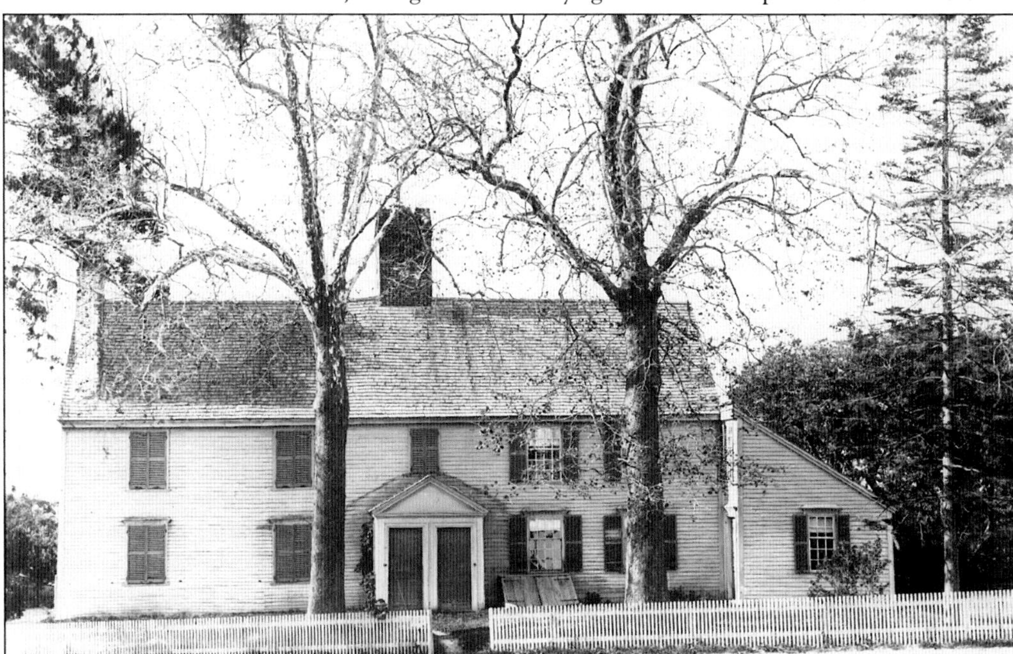

A late-nineteenth-century photograph of the Holten house. In the eighteenth century this was the home of Dr. Samuel Holten, a patriot of the Revolution who served as president of the Continental Congress and was a signer of the 1778 Articles of Confederation. The house is now preserved by the General Israel Putnam Chapter, Daughters of the American Revolution.

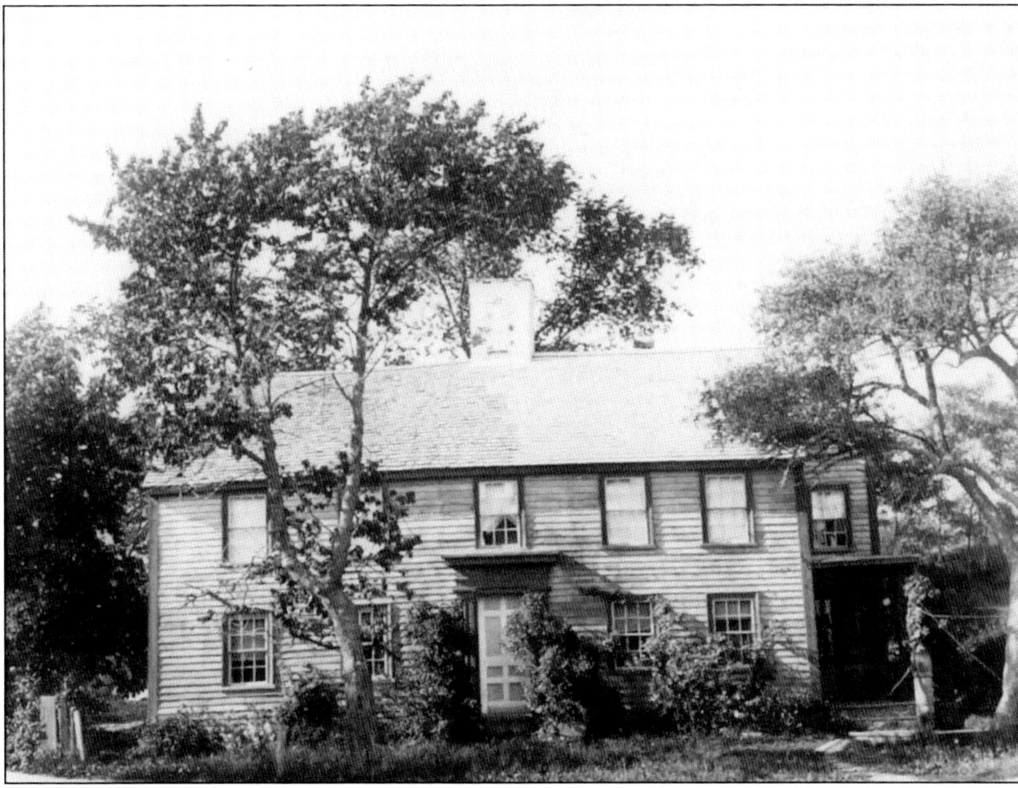

The 1692 home of John Holten, cooper. Located at 27 Centre Street, the house exhibits a "Beverly projection" to the right of the main house.

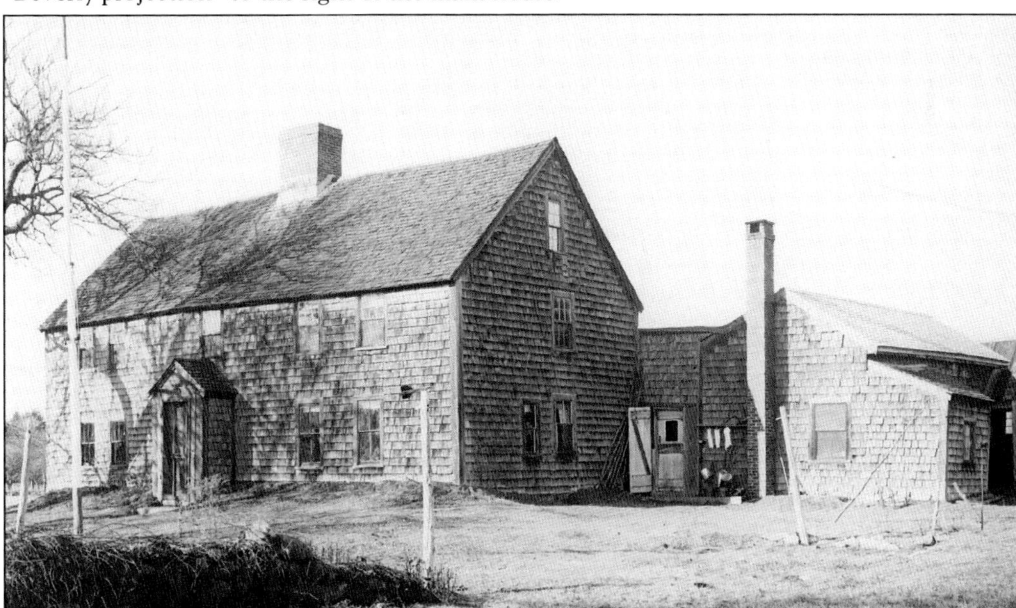

The *c.* 1700 "First Period" Ambrose Hutchinson house. This dwelling sits beside Forest Street, which was an ancient Indian trail.

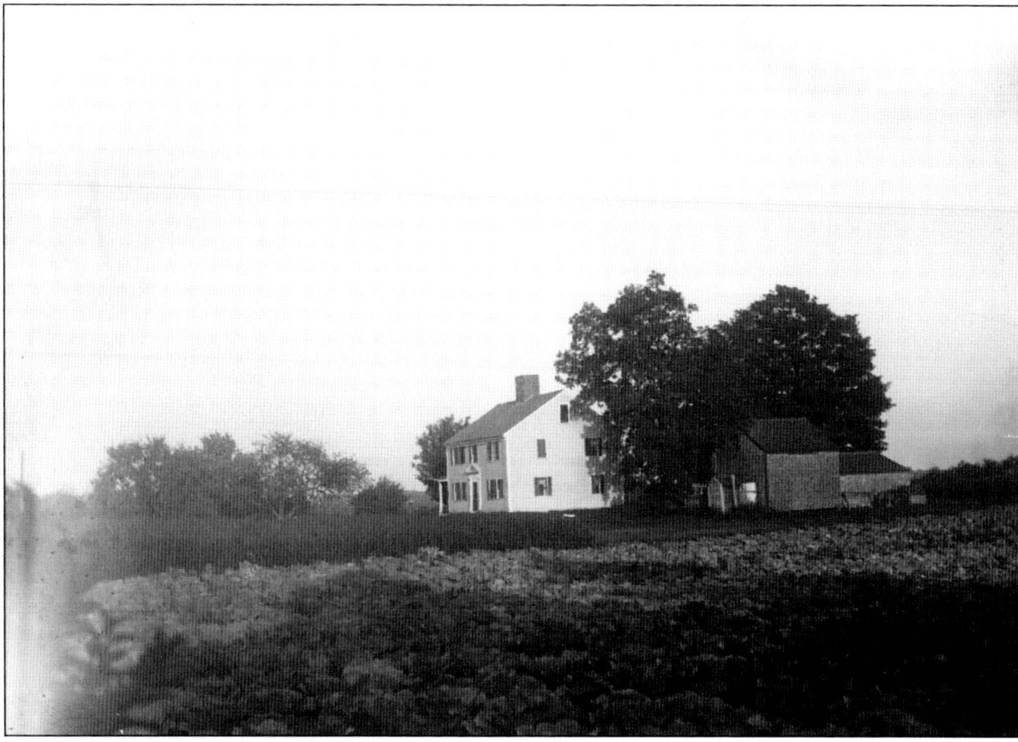

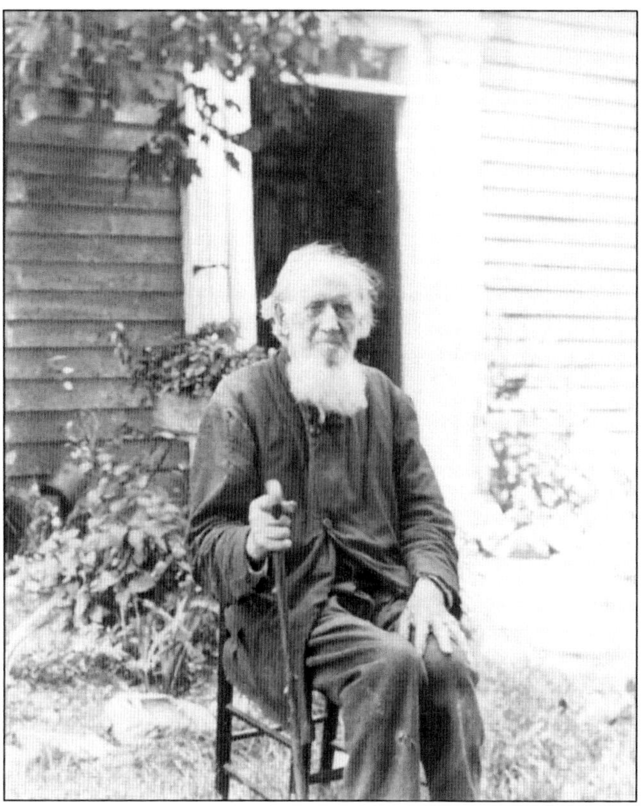

Various branches of the Pope family had once settled on extensive farms in the area surrounding the Newburyport Turnpike (Route 1) and the Essex Turnpike (Route 114). This house, which is no longer standing, was built in 1802 by Amos Pope, a noted mathematician, publisher of almanacs, and farmer.

Jasper Pope (1802–1887) rests in a favorite chair in front of his eighteenth-century farmstead, which was located just west of the Newburyport Turnpike.

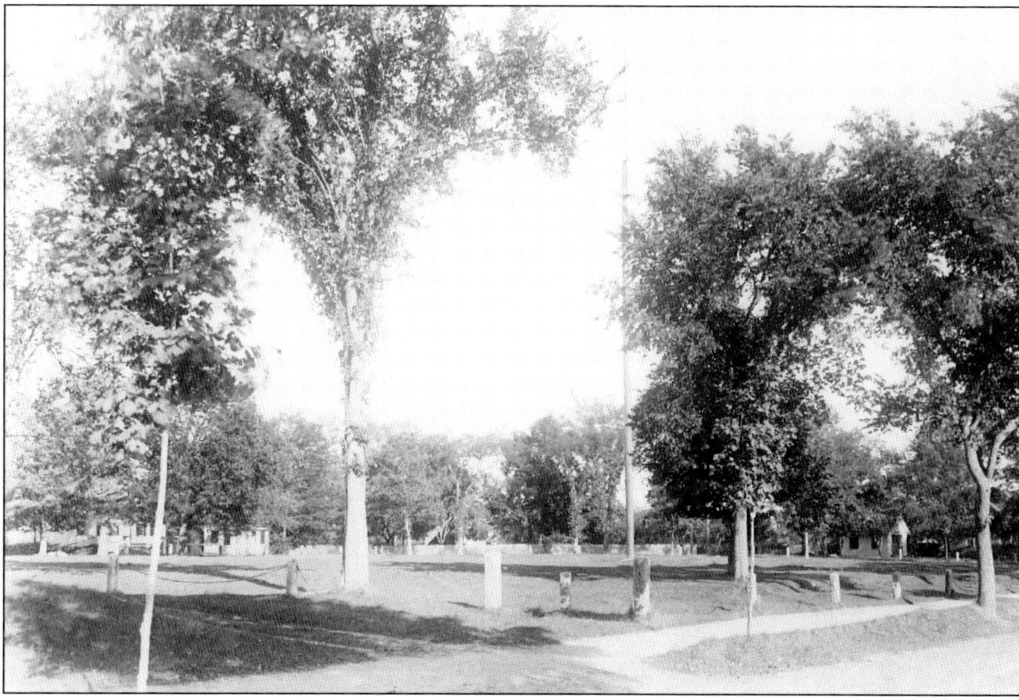

The Village Training Field at 85 Centre Street was left in 1719 to the inhabitants of Salem Village by Nathaniel Ingersoll. Here Danvers Minute Men gathered to march to the Lexington Alarm of April 19, 1775. At the right of this 1890 photograph the Fire Company Number 5 Hose House can be seen.

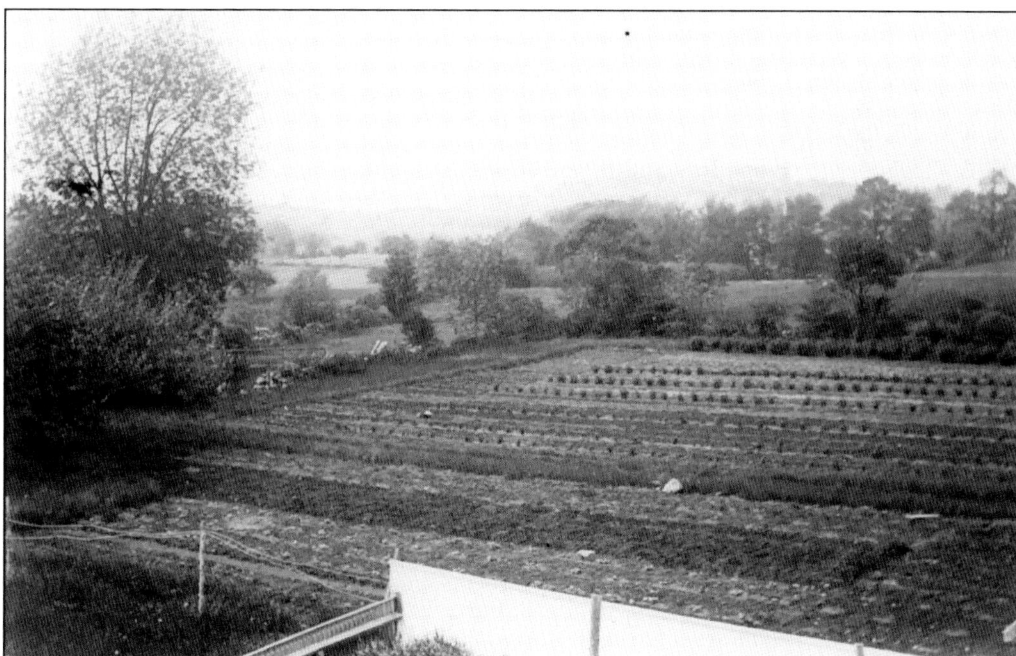

This glass-plate northwest view of the backyard of a residence on Centre Street reveals a well-tended vegetable garden.

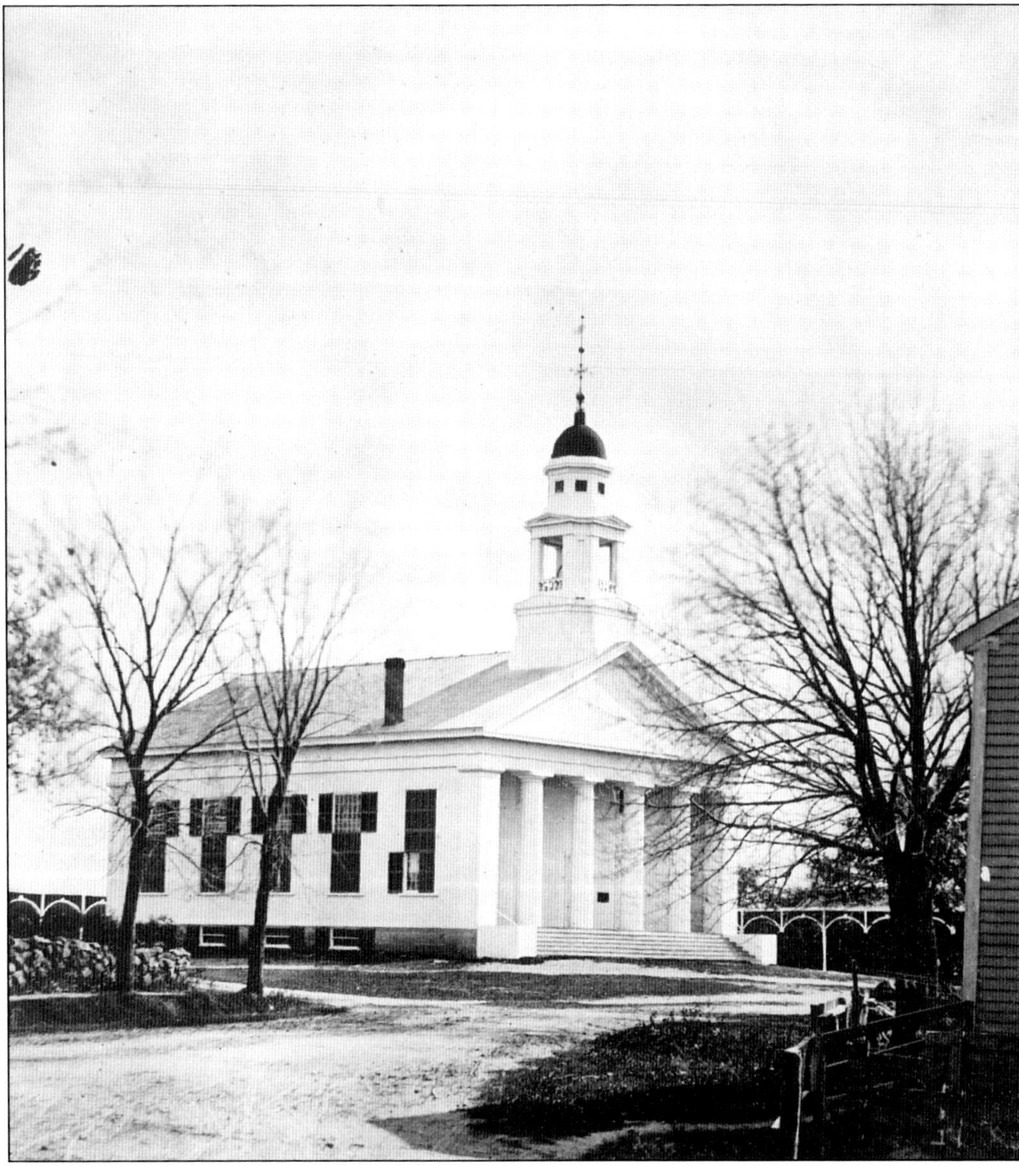

The spiritual and cultural center of Salem Village was the First Church, Congregational. Religious services had commenced at the village in 1672 and in 1689 an independent covenanted church was established. This Greek Revival-style edifice on the corner of Centre and Hobart Streets was the fifth meetinghouse of the congregation and the fourth on this site. This structure was dedicated in November 1839, and in this 1866 photograph one can see carriage sheds on either side of the building.

A floor plan of the 1839 church indicates pew locations and costs, with the names filled in to note the families who purchased them.

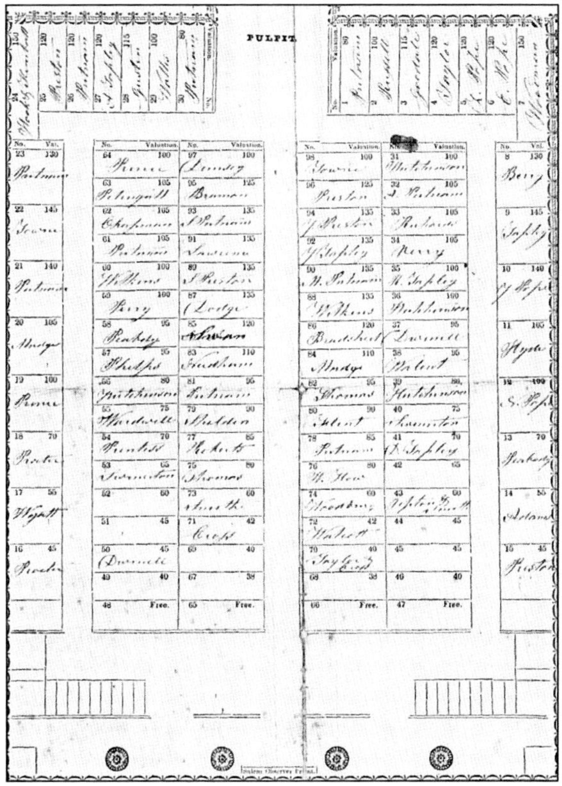

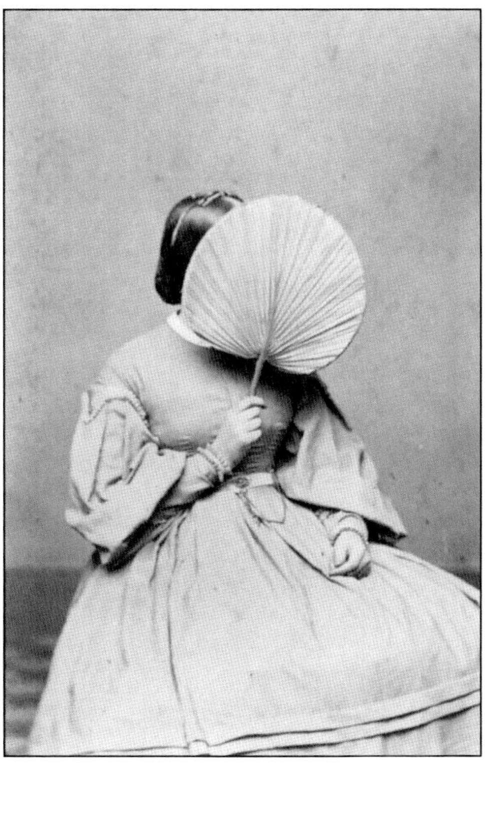

A curious early 1860s carte-de-visite photograph of a camera shy Mary Braman. Mrs. Braman (1805–1898) was the wife of Reverend Milton Parker Braman, who ministered to the church from 1826 to 1861.

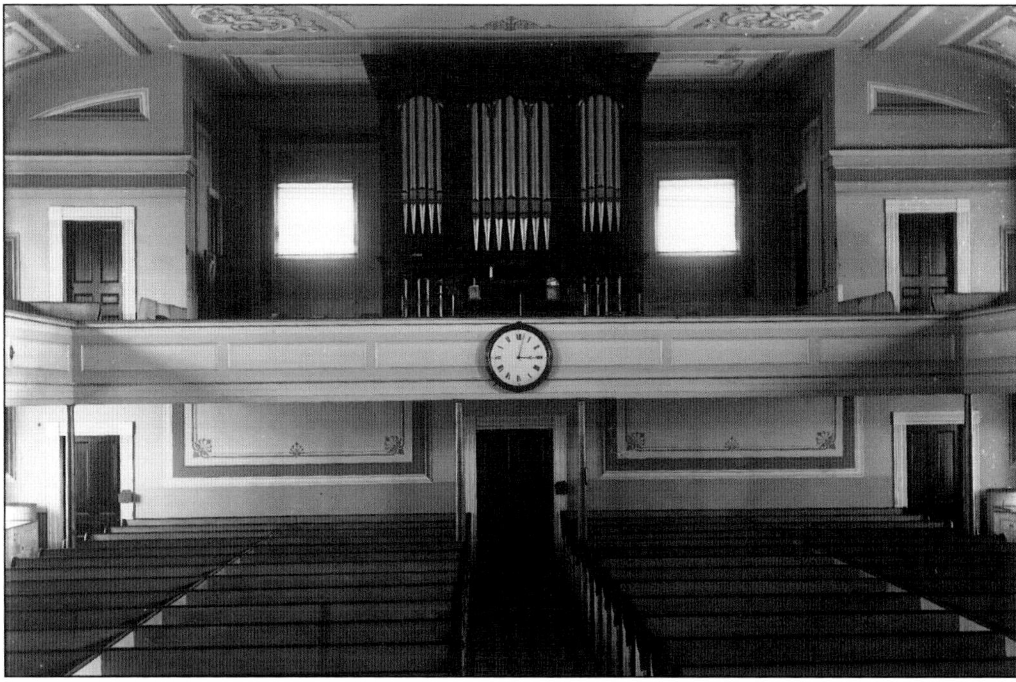

Looking toward the church entrance, this *c.* 1880 photograph of the First Church reveals the interior prior to an 1888 remodeling. In January 1890 a spectacular fire destroyed the church.

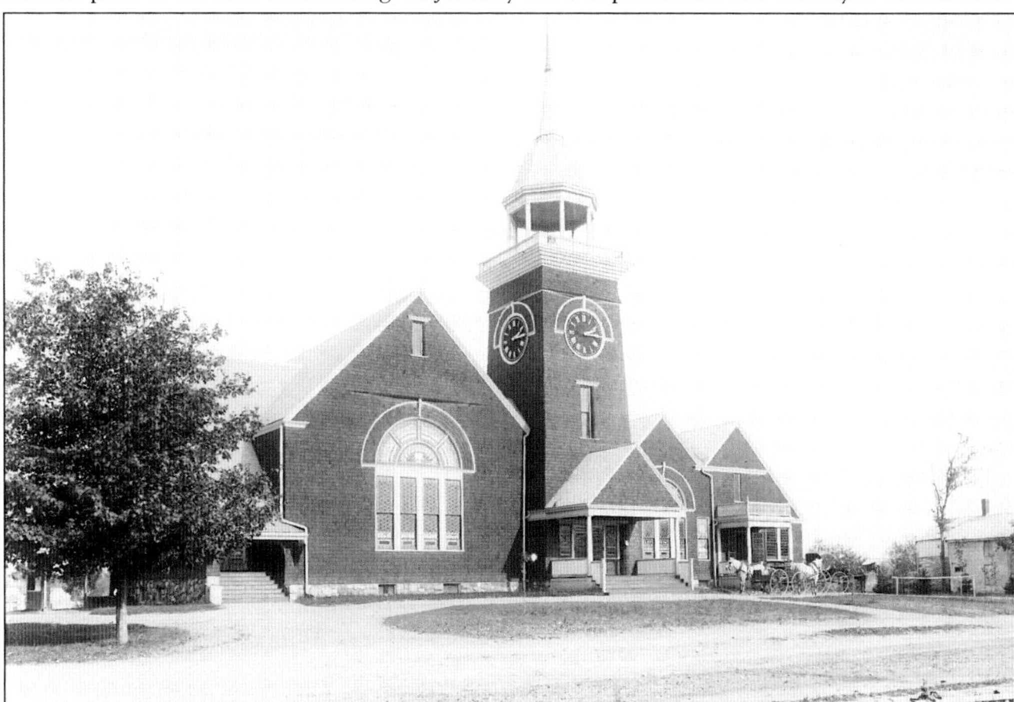

The sixth edifice occupied by the First Church was this shingle-style building erected in 1890 from the plans of architect Arthur Vinal. In May 1978 this church suffered a fire and was torn down.

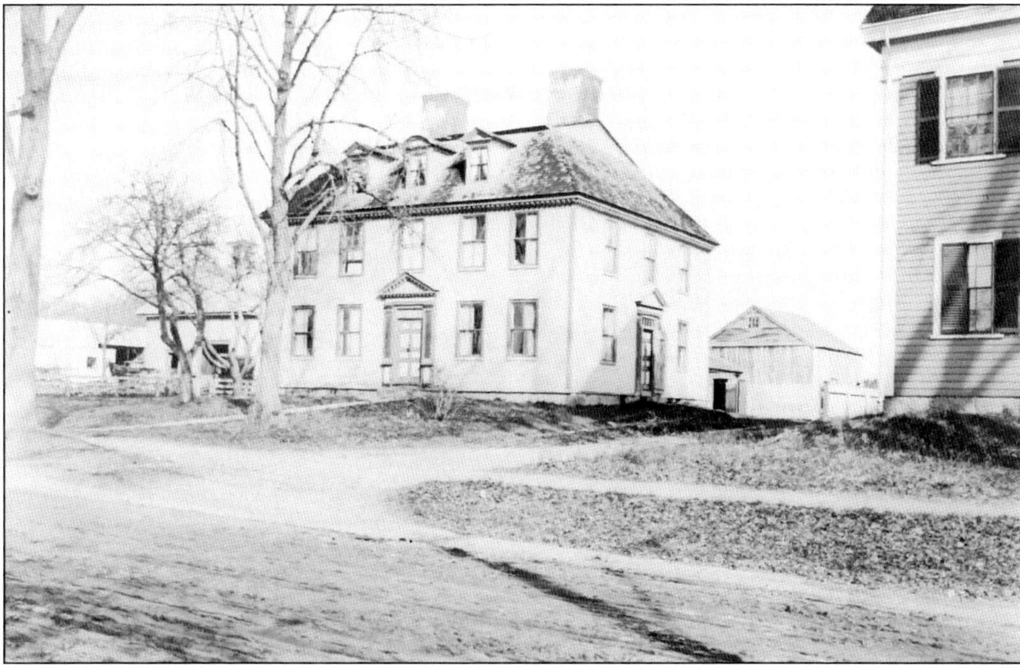

Built in the Georgian style in 1784 for Reverend Benjamin Wadsworth, this gable-on-hip-roofed house at 73 Centre Street replaced the old parsonage, which had been associated with the witchcraft events.

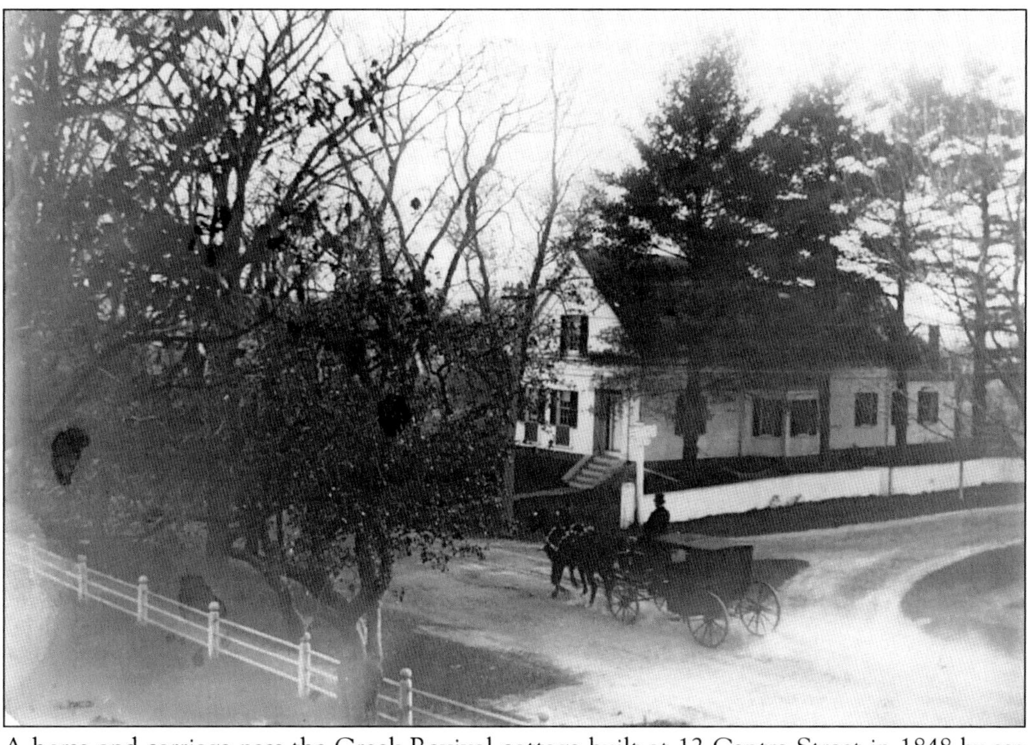

A horse and carriage pass the Greek Revival cottage built at 12 Centre Street in 1848 by sea captain Philemon Putnam.

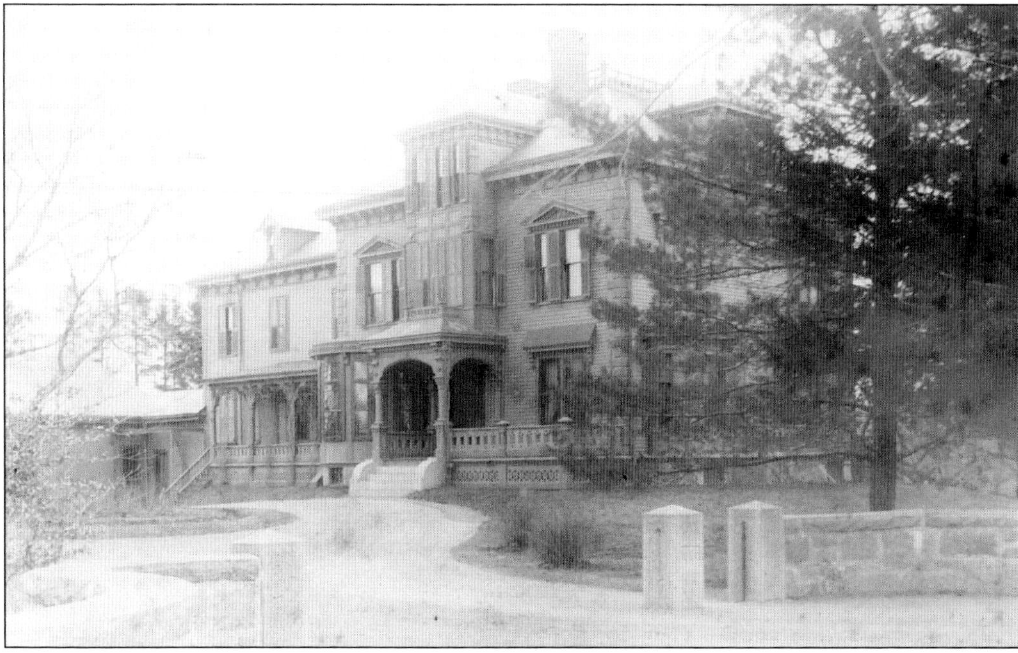

Augustus Mudge, shoe manufacturer and state senator, built this imposing residence in 1880 on Centre Street. Called "Stonewall," the house was demolished in the late 1960s when Route I-95 cut through Danvers.

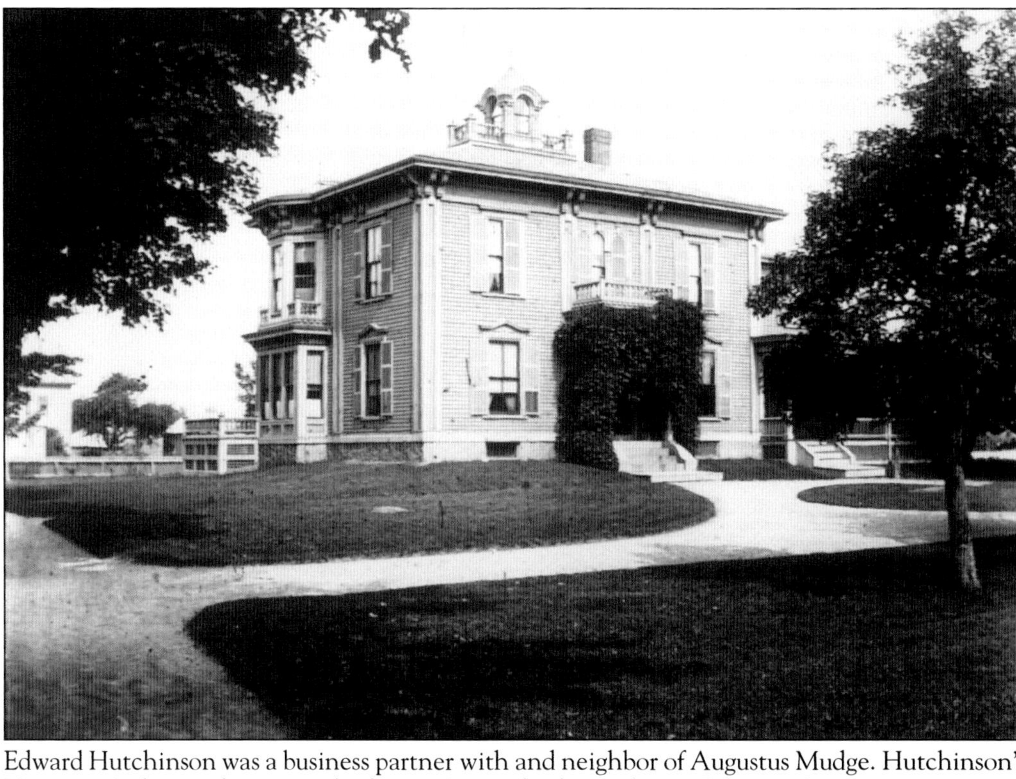

Edward Hutchinson was a business partner with and neighbor of Augustus Mudge. Hutchinson's Victorian Italianate house was built in 1878, and is located at 105 Centre Street.

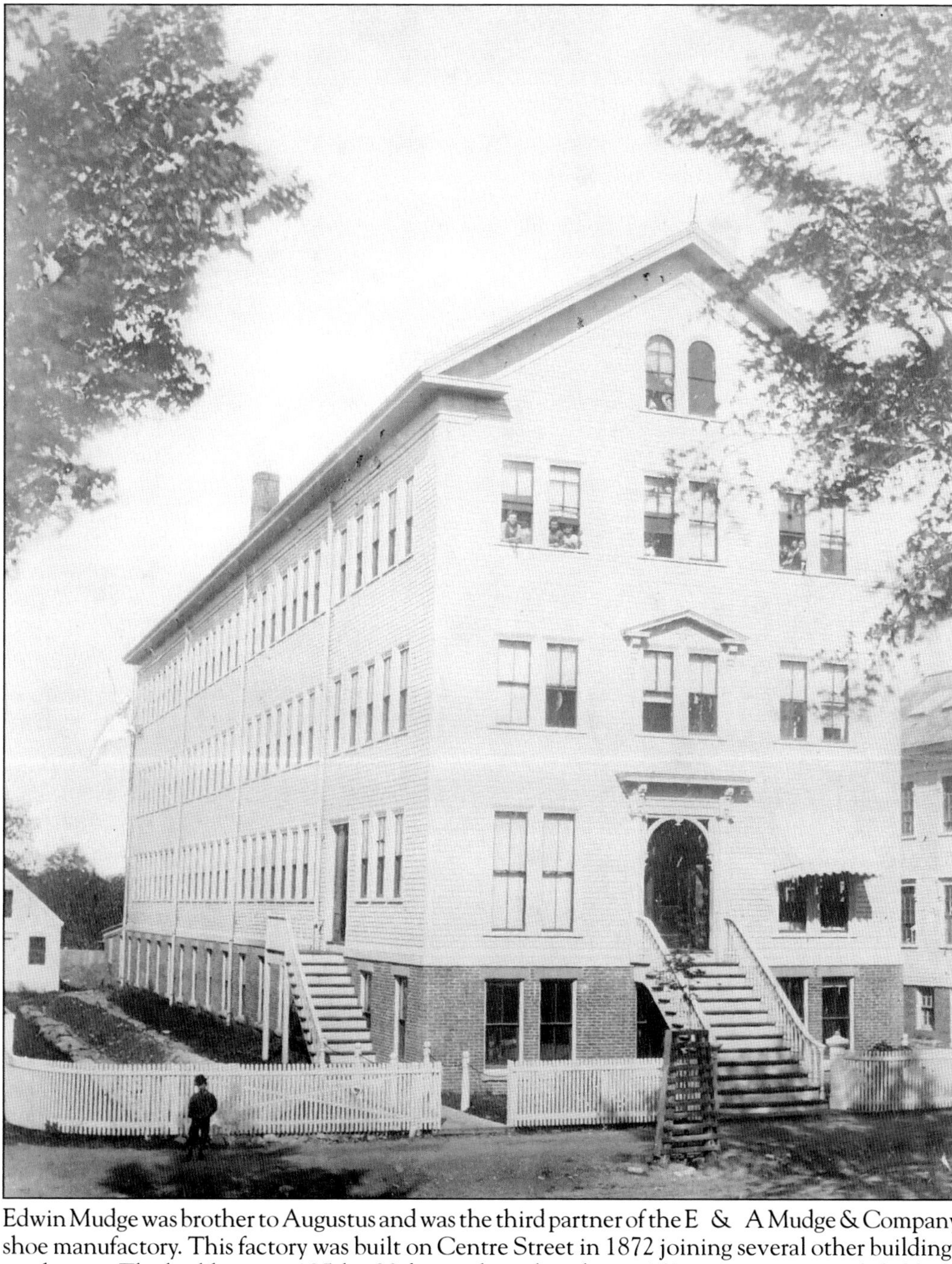

Edwin Mudge was brother to Augustus and was the third partner of the E & A Mudge & Company shoe manufactory. This factory was built on Centre Street in 1872 joining several other buildings on the site. The building was 125-by-33 feet and employed over 150 men, women, and children. Adults could earn between $1 and $4 per day, and the daily output was 1,500 pairs of shoes, chiefly ladies side-lace boots. This building caught fire and burned down on June 4, 1885.

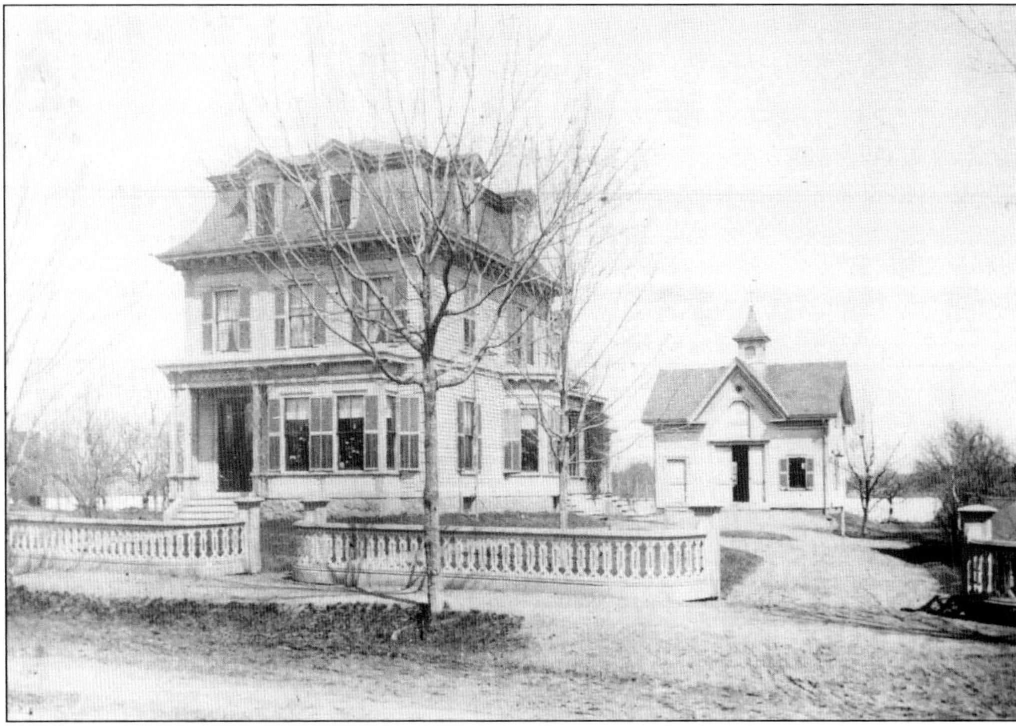

Though some houses in the Centre Street neighborhood were grand like the 1872 Second Empire-style house of Alfred Hutchinson (above), most were fairly modest dwellings like the house at 209 Centre Street (below).

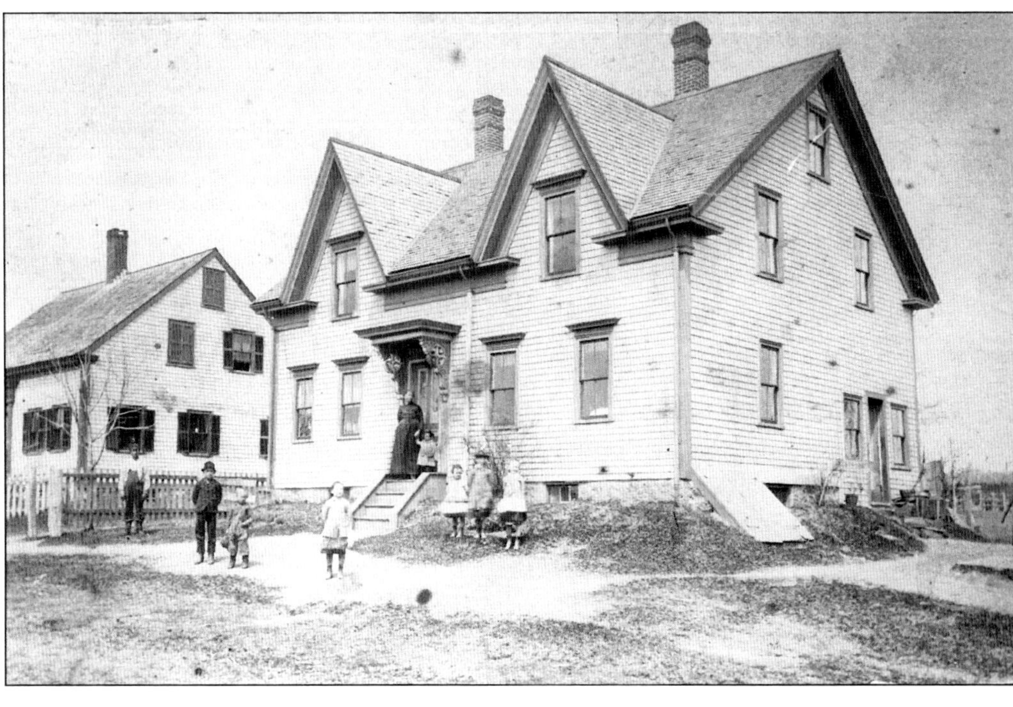

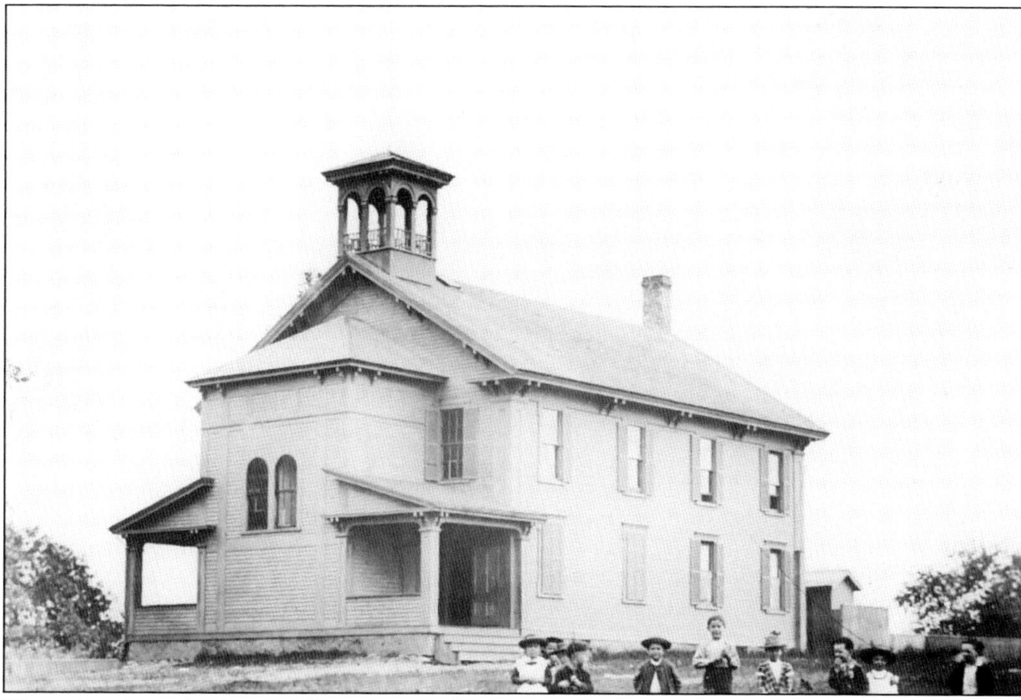

This school was built in 1857 near 1 Collins Street, but remained unused due to controversy between the villages at Danvers Centre and Tapleyville over the need for a new school district. It was moved in 1865, used as a shoe factory for a time, and was eventually converted to a residence at 53 Locust Street.

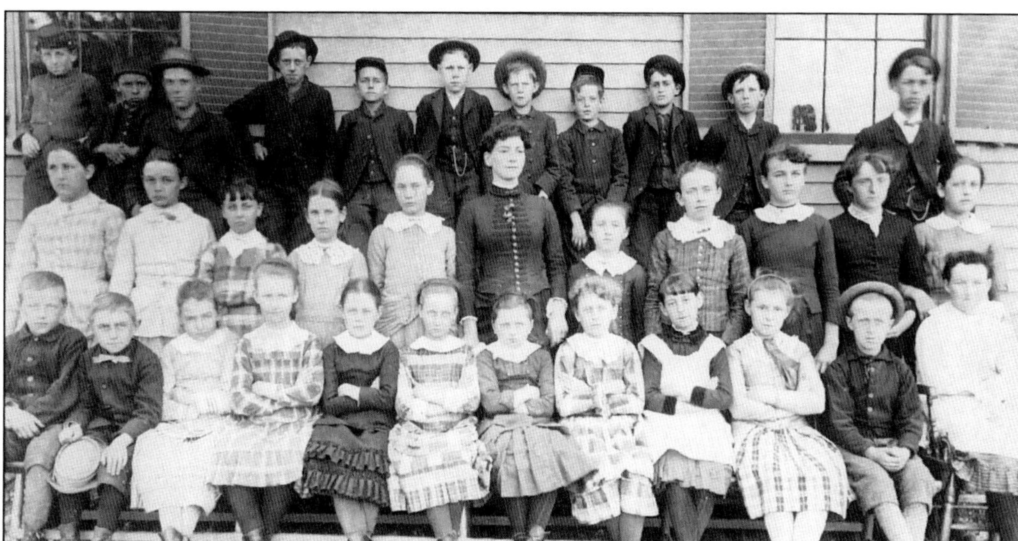

This is an 1870s class photograph of the grammar schoolchildren in District Number 5 in Danvers Centre.

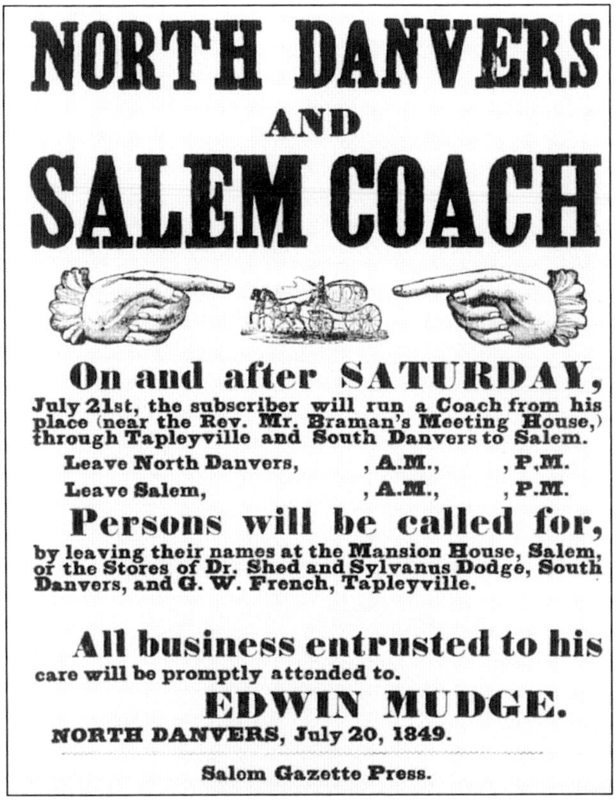

An 1849 broadside advertisement for the North Danvers and Salem Coach.

This rare one-sixth-plate Daguerreotype was made in the 1850s. Taken near the front of the First Church (at right), the subject is a Concord-type coach with lettering on the side which reads, "Tapleyville, Danvers & Salem."

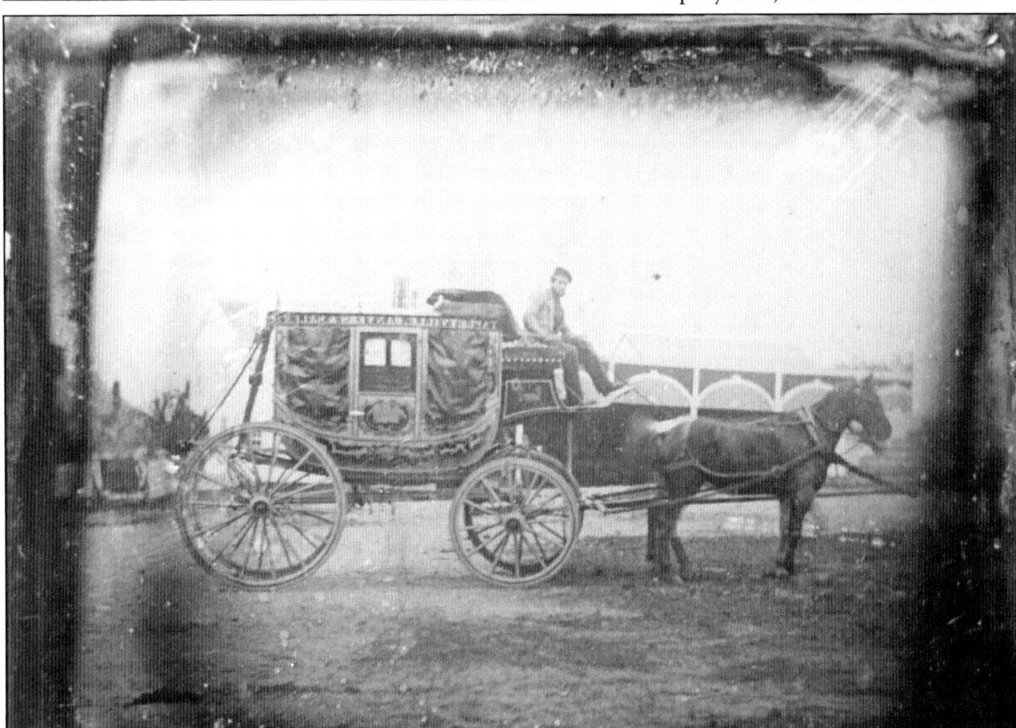

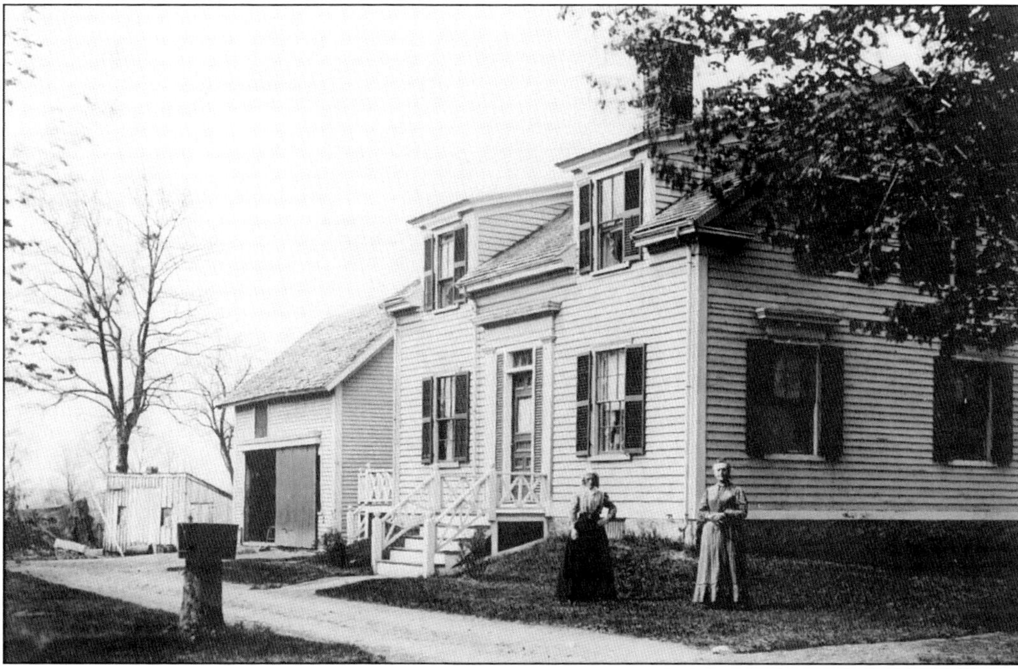

A modest 1854 Greek Revival house at 100 Centre Street, shown here in the 1890s.

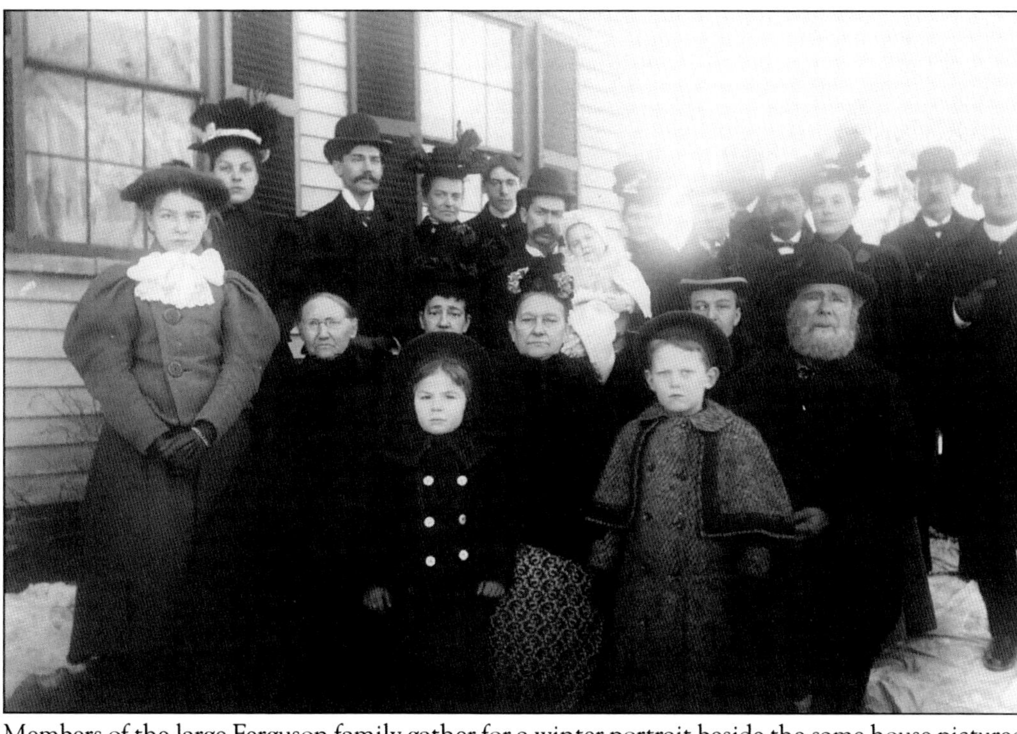

Members of the large Ferguson family gather for a winter portrait beside the same house pictured at the top of the page.

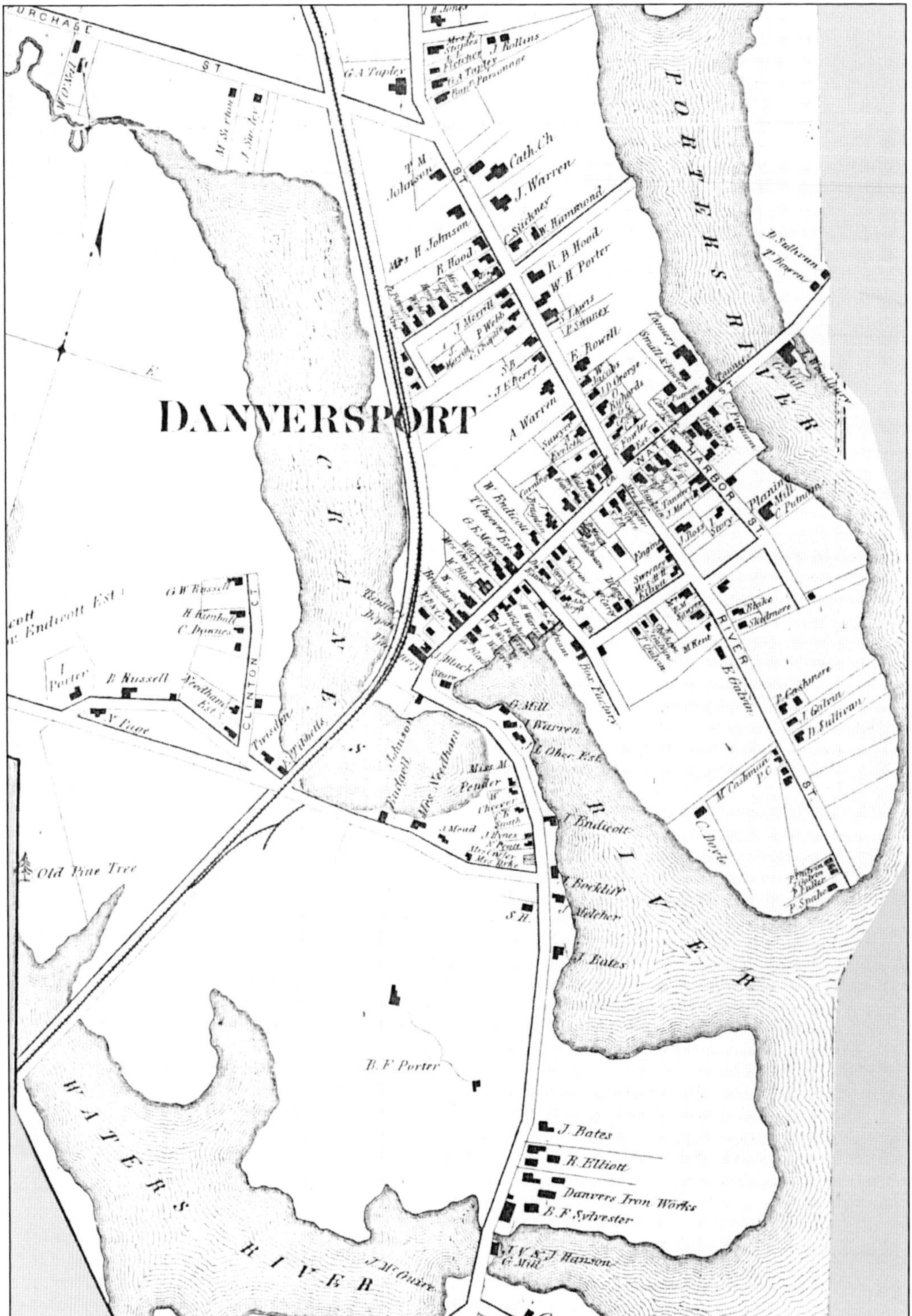

A map of 1872 Danversport.

Four

Danversport

For generations before European settlement this area was an encampment site for Native Americans. In 1632 John Endecott, the first governor of the Massachusetts Bay Colony, was granted many acres of land here and established his extensive Orchard Farm. The three saltwater rivers—the Porter, Crane, and Waters—were used by settlers for travel, trade, and as a food source.

By the 1750s the first of many tidal mills was built upon the riverbank, quickly followed by a new road and bridges which linked North Danvers to Salem. Understanding the economic advantage of this important route to Salem and the ocean, inhabitants of what became known as "New Mills Village" agreed to pay for the costly maintenance of this road system so as not to burden their fellow Danvers townsmen. The late eighteenth and the early nineteenth century saw the prospering of shipbuilding, brick manufacturing, and leather and wood processing here. Just before the new railroad system arrived, "Danversport," as it was now being called, was receiving over 150 cargo-laden schooners and sloops annually. Huge amounts of bricks and locally grown produce were shipped from the wharves of Danversport. By the end of the nineteenth century the old Yankee-English stock was being supplemented by newer waves of immigrants from southern Europe, many of whom found work in the brick and the rapidly growing leather and tanning industries in this section of town.

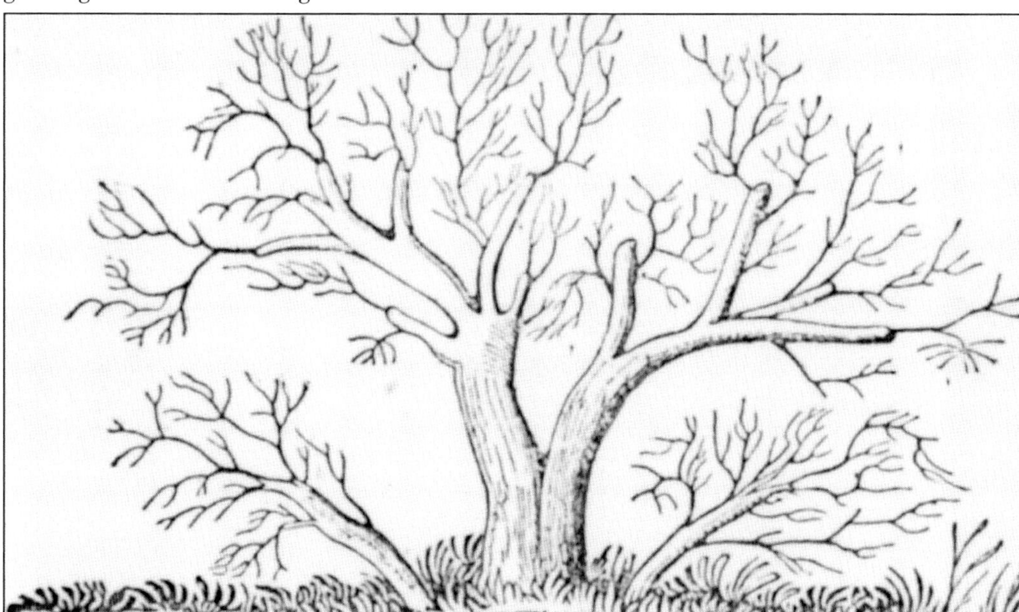

A woodcut engraving from the 1840s of the John Endecott pear tree.

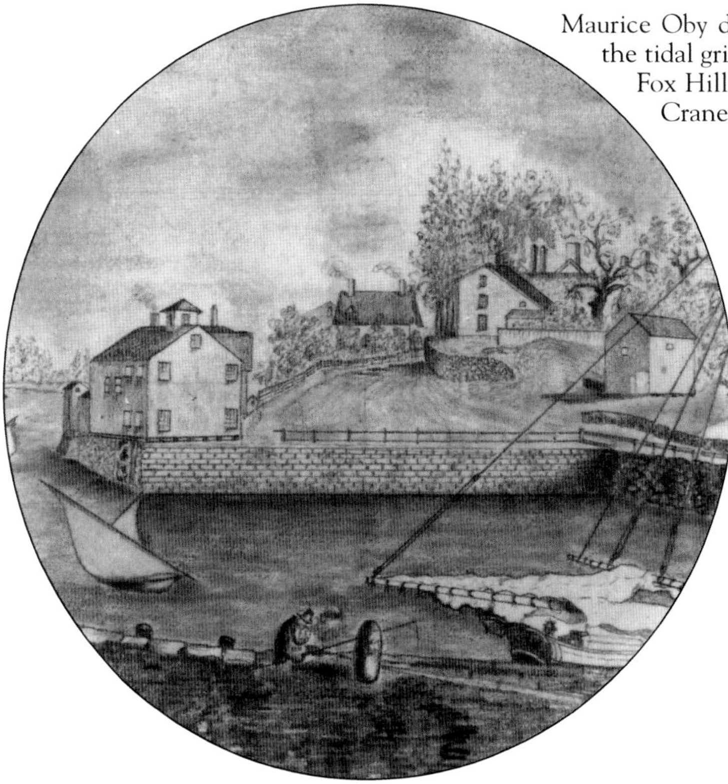

Maurice Oby drew this c. 1853 sketch of the tidal gristmill on Water Street with Fox Hill in the background and the Crane River in the foreground.

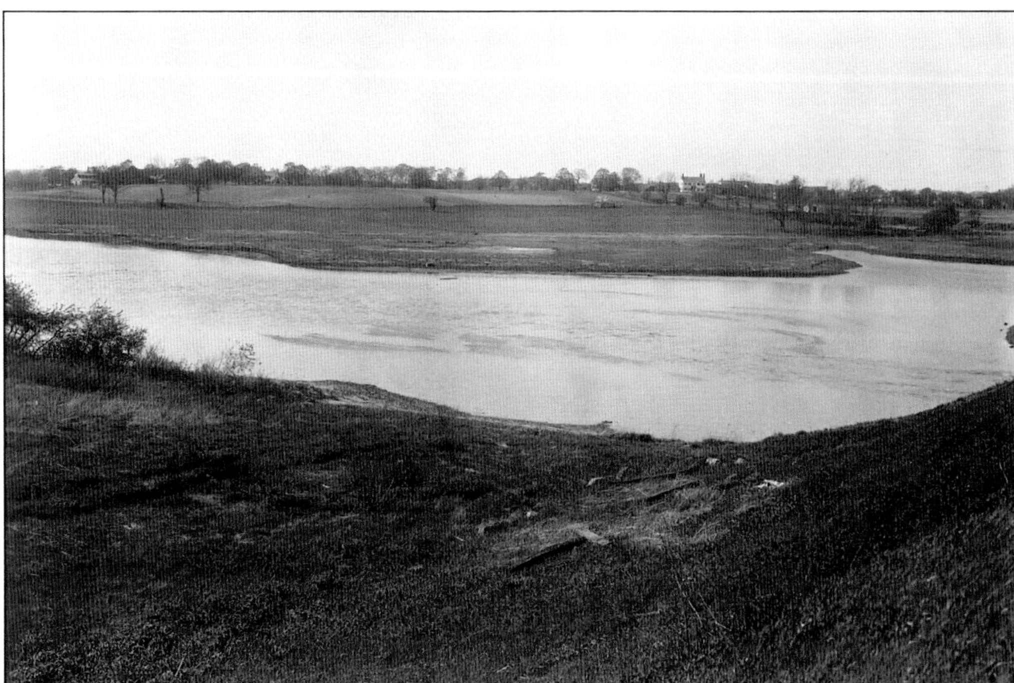

This is a view looking northeast across the Waters River toward the site of Governor Endecott's original house.

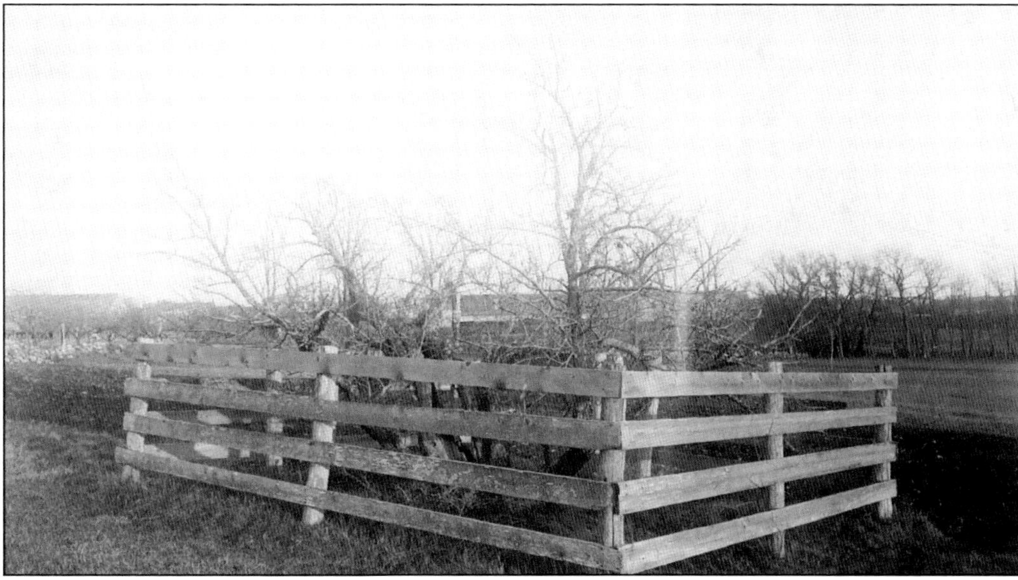

Photographer E.W. Merrill took this shot in 1894 of the Endecott pear tree. A survivor from Endecott's c. 1632 orchard, the tree was (and still is) cherished as a living link to the seventeenth century.

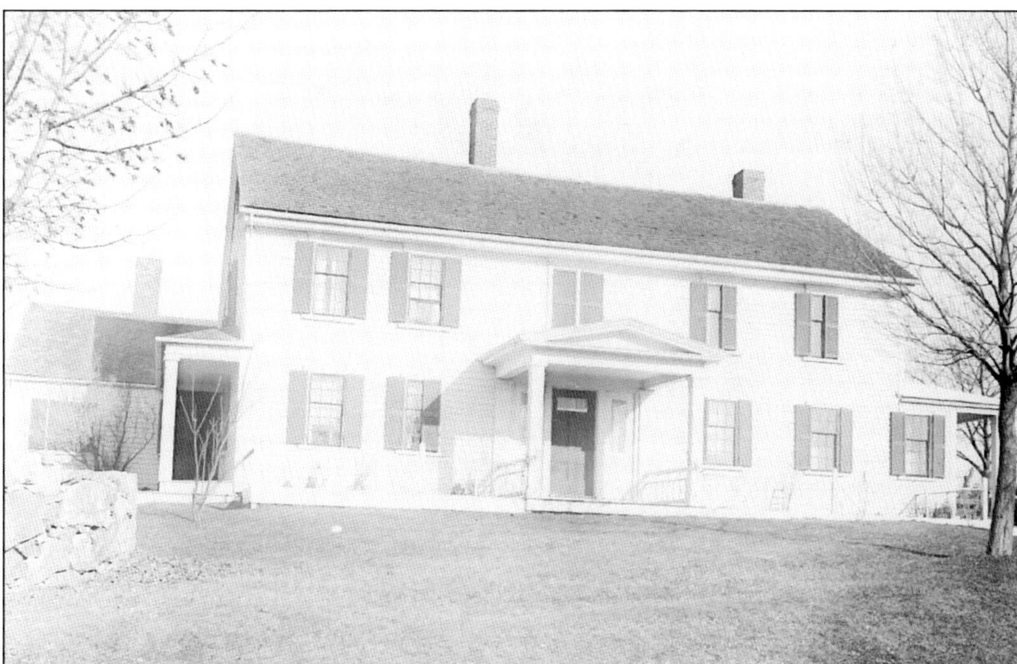

The c. 1681 home of Zerubbabel Endecott, physician son of Governor Endecott, stood on Endicott Street until 1973. The frame to this "First Period" house is now preserved at the Nurse Homestead at 149 Pine Street.

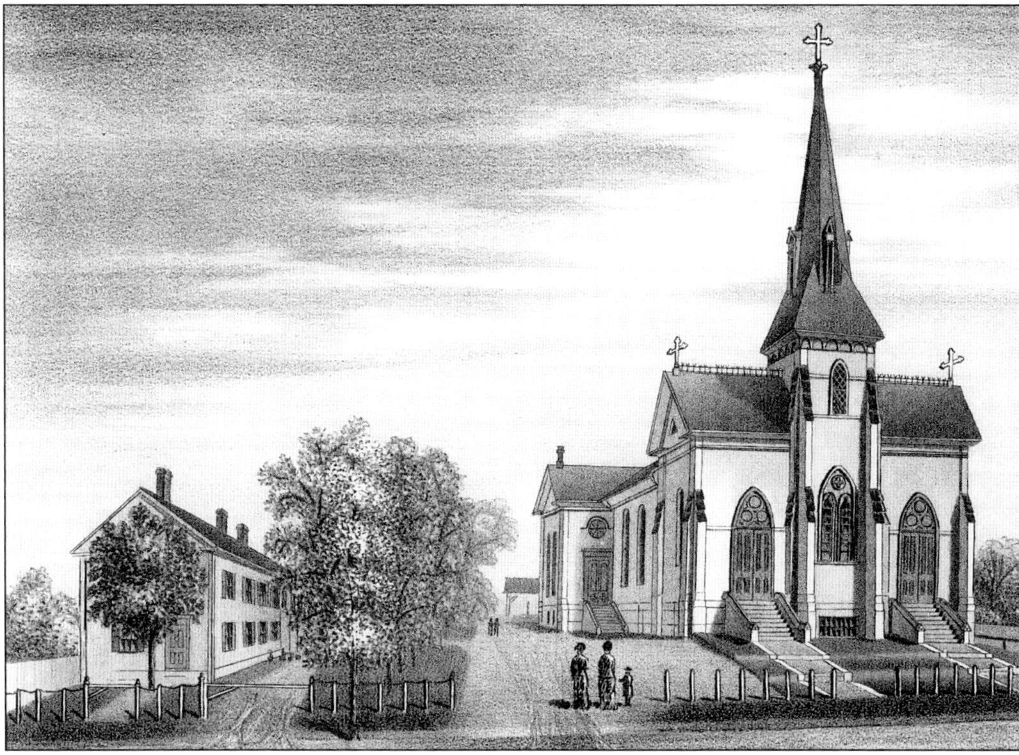

An 1884 engraving of the church on High Street, originally built in 1833 for use by the Universalist congregation. This was the location of many anti-slavery meetings. In 1859 the church became the home of the Roman Catholic community and was named St. Mary of the Annunciation. In the 1930s the structure was torn down to make way for Route 128.

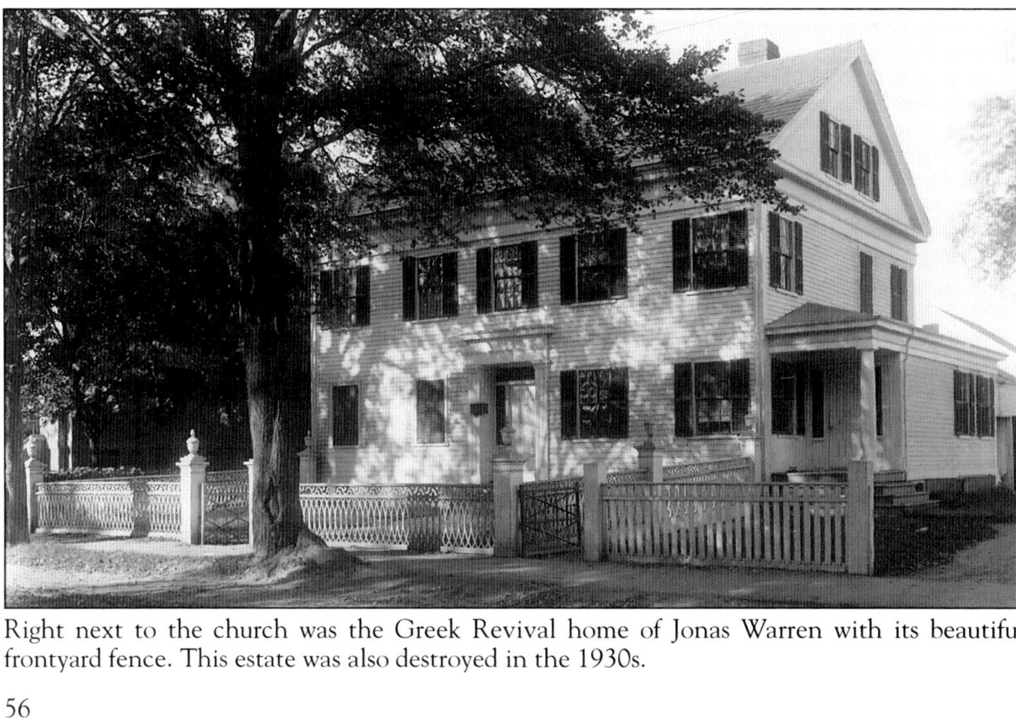

Right next to the church was the Greek Revival home of Jonas Warren with its beautiful frontyard fence. This estate was also destroyed in the 1930s.

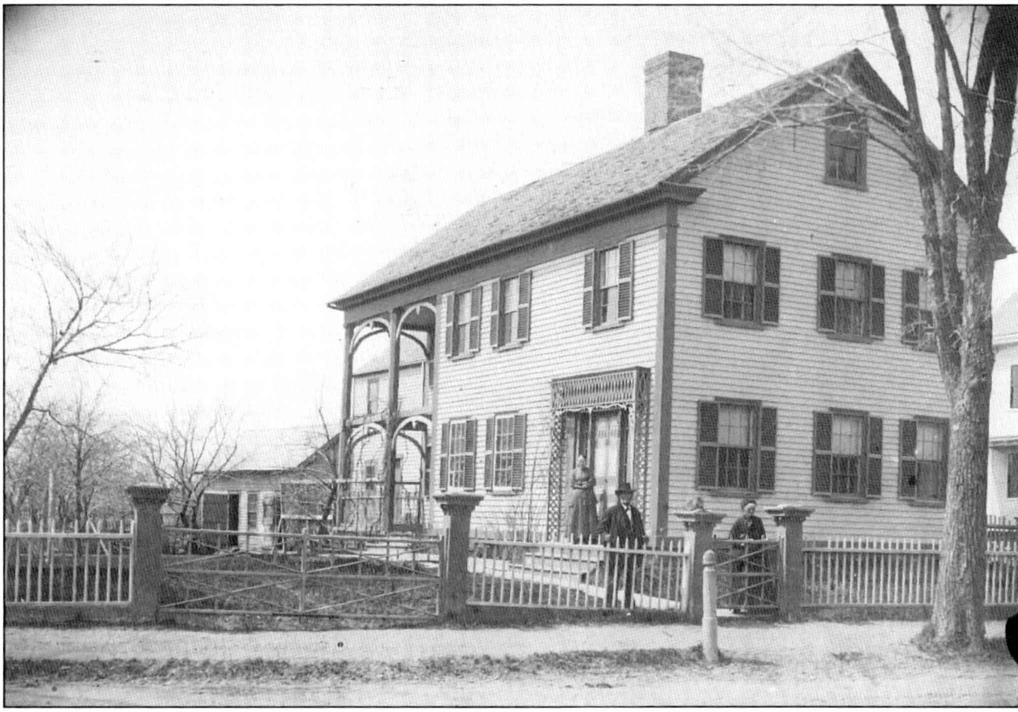

George Porter, carpenter, built this home for himself at 145 High Street in 1842.

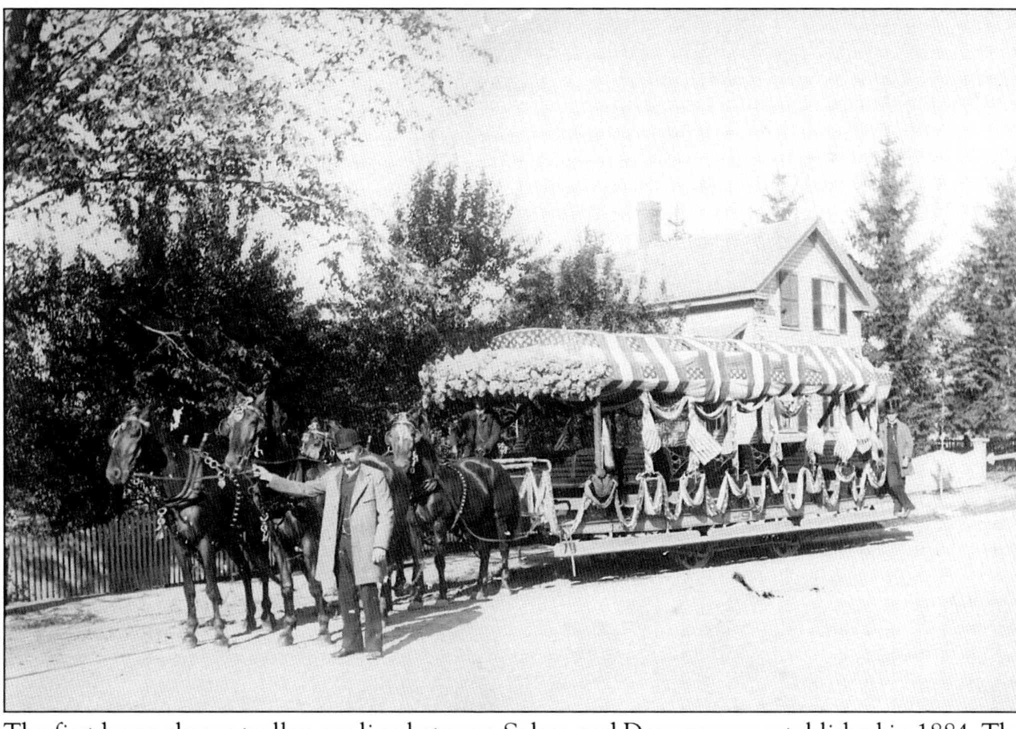

The first horse-drawn trolley-car line between Salem and Danvers was established in 1884. The trolley route was over Water and High Streets in Danversport into Danvers Plains. This trolley is all decked out in a patriotic motif, possibly for a Fourth of July celebration.

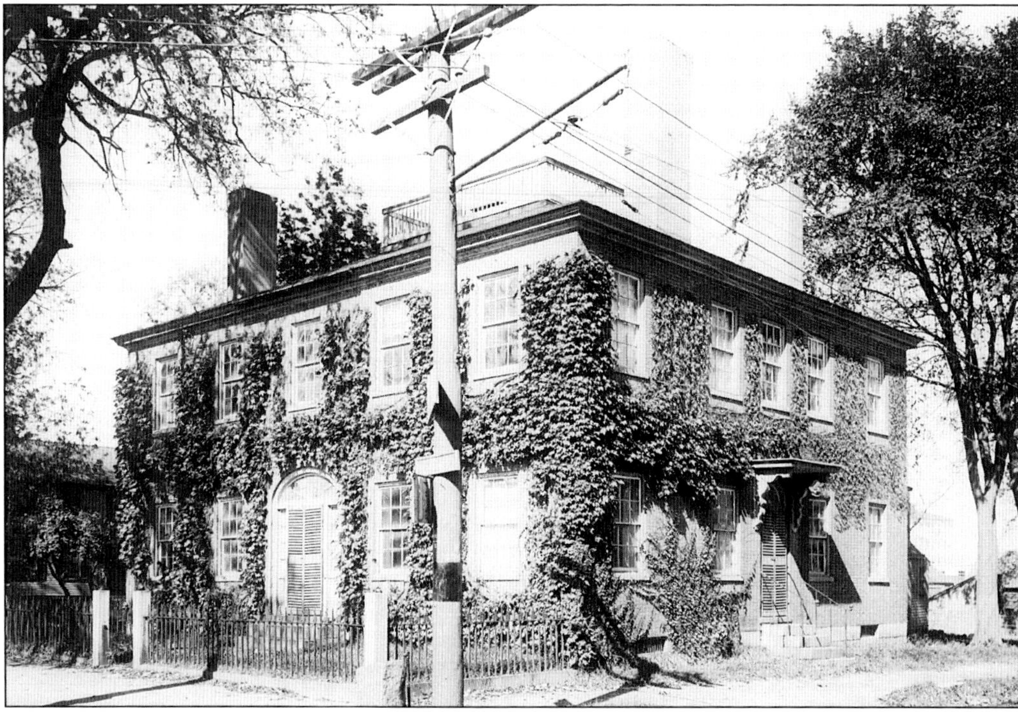

The 1809 Federal-style brick house at 166 High Street was built for mill and tannery owner Samuel Fowler Jr.

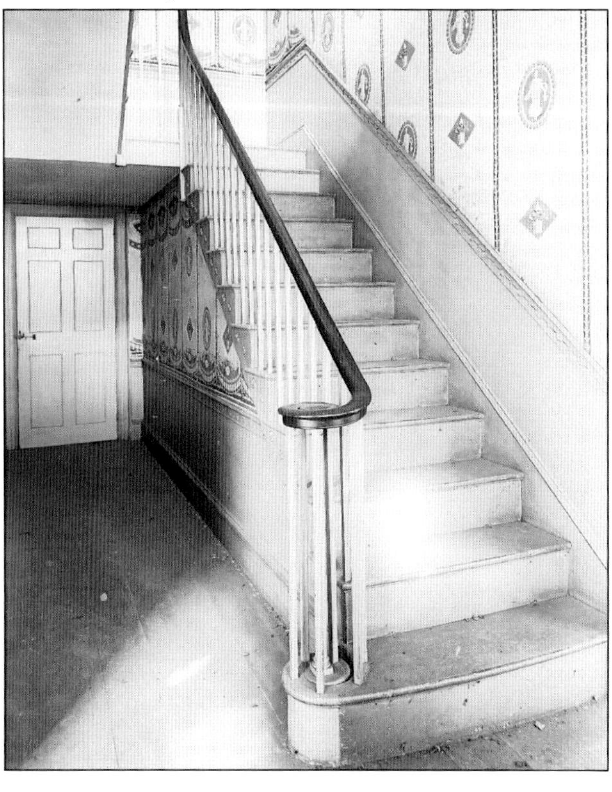

A view of the stairway and early wallpaper in the Fowler house.

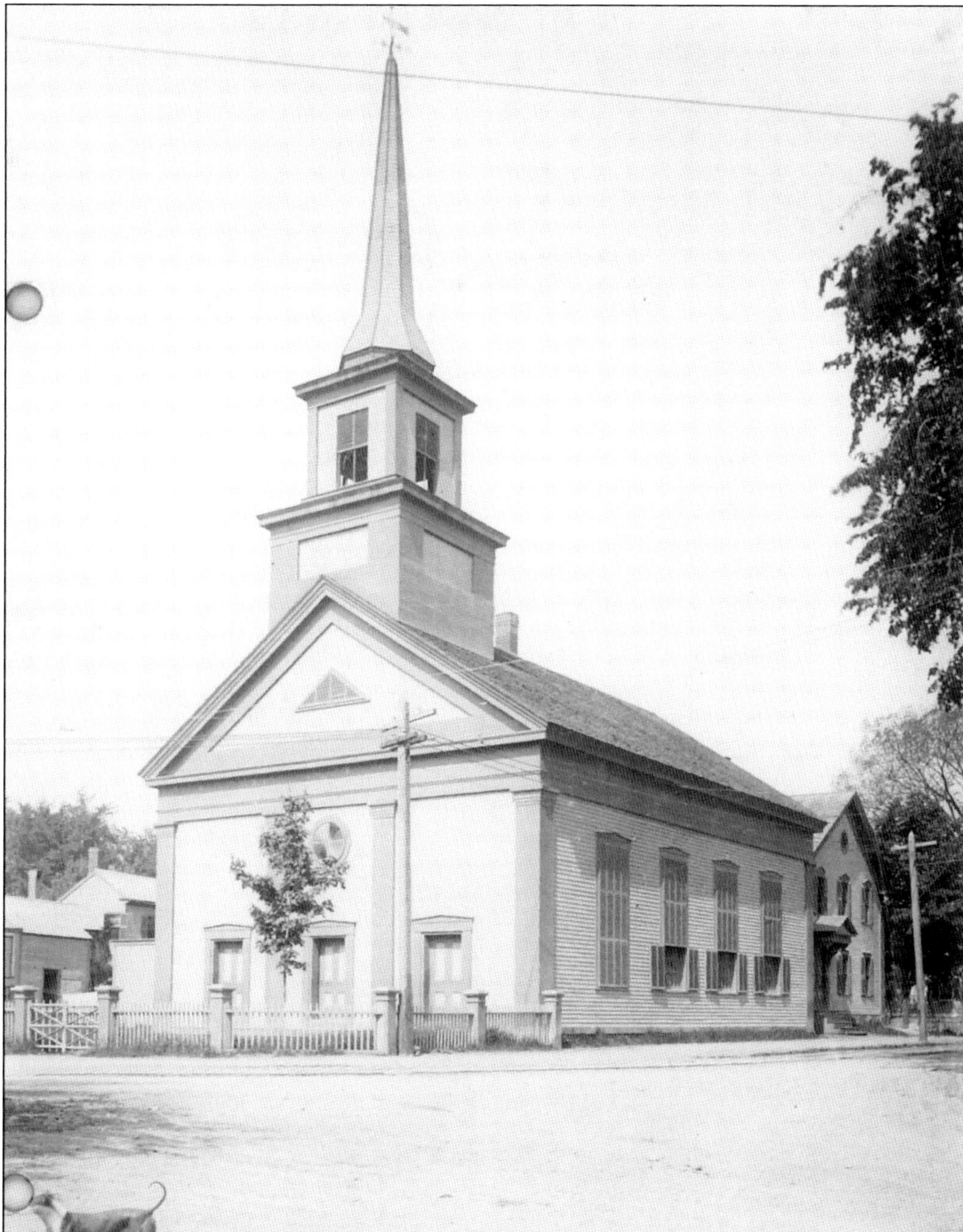

The First Baptist Society in Danvers was formed in 1781. This Greek Revival church at the corner of High and Water Streets was built for the congregation in 1848, and is now Danvers' earliest surviving church structure.

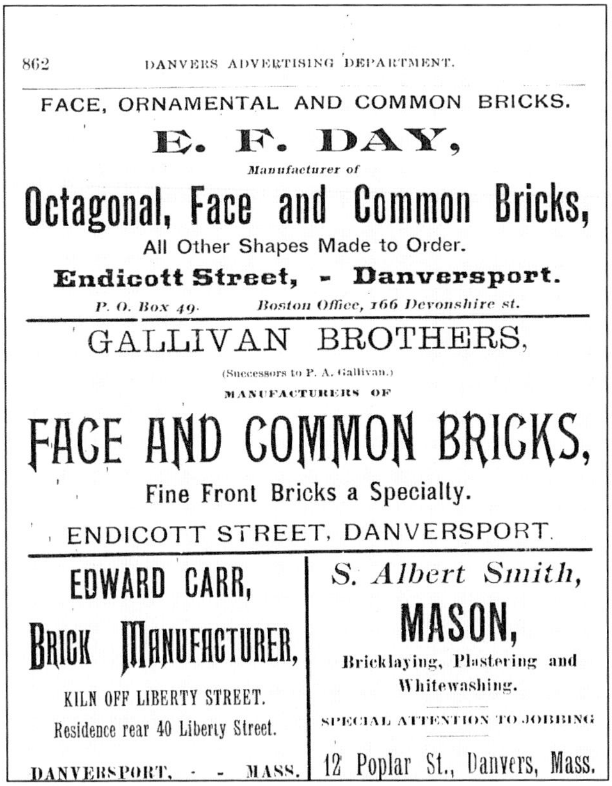

862 DANVERS ADVERTISING DEPARTMENT.

FACE, ORNAMENTAL AND COMMON BRICKS.

E. F. DAY,

Manufacturer of

Octagonal, Face and Common Bricks,

All Other Shapes Made to Order.

Endicott Street, - Danversport.

P. O. Box 49. Boston Office, 166 Devonshire st.

GALLIVAN BROTHERS,

(Successors to P. A. Gallivan.)

MANUFACTURERS OF

FACE AND COMMON BRICKS,

Fine Front Bricks a Specialty.

ENDICOTT STREET, DANVERSPORT.

EDWARD CARR,

BRICK MANUFACTURER,

KILN OFF LIBERTY STREET.

Residence rear 40 Liberty Street.

DANVERSPORT, - - MASS.

S. Albert Smith,

MASON,

Bricklaying, Plastering and Whitewashing.

SPECIAL ATTENTION TO JOBBING

12 Poplar St., Danvers, Mass.

Business advertisements in an 1890s directory indicate the many brick manufactories operating at that time in Danversport.

The extensive Calvin Putnam Lumber Company on Harbor Street included a planing mill and wharves for the delivery of wood by ship. One of the Putnam wagons is shown here preparing to deliver new shingles.

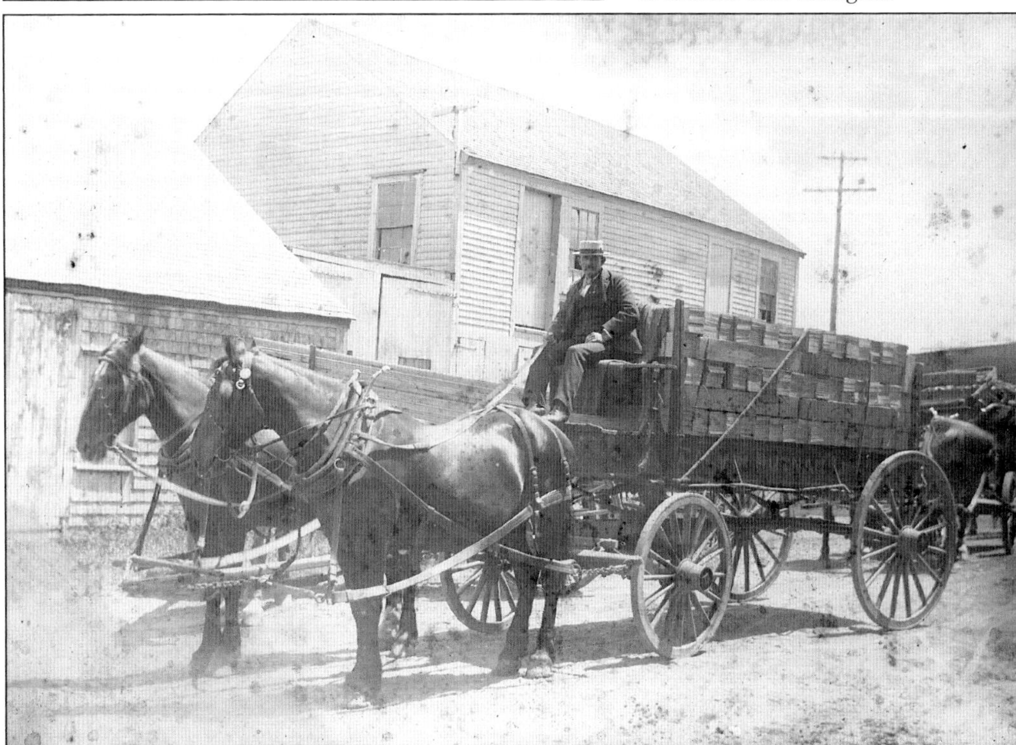

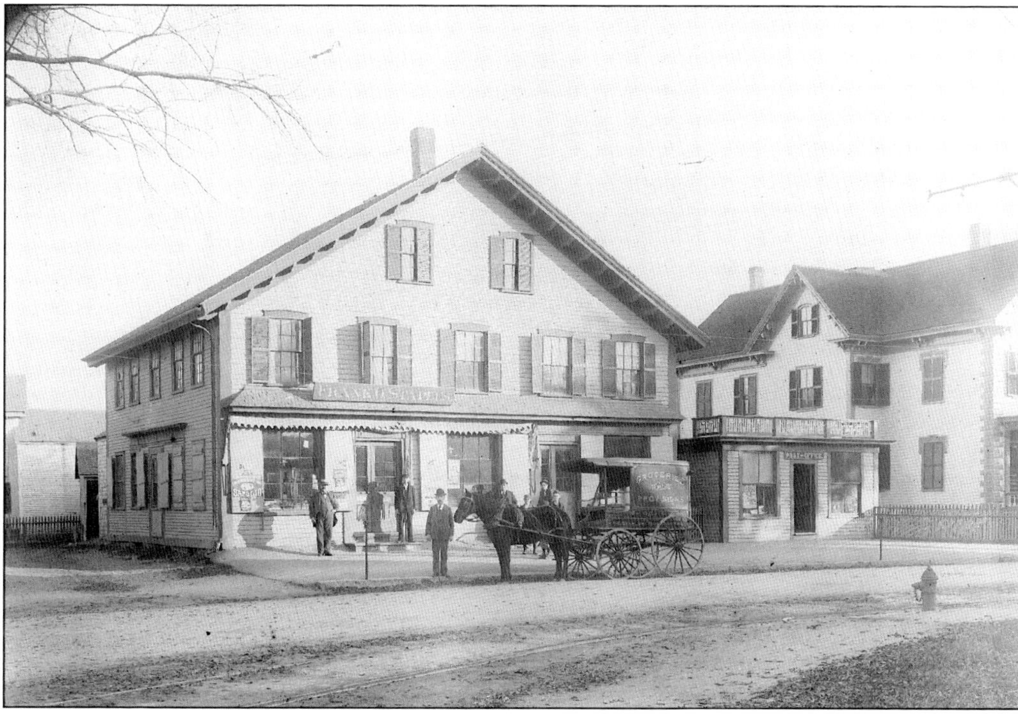

Frank Staples' grocery and provision store was located on Water Street across from the Baptist church. The Danversport Post Office occupies the one-story building in this 1894 photograph by A.O. Elwell.

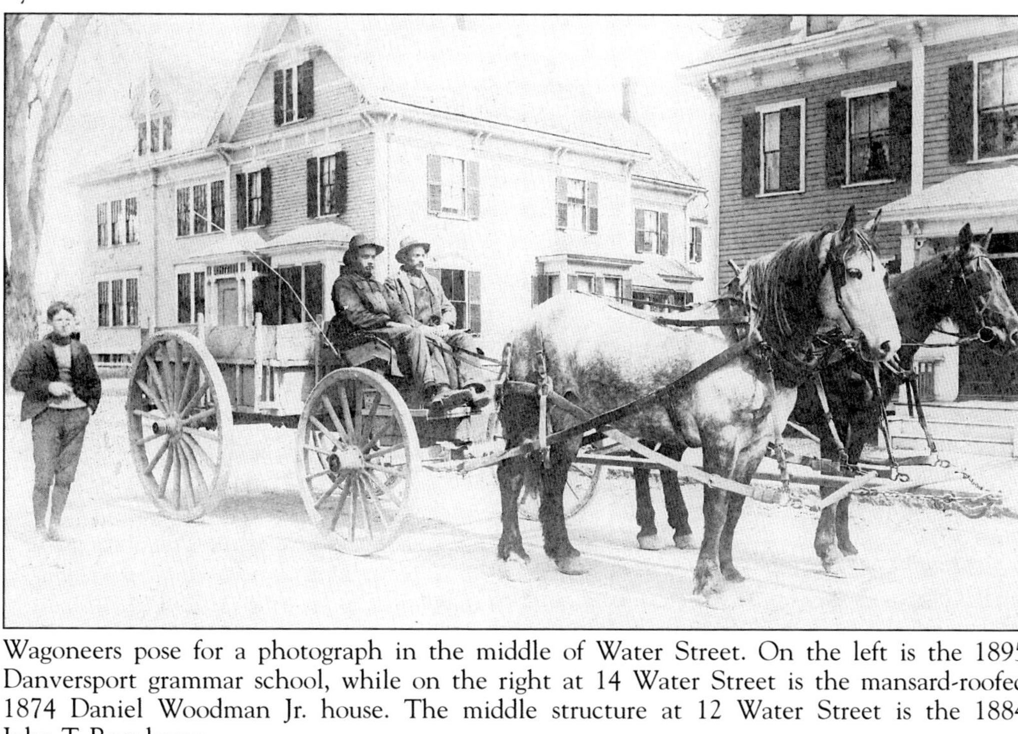

Wagoneers pose for a photograph in the middle of Water Street. On the left is the 1895 Danversport grammar school, while on the right at 14 Water Street is the mansard-roofed 1874 Daniel Woodman Jr. house. The middle structure at 12 Water Street is the 1884 John T. Ross home.

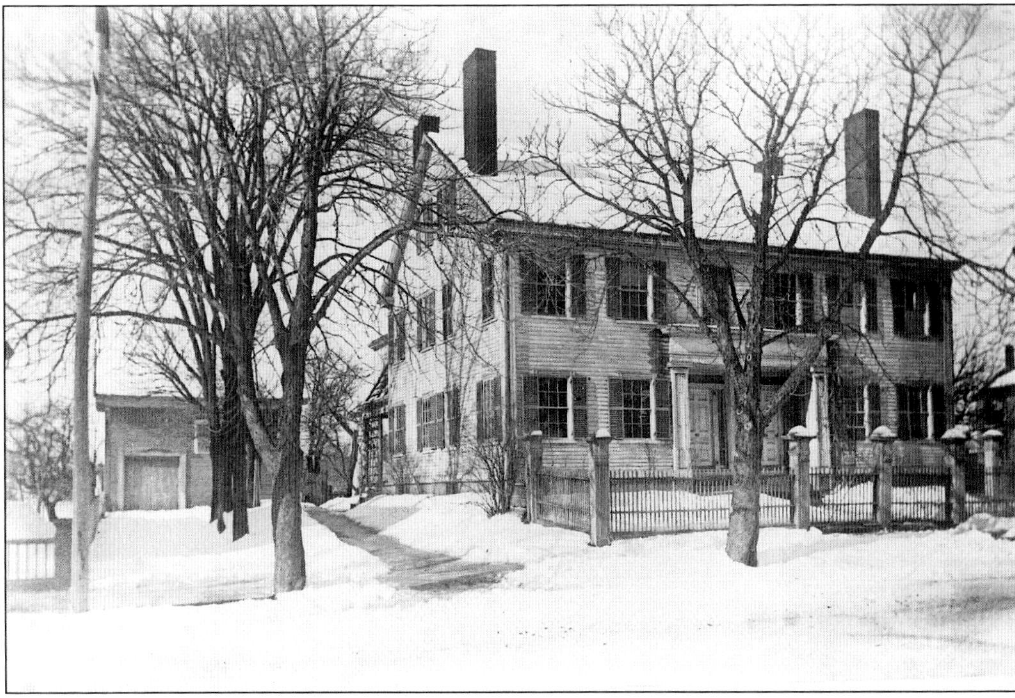

This double house with its impressive entablature headed and recessed double entrance was built in 1834 for brothers William and Moses Jr. Black. Today it is 25 and 27 Water Street.

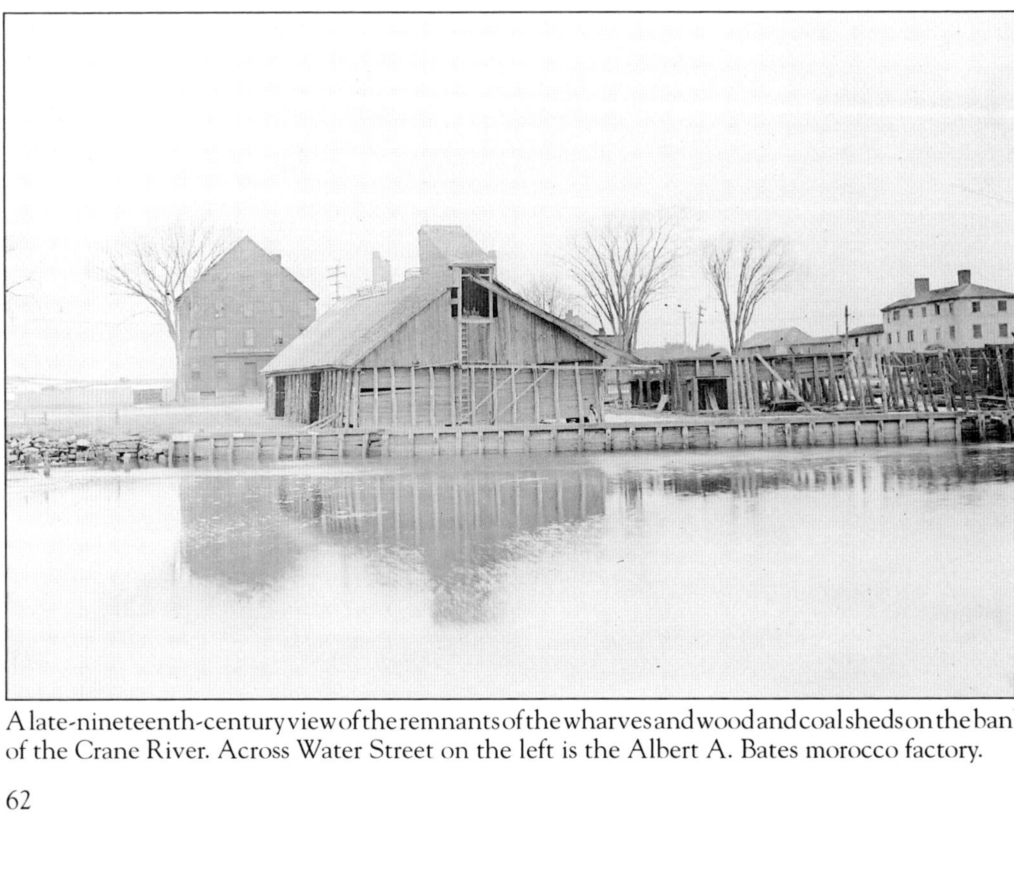

A late-nineteenth-century view of the remnants of the wharves and wood and coal sheds on the bank of the Crane River. Across Water Street on the left is the Albert A. Bates morocco factory.

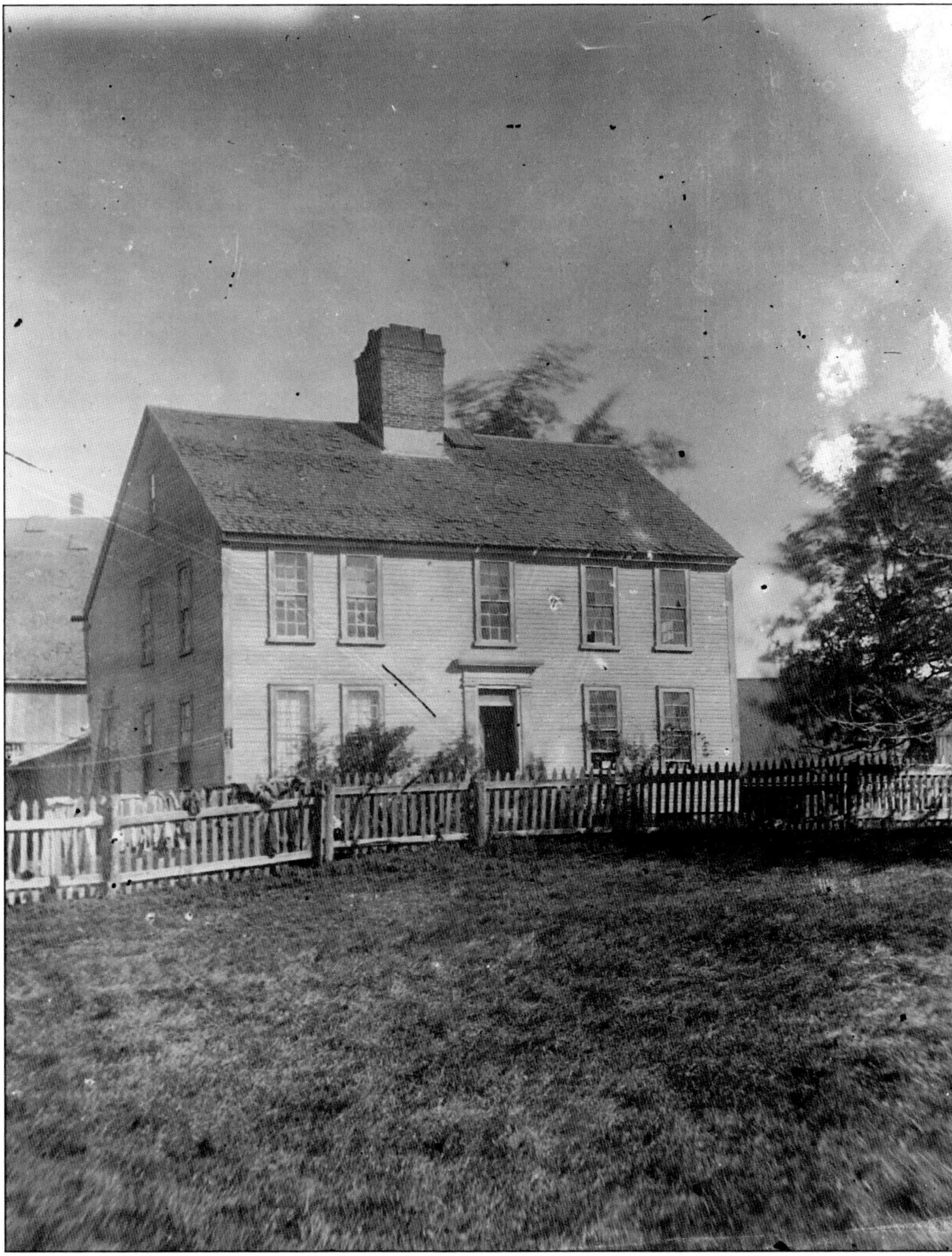

A *c*. 1860 view of the Israel Hutchinson house near 35 Water Street. Hutchinson was a miller and veteran of the French and Indian and the Revolutionary Wars. In April 1775 he was captain of a Danvers Minute Company and he and his men saw fierce action during the Lexington Alarm of April 19. The bodies of several of the slain Danvers men were brought back here following the battle. Hutchinson was colonel of the 27th Continental Regiment which served with General Washington during the critical period of 1776 and early 1777. The Hutchinson house was torn down in 1889.

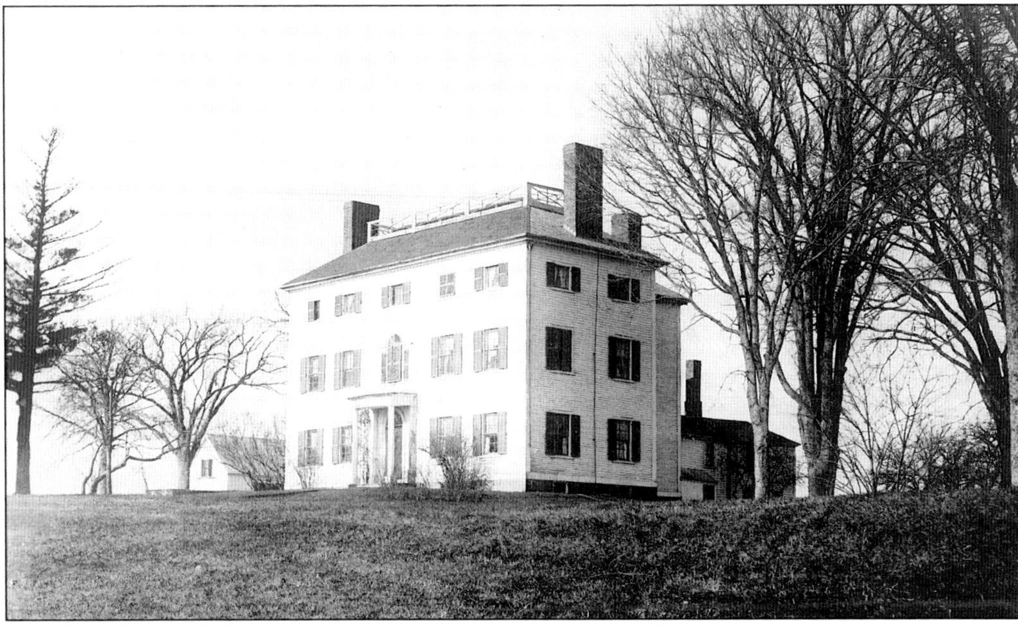

Nathan Read, inventor and industrialist, had this Federalist-style house built traditionally from the design of Samuel McIntire in about 1798. The building was the victim of arson in 1966.

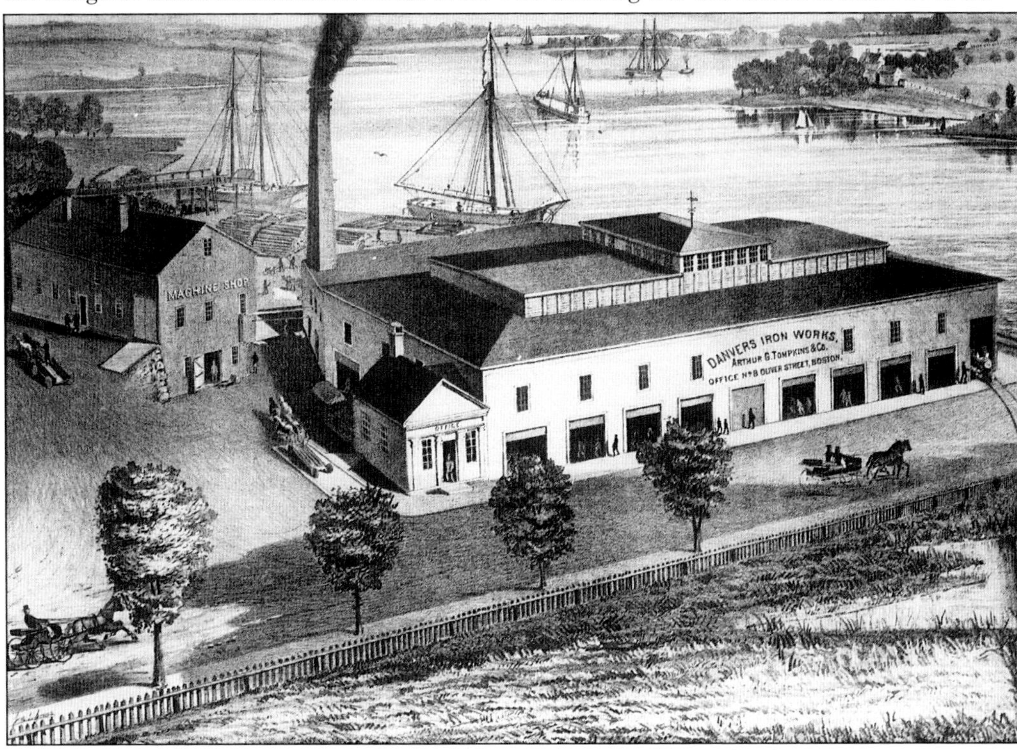

Read invented and patented a nail-cutting machine in 1799. At this location on the Waters River, he established the Salem Iron Factory including an iron foundry, nail shop, and anchor factory. Later known as the Danvers Iron Works, the business produced iron rods and sheet iron into the twentieth century. This engraving dates from 1884.

This is a Daguerreotype of Matthew Hooper (1792–1858). Hooper was a carpenter who prospered in business ventures and eventually purchased the iron works. His new mansion house was built in 1853 in the Italianate style and included a cupola on a hipped roof.

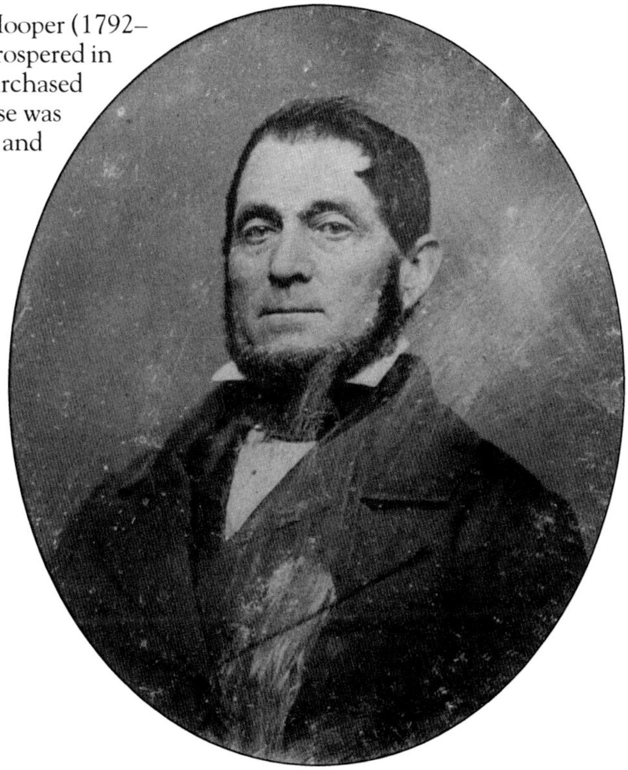

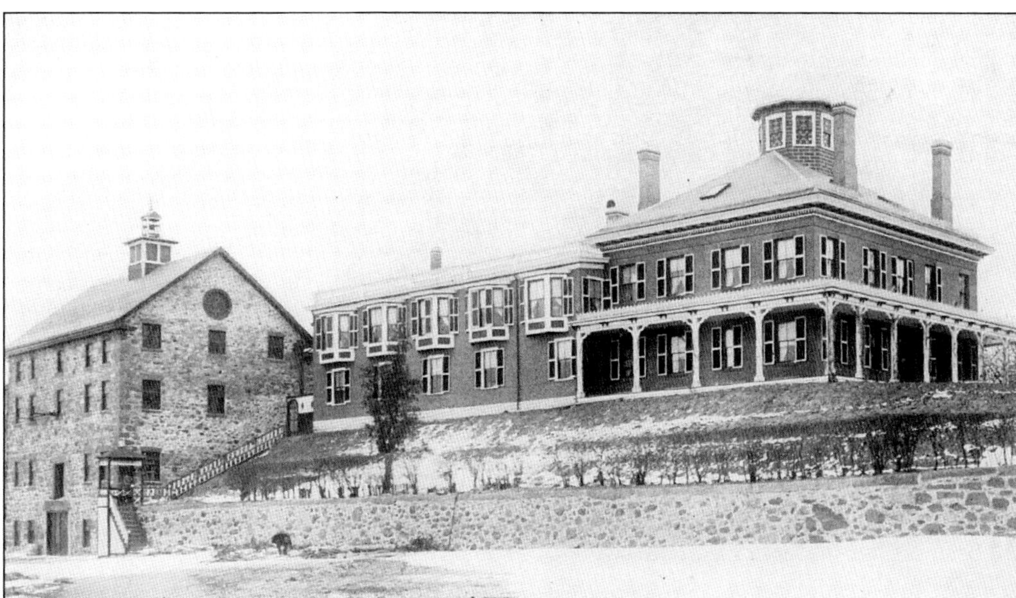

The Hooper estate included an immense stone barn to its rear (see also p. 15). In 1883 William Penn Hussey acquired the estate and expanded the dwelling to include a grand piazza and a two-story addition to the rear as seen in this *c.* 1899 photograph.

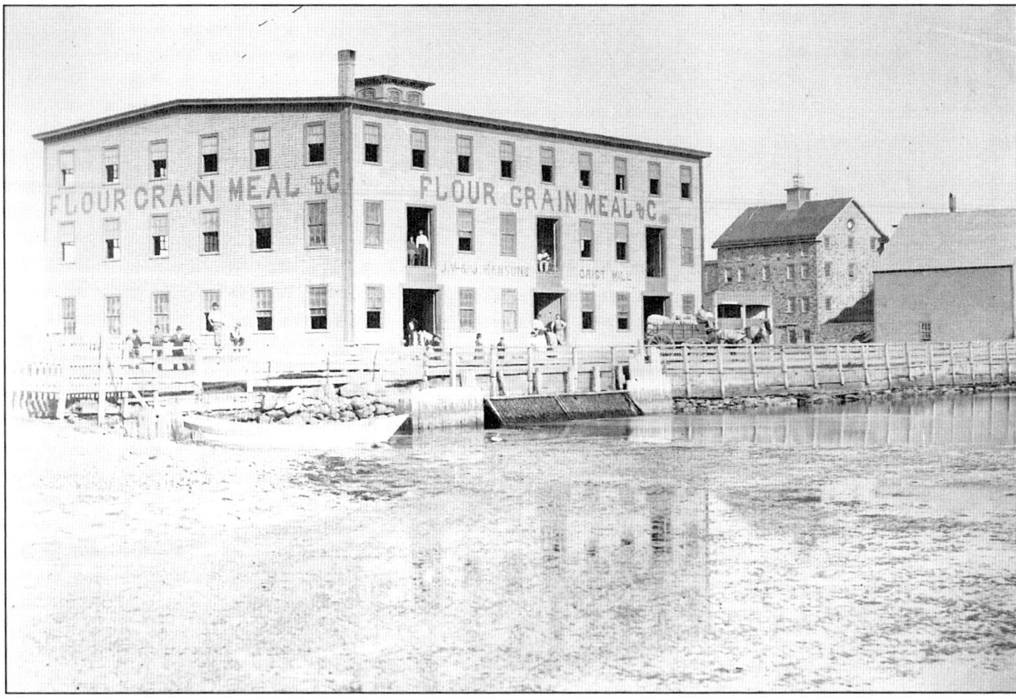

This 1881 photograph by Lefavour & Clough of Beverly features the J.V. & J. Hanson tidal mill, built on pilings at the bridge over the Waters River. The Hooper-Hussey stone barn can be seen in the background. In 1896 the mill was destroyed by fire.

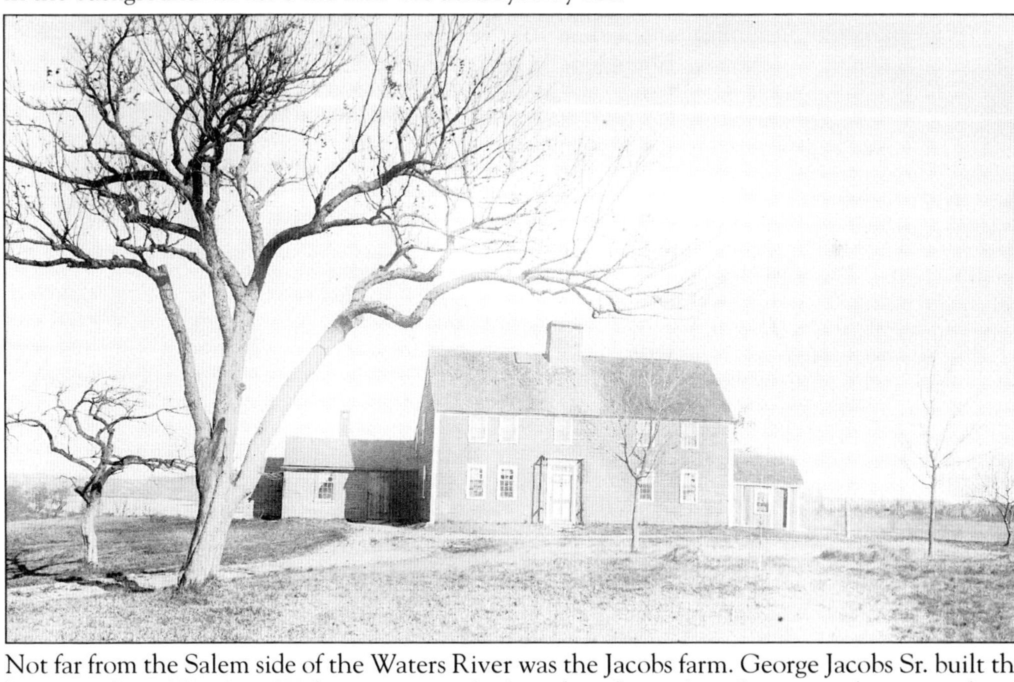

Not far from the Salem side of the Waters River was the Jacobs farm. George Jacobs Sr. built the house in the 1650s. In 1692 he was accused of witchcraft, tried, and convicted; as a result, on August 19, 1692, he was hanged. The house remained in the family into the twentieth century. It was the victim of neglect and fire, succumbing around 1940.

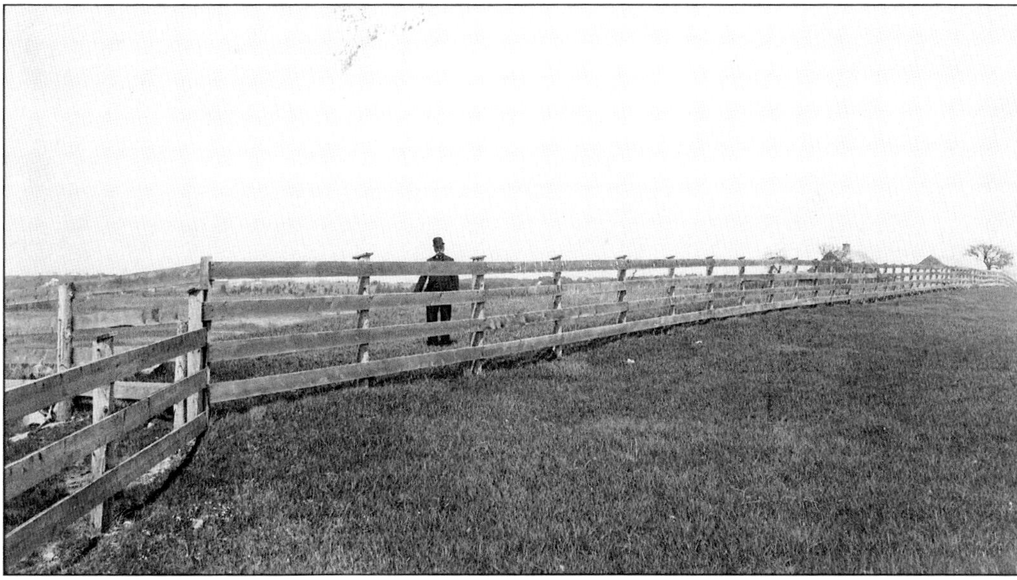

The Jacobs family secretly stole George's body from the place of execution and brought it to his farm for burial. In this 1890s photograph a descendant of Jacobs points to the burial location, not too far from the house. The remains were disturbed during later house construction. They now rest at the Nurse burial ground on Pine Street.

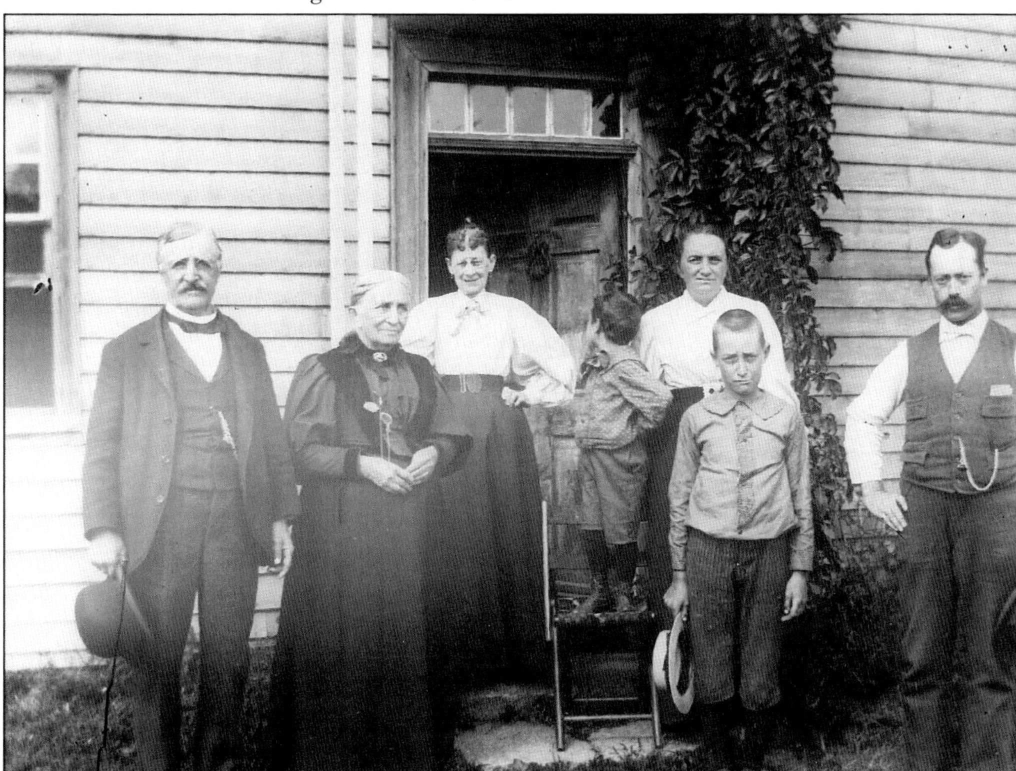

A print from a glass-plate negative captures William Allen Jacobs (left), his wife Frances, and other members of the family in front of the doorway of the old Jacobs homestead.

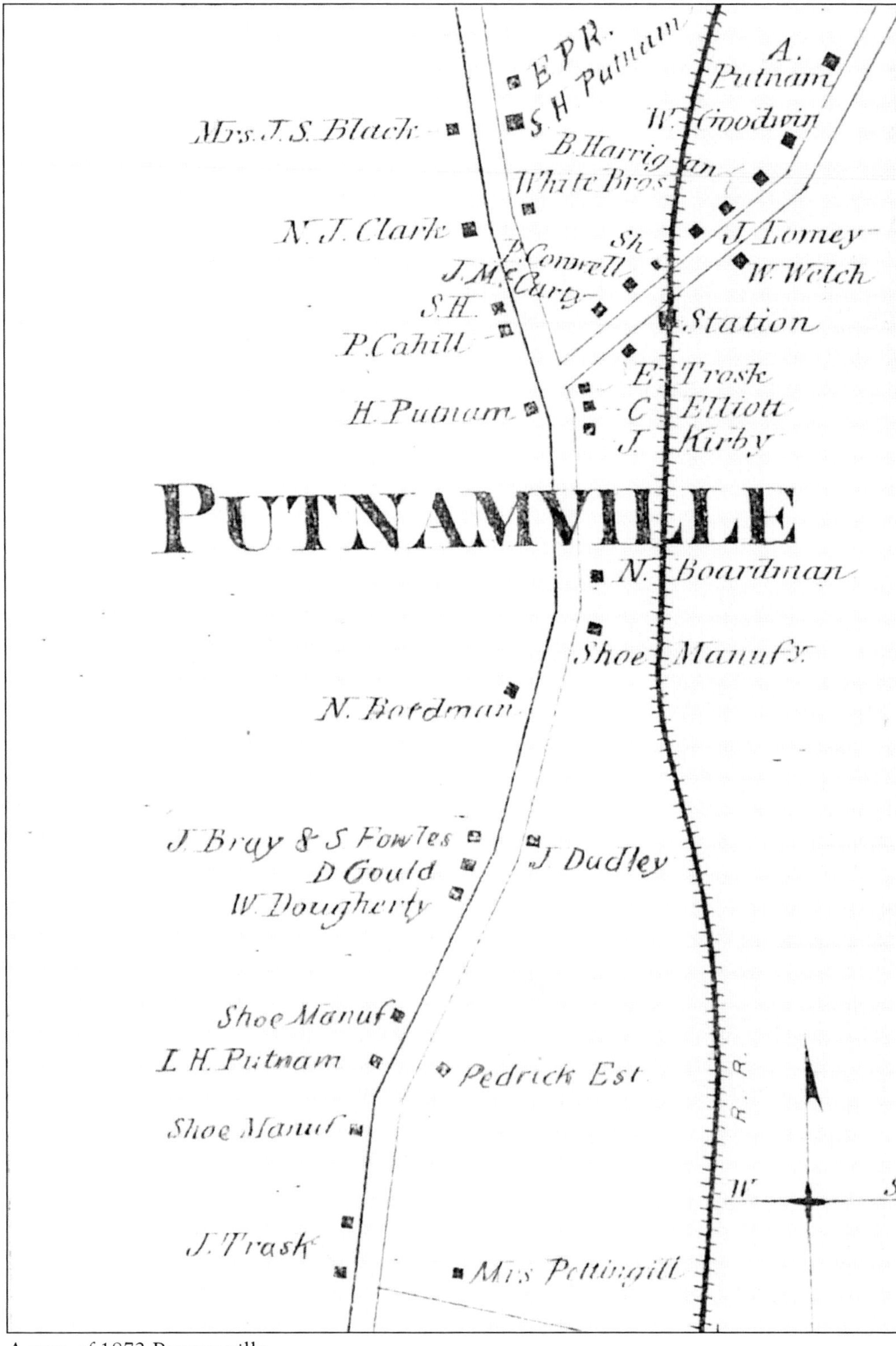

A map of 1872 Putnamville.

Five

Putnamville

This territory, north of Lindall Hill and primarily located on Locust Street, began its period of seventeenth-century European settlement as an area of scattered farms. Around the time of the Revolution, Zerubbabel Porter, owner of a leather-currying shop, hired several men to make shoes from his excess leather. Gradually expanding his business, Porter hired more workmen and sold the resulting shoes, not to local consumers, but by specializing and expanding his market outside the immediate area. He packed his thick, sturdy brogan shoes in barrels and exported them to what became a thriving southern market where such shoes were in demand for use by slaves.

Eventually six other shoe factories were established in this section of town, including a major business owned by entrepreneur Elias Putnam. With this growth, a box factory and other businesses were attracted to the area. Referred to as "Putnamville," the village became the most prosperous one in Danvers during the first quarter of the nineteenth century.

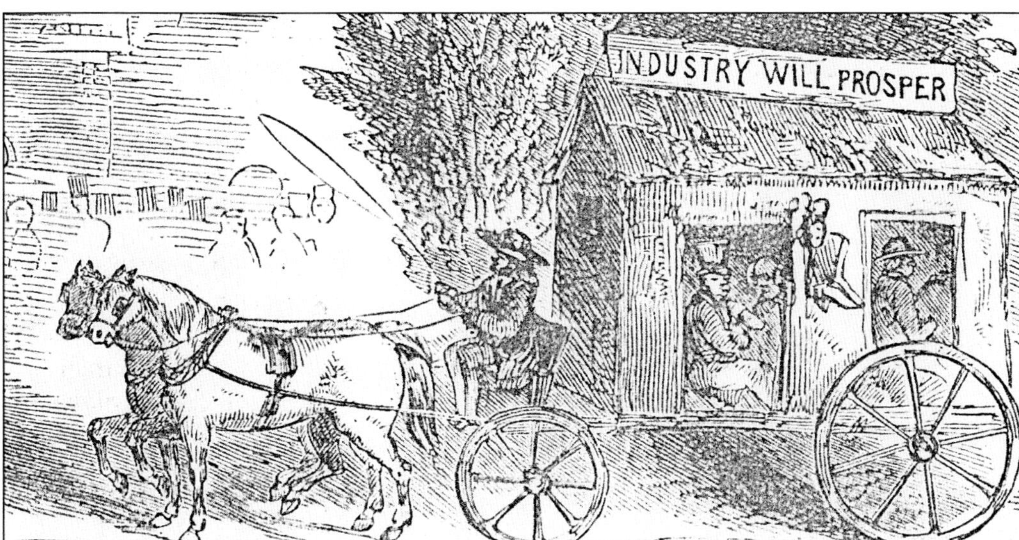

A portion of an 1852 engraving of the Danvers centennial parade representing the town's historic shoe industry.

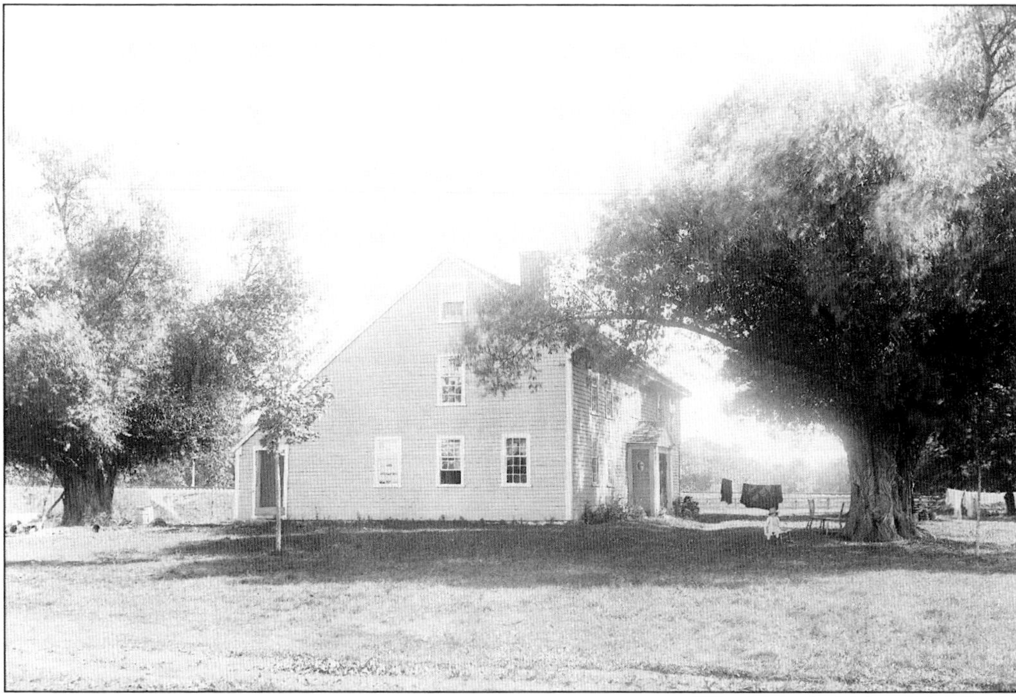

With a saltbox-shaped roof and a rare plaster coving under the front eaves, the 1660s-era Daniel Rea house off Locust Street is a fine example of the town's earliest architecture.

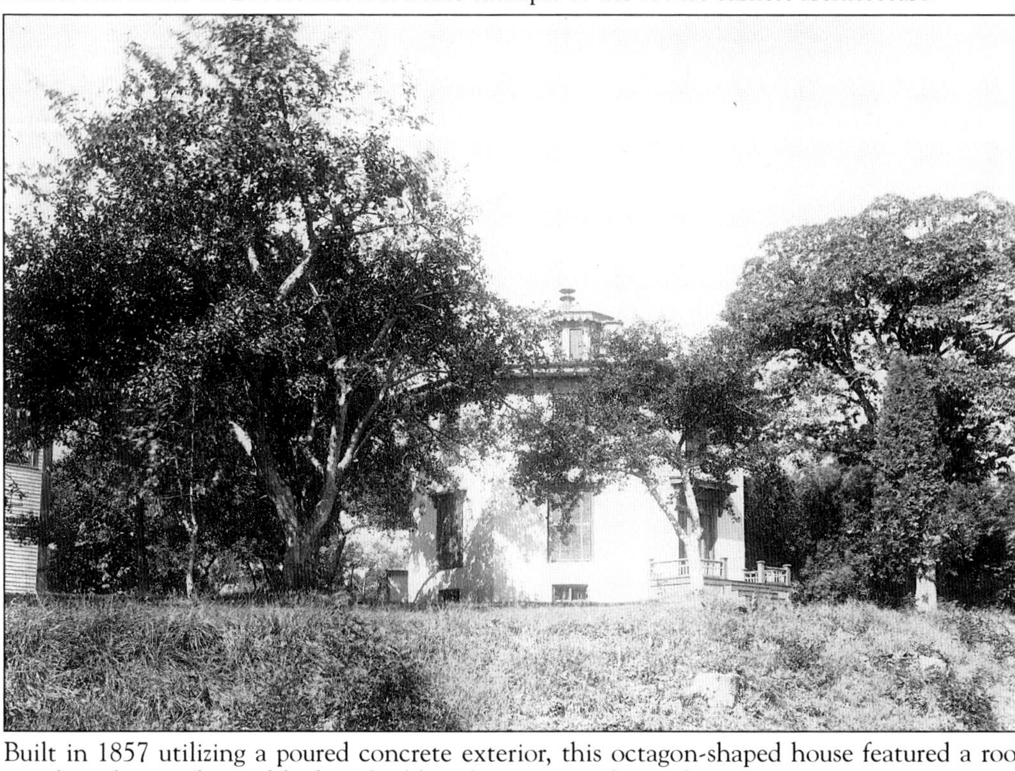

Built in 1857 utilizing a poured concrete exterior, this octagon-shaped house featured a roof cupola and many forward-looking building features. It is located at 148 Locust Street.

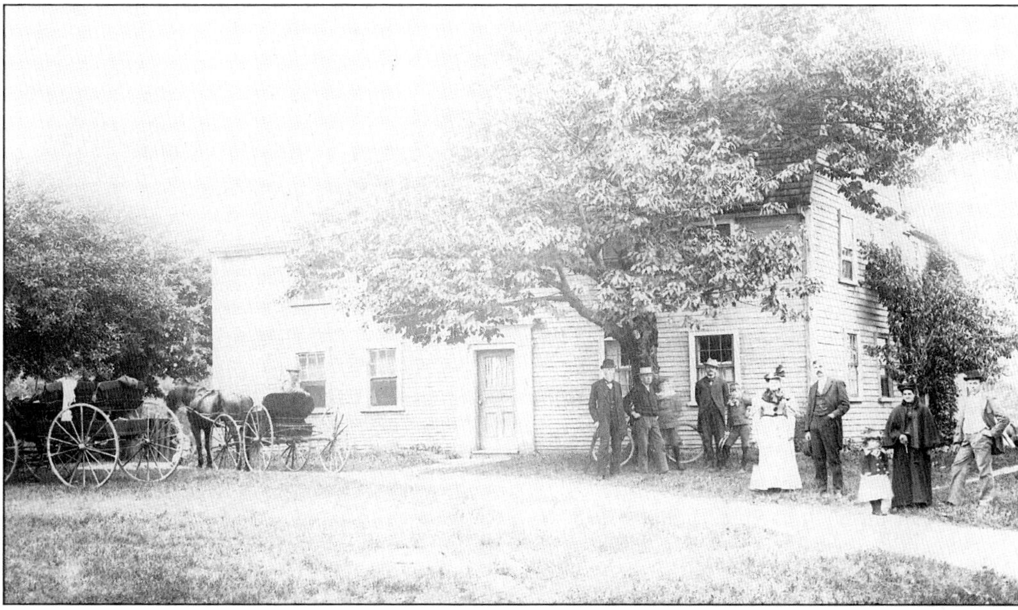

Members of the Porter family reunion in the 1890s gather around the early-eighteenth century gambrel-roofed birthplace of General Moses Porter. Fighting in the Revolution as a teenager, Porter served the young Republic as a soldier and officer in numerous important posts and positions for forty-seven years. The Locust Street house was torn down in 1902.

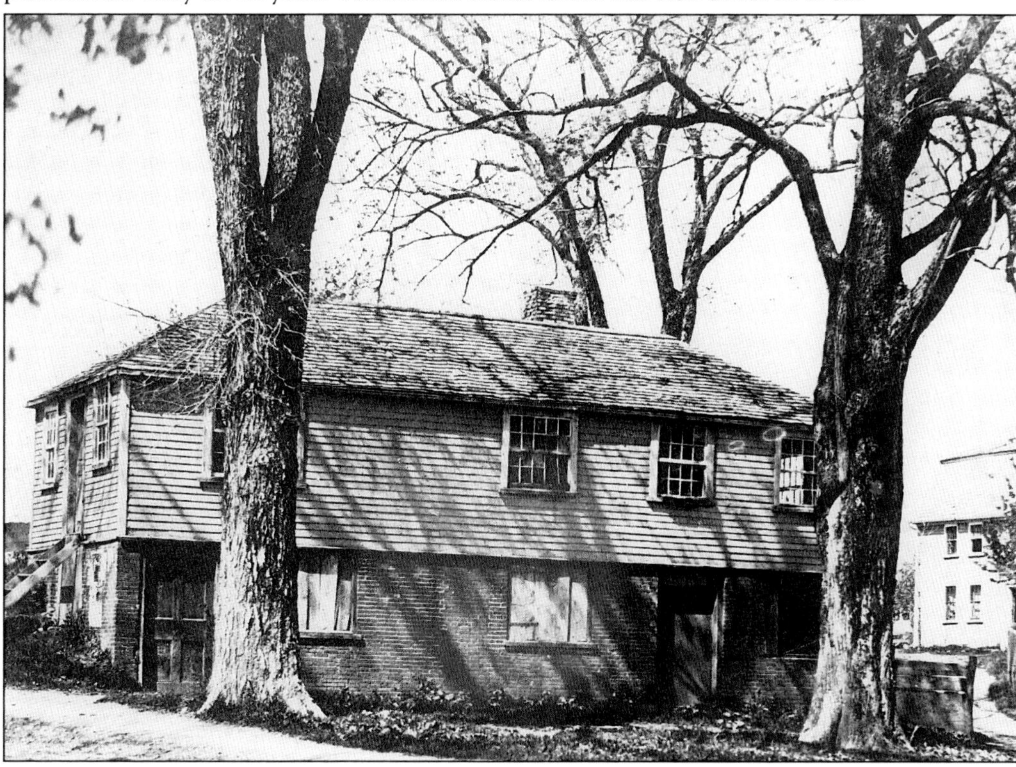

Just a short distance from the Porter house (in the right background) was the currying shop and shoe factory managed by Zerubbabel Porter.

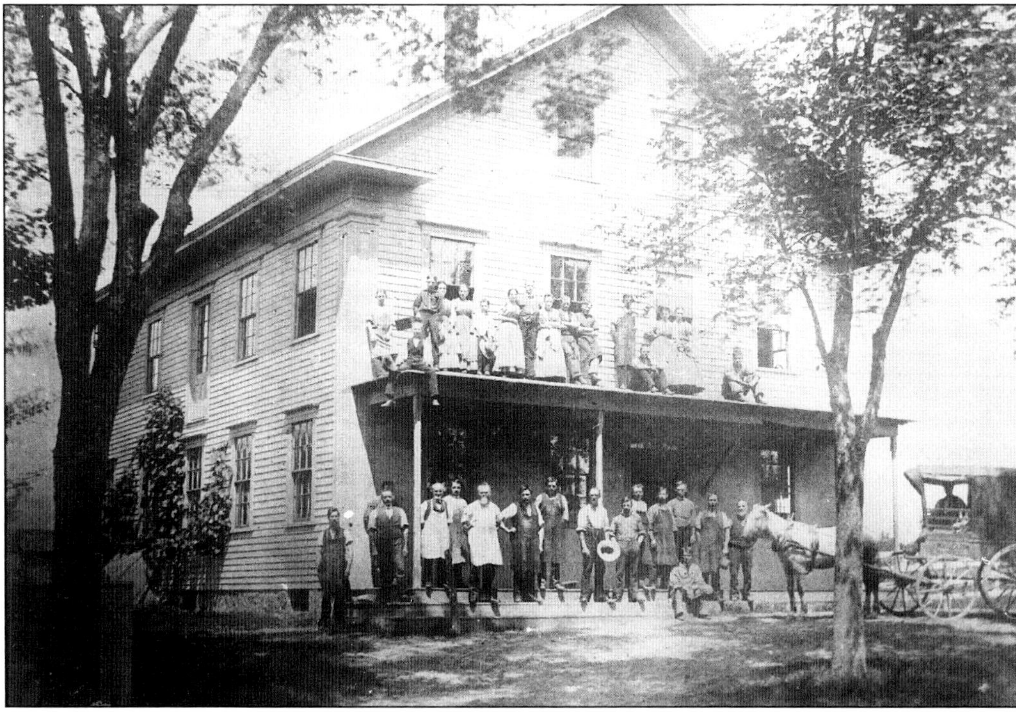
Workers of the Israel H. Putnam shoe factory on Locust Street pose for a photograph in the 1870s.

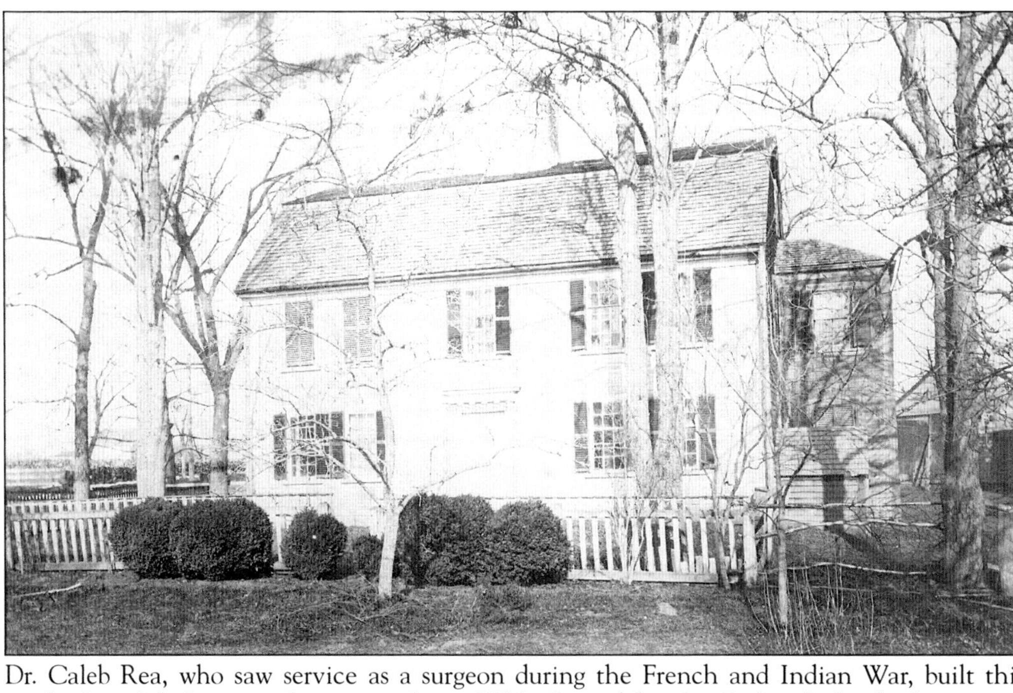
Dr. Caleb Rea, who saw service as a surgeon during the French and Indian War, built this gambrel-roofed Georgian house in about 1756. Owned by the Pederick family for several generations, the house, located at 159 Locust Street, was used as a summer residence in 1907 by Vice-President Charles W. Fairbanks. It is shown here in 1880.

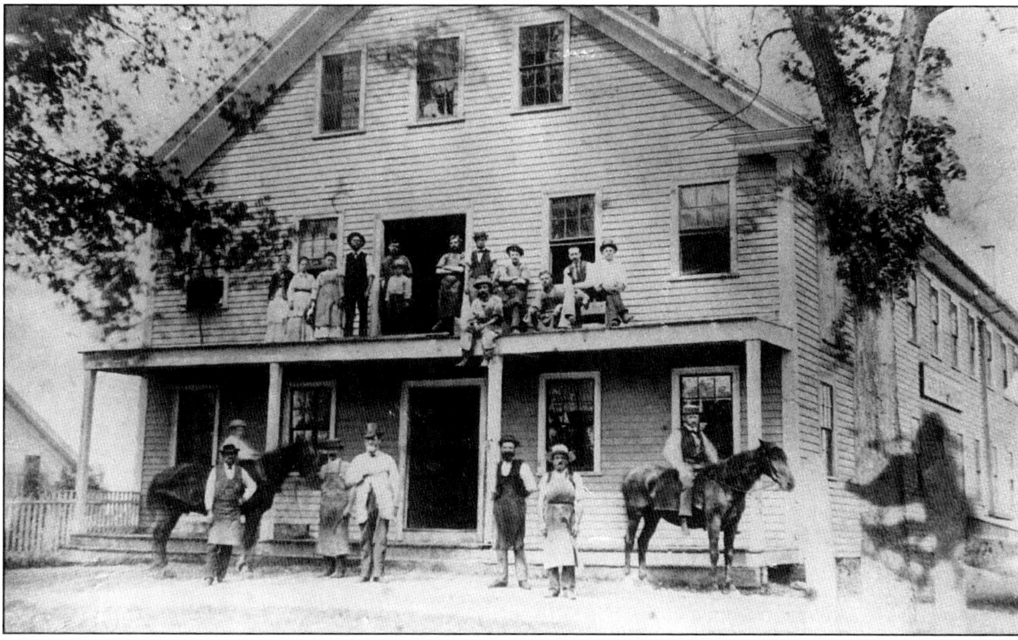

Yet another shoe factory in Putnamville was that of the White Brothers. It was located on Locust Street above Wenham Street, and is shown here in 1870.

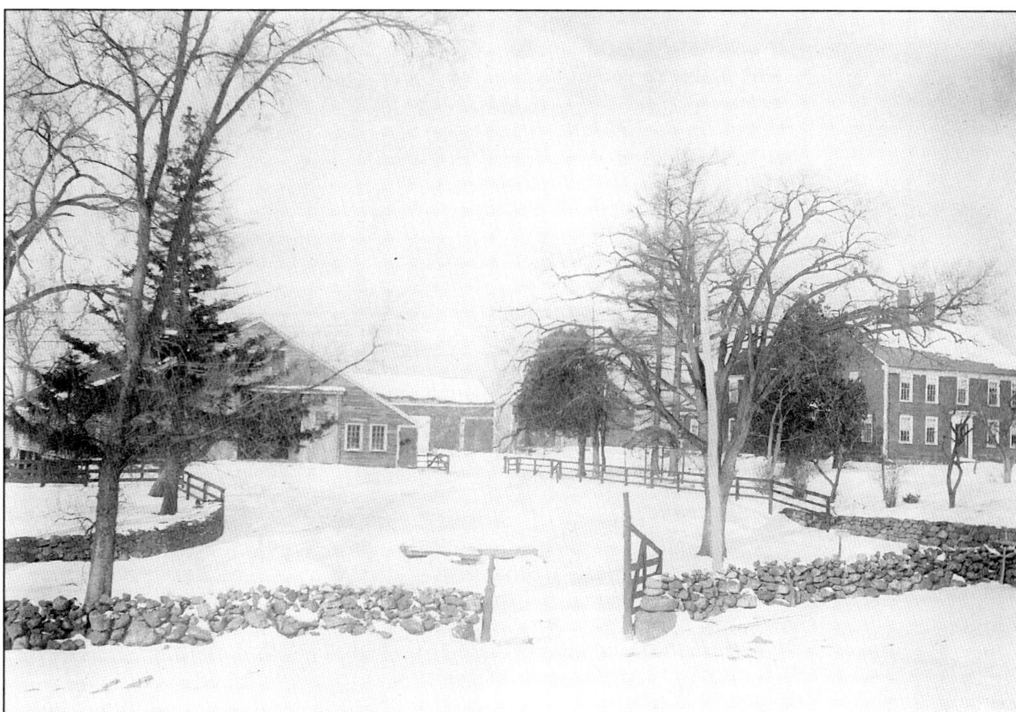

This house and farm on upper Locust Street was the birthplace of shoe manufacturer and state senator Elias Putnam (1789–1847) and later home of shoe manufacturer John A. Sears. The estate was one of several that was obliterated in 1955 with the building of the Putnamville Reservoir.

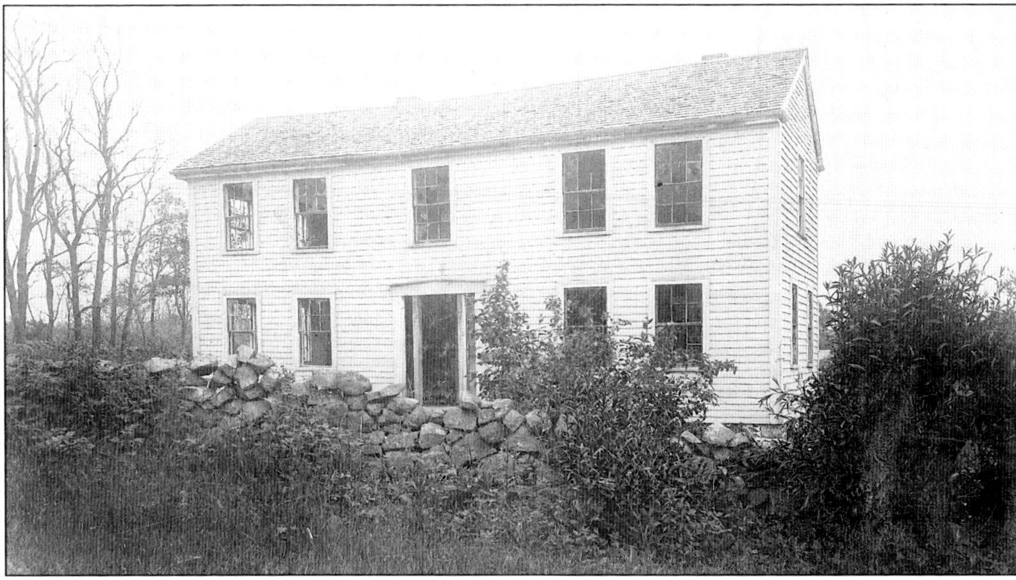

Originally an ell to the Putnam-Sears house, this was the birthplace in 1831 of Grenville Mellen Dodge. Dodge was an engineer, a brigadier general during the Civil War, chief engineer to the Union Pacific Railroad, and assisted in the creation of the Transcontinental Railroad. Moved once as shown in this 1890 photograph, the structure was later relocated to the Choate estate on Locust Street.

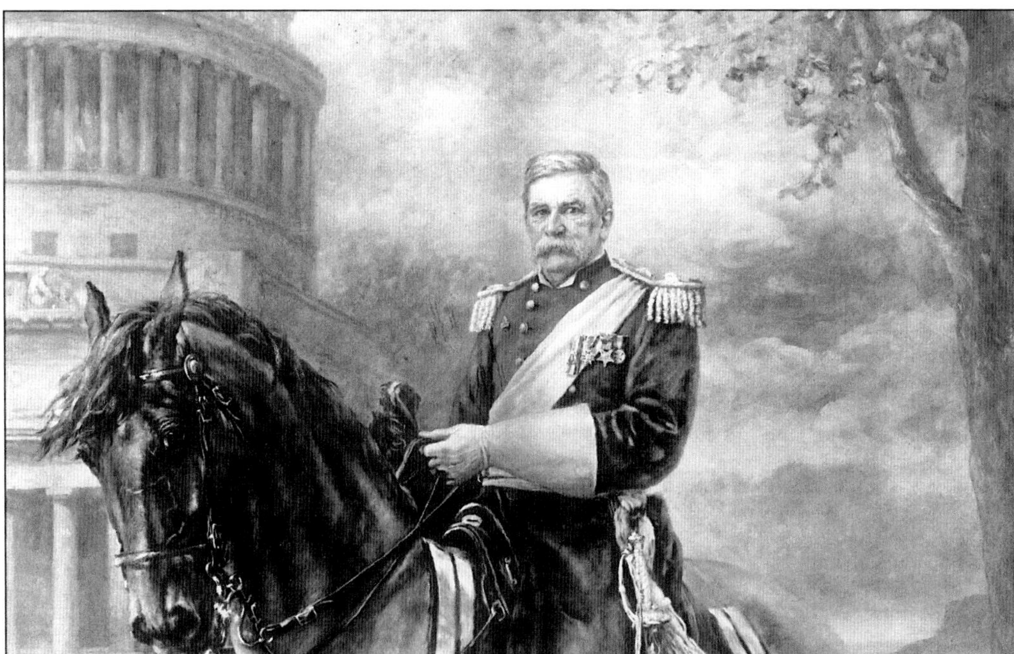

A detail from an engraving featuring Dodge as grand marshal at the ceremonies opening President Ulysses S. Grant's tomb in New York on April 27, 1897. Dodge led a remarkable career as a railroad builder, financier, and politician. An active Republican, he was a congressman and intimate to Grant and William T. Sherman. Dodge's visits to Danvers were always notable events.

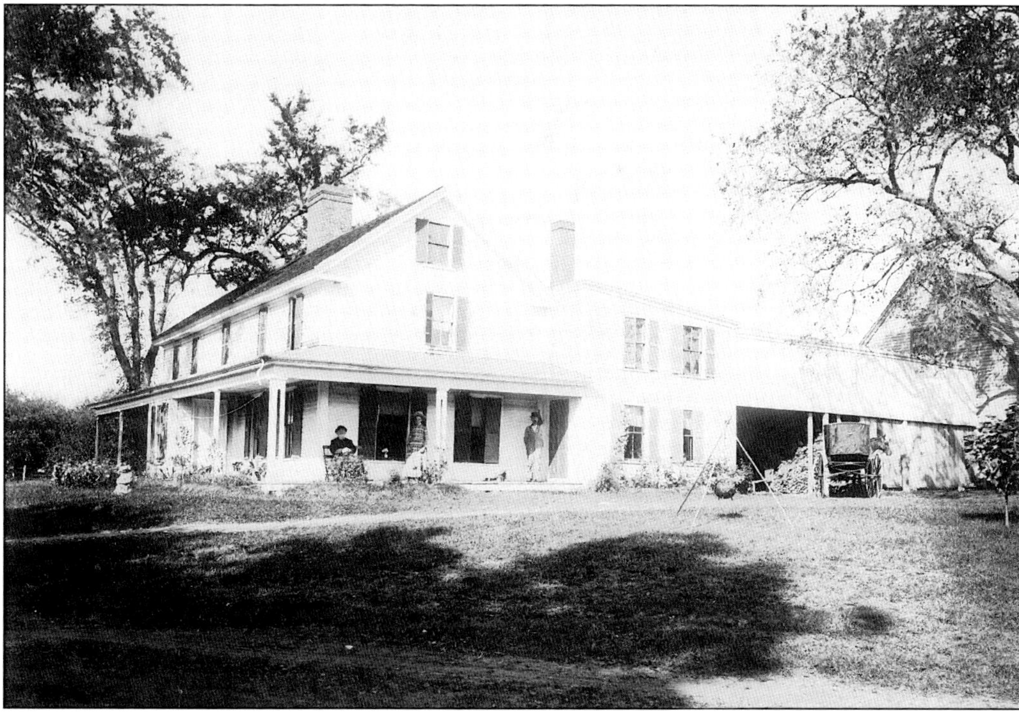

This 1891 view of the *c.* 1664 Joseph Porter house at 487 Locust Street reveals a string of attachments to its rear including a carriage shed and barn.

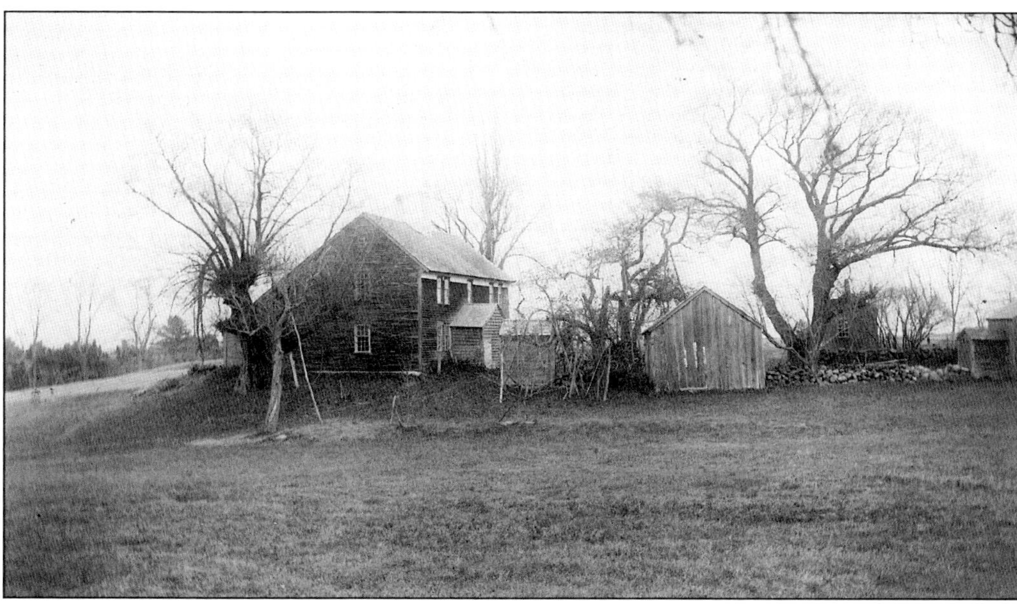

The rugged, rustic farmhouse of Deacon Benjamin Putnam was built prior to 1700. Photographed in November 1887, the homestead includes numerous outbuildings. Located on North Street, the house was destroyed by fire in 1900.

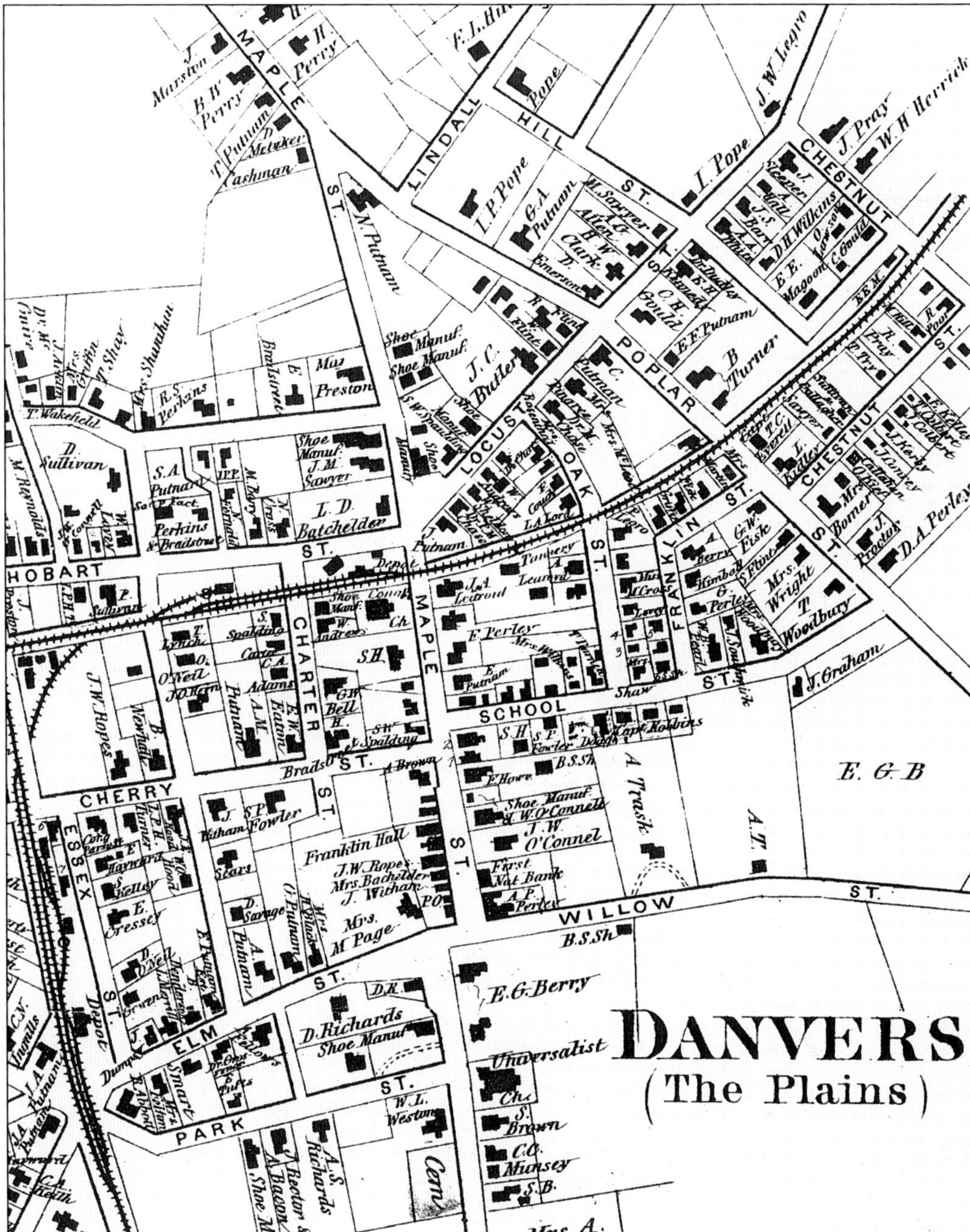

The central portion of Danvers Plains as it appears on an 1872 map.

Six

Danvers Plains

This geologically flat area today spreads out from a point where Elm, Maple, Conant, and High Streets converge. Slowly developing from the eighteenth century, by 1850 this area became the most commercial and active village in Danvers. Its prominence began due to its location at the intersection of the active Topsfield and Ipswich Roads. At this crossroads two country stores, a tavern, and several other buildings had been established. By the mid-1830s the neighborhood was in the midst of a growth spurt with over a dozen shoe manufactories established here. Ancillary businesses were also attracted to this locale, which led to new residential streets and the establishment of two banks and several churches.

The newly created mid-nineteenth-century Eastern Railroad and the later Danvers Railroad bisected the Plains Village, adding to its economic and building growth. In the 1880s horsecars connected the village to other towns, and in the 1890s the more efficient electric trolley cars took over the horsecar routes. By 1895 the territory encompassing Danvers Plains possessed both half of the town's total population and half its businesses.

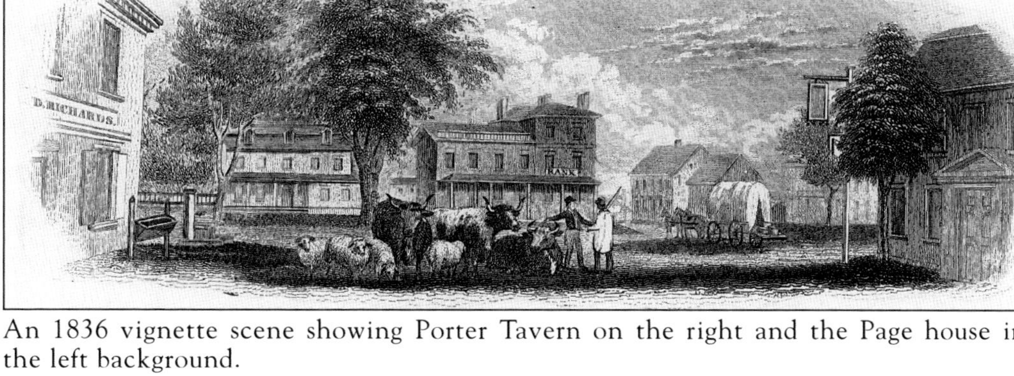

An 1836 vignette scene showing Porter Tavern on the right and the Page house in the left background.

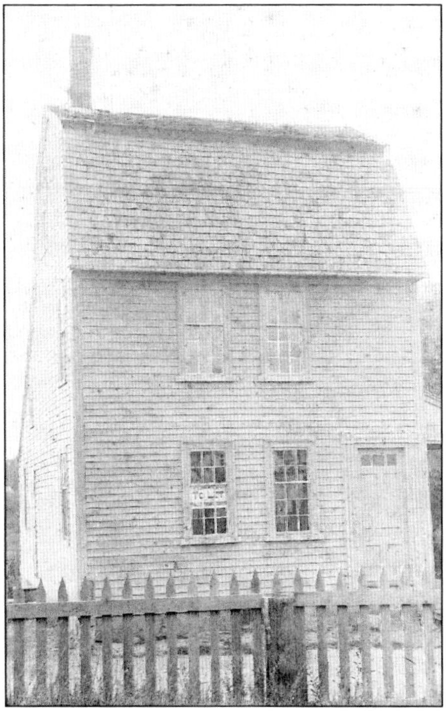

One of two surviving sections of the 1745 John Porter tavern originally located at High and Conant Streets (the other is now at 63 Elm Street). This section was first moved around 1838 to Cherry Street, and later to this location on Bell Street. The tavern was a major house of entertainment. Its original site was purchased in the 1830s by Eben Berry.

A winter afternoon in the 1860s. This stereograph view looks down Elm Street from the frontyard of the Page house (right). To the left is the Daniel Richards barn and his 1842 house at 28 Elm Street.

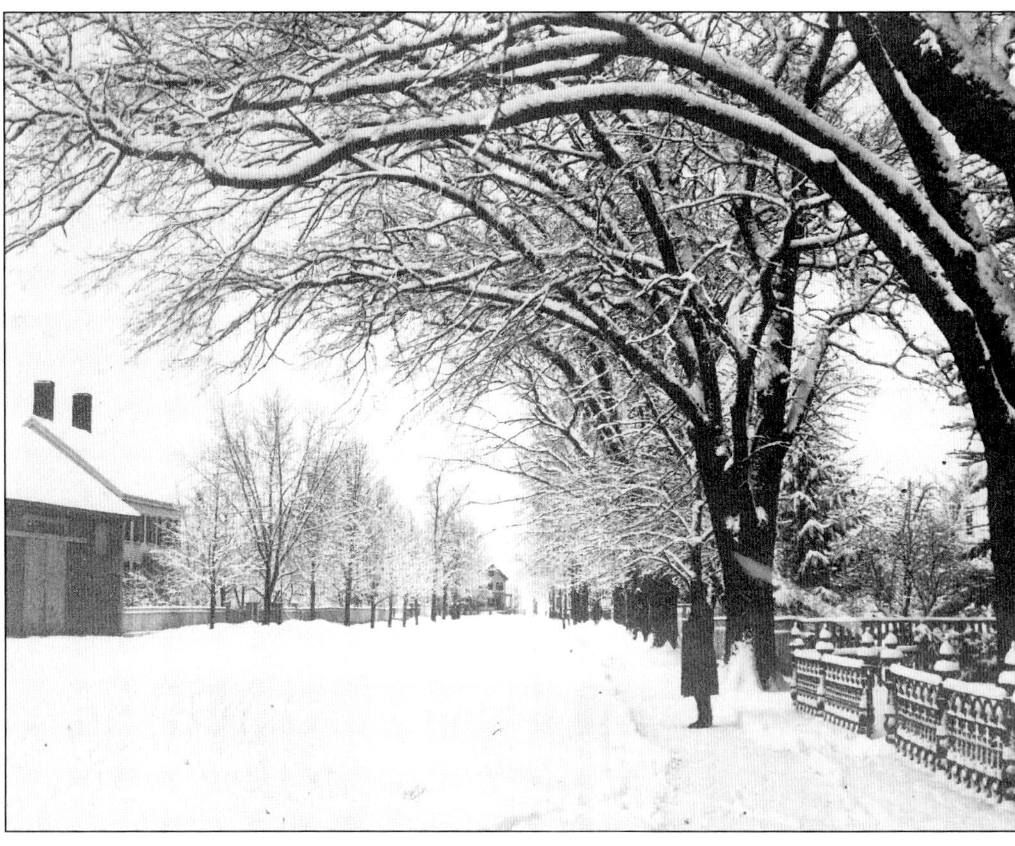

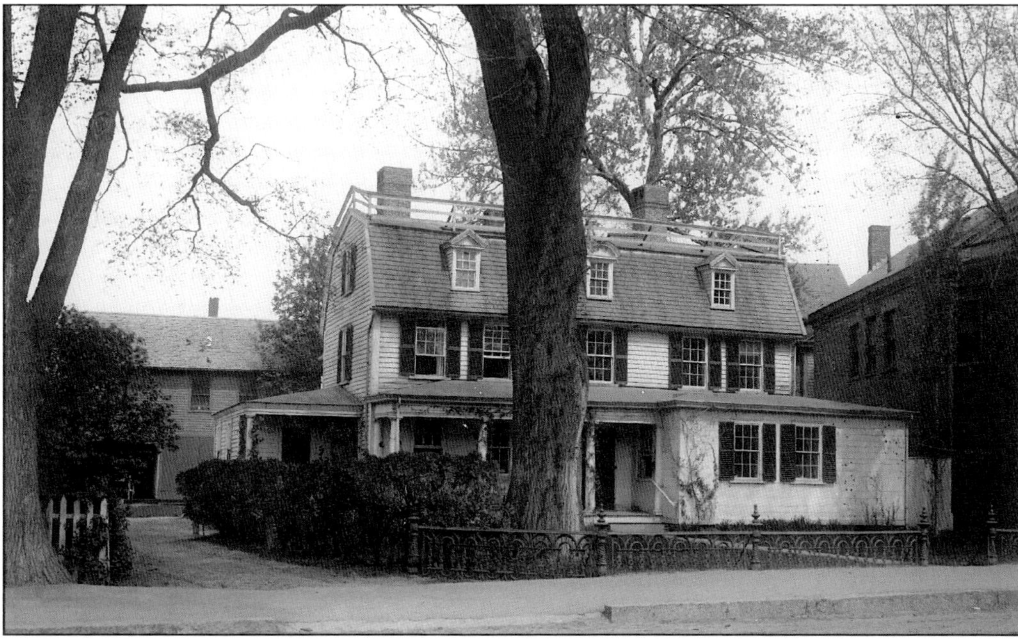

Jeremiah Page moved to Danvers in the 1740s, lured by rich clay deposits. He prospered as a brickmaker and built this Georgian house in 1754. Page was captain of a Danvers militia company. Part of his house was used as an office in 1774 by Governor Thomas Gage. In 1775 Page and his men fought the governor's troops at the Lexington Alarm.

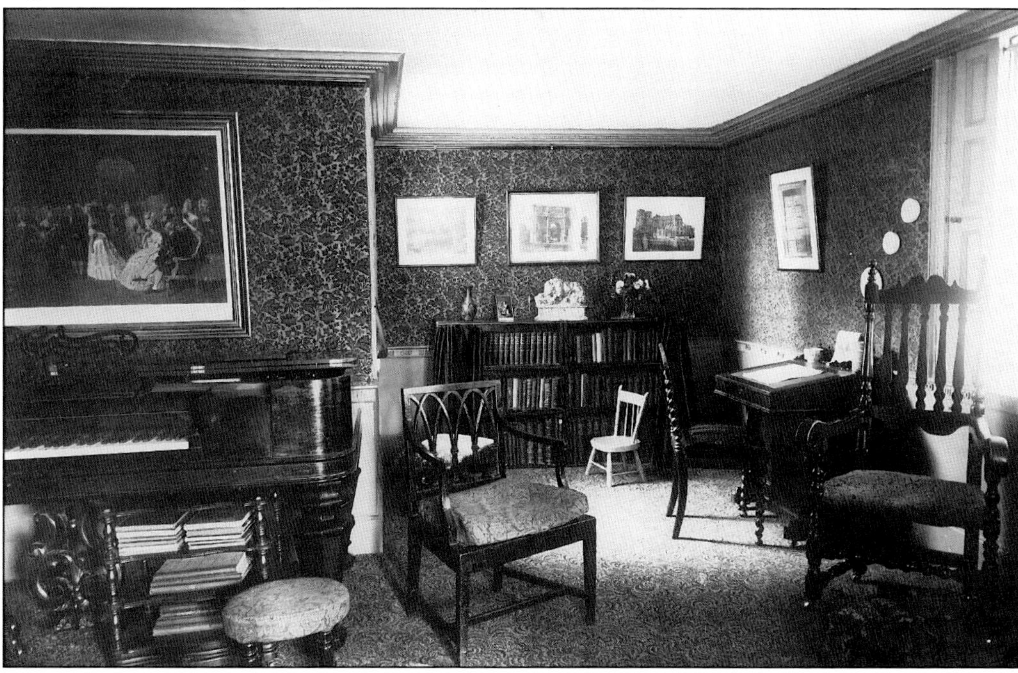

Jeremiah's son John added a piazza and expanded the east parlor toward the street in the 1830s. By the time this photograph was taken of the parlor, Anne Page, John's daughter and a well-known educator, resided here. Upon her death in 1913, the Danvers Historical Society purchased the house and moved it from Elm Street to its present location on Page Street.

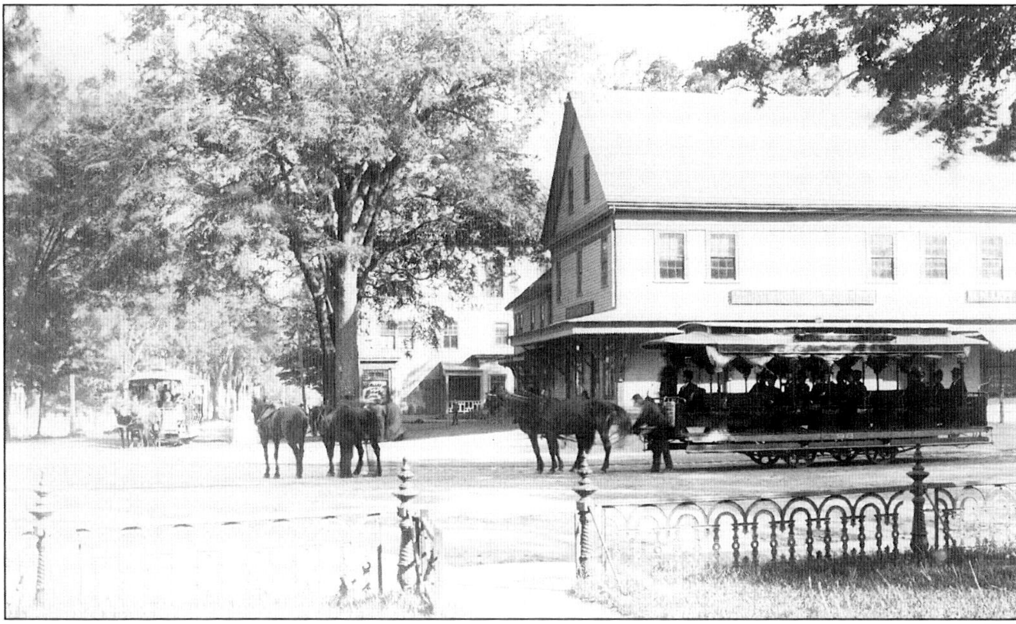

On June 12, 1892, this photograph was snapped from the Page house piazza. Horsecars were first introduced to Danvers in 1884, but were superseded in December 1892 by electric cars. As the trolley on Elm Street is being hitched with a new team of horses, another trolley is approaching from High Street. The Daniel Richards store is in the background.

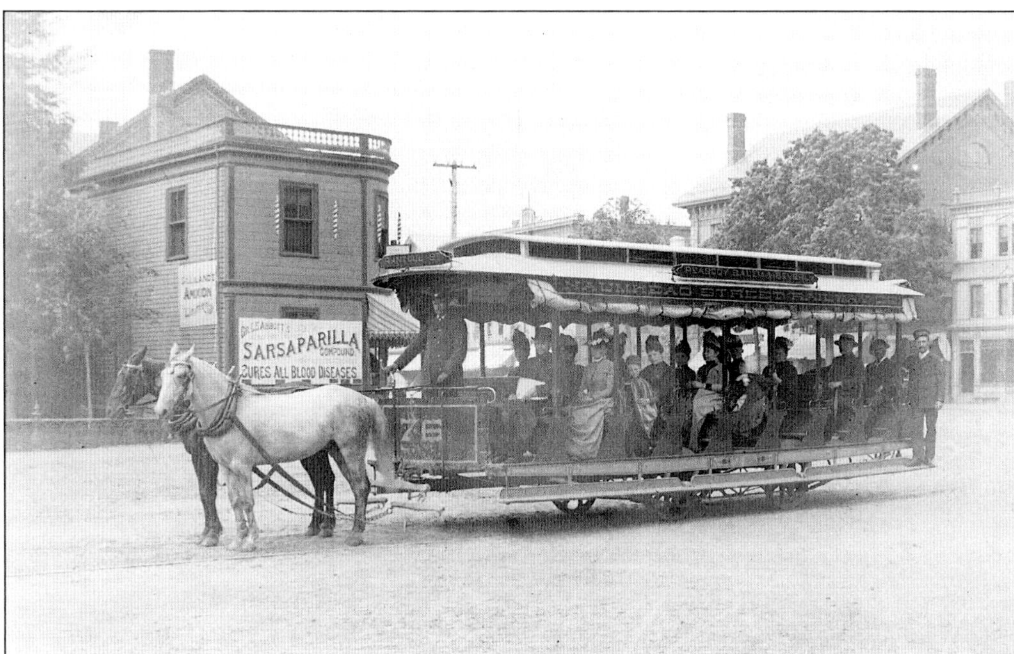

A car of the Naumkeag Street Railway Company pauses on Elm Street. At the far left is the Page house yard, while in the background on Maple Street one can see the three-story brick First National Bank, formerly the Village Bank.

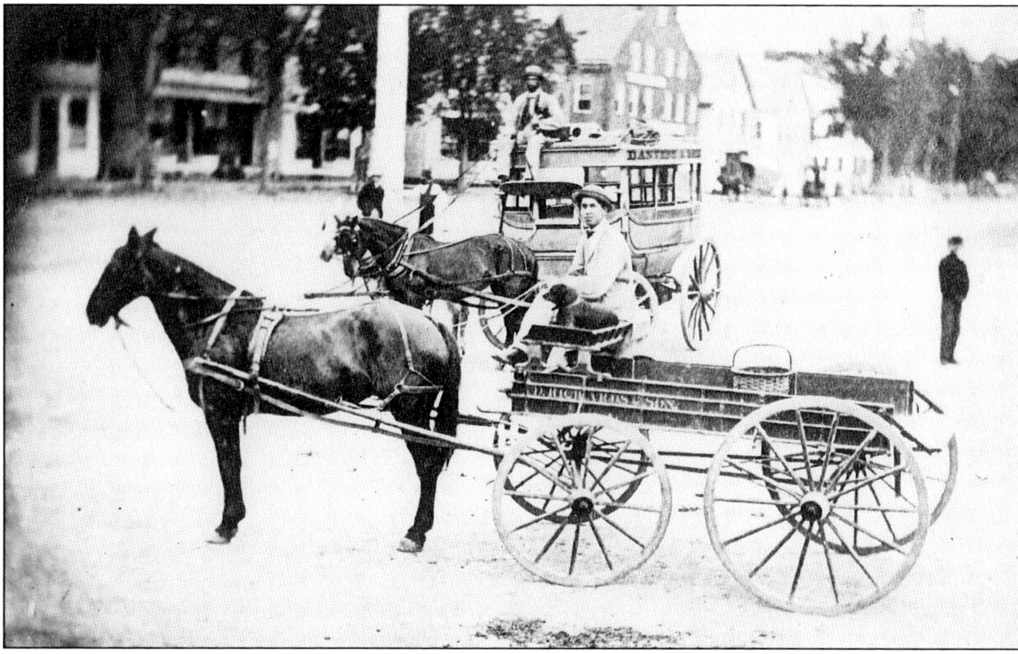

In this c. 1866 view of Maple Street looking toward the brick Francis Noyes shoe manufactory (32–34 Maple Street), a young man sits aboard the delivery wagon for the Daniel Richards grocery store. Near the square's flagpole, the Danvers and Salem stagecoach is poised. This mode of public conveyance predated the trolley line.

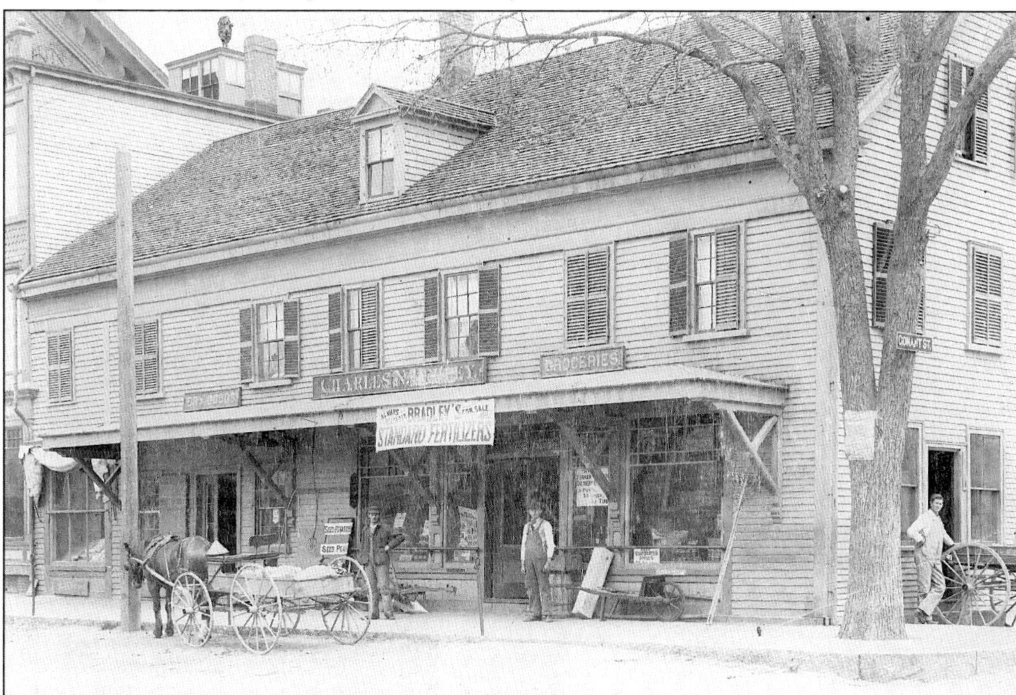

Yet another popular grocery, this one on the corner of Maple and Conant Streets, was the Charles N. Perley store. This market operated from 1800 until 1941.

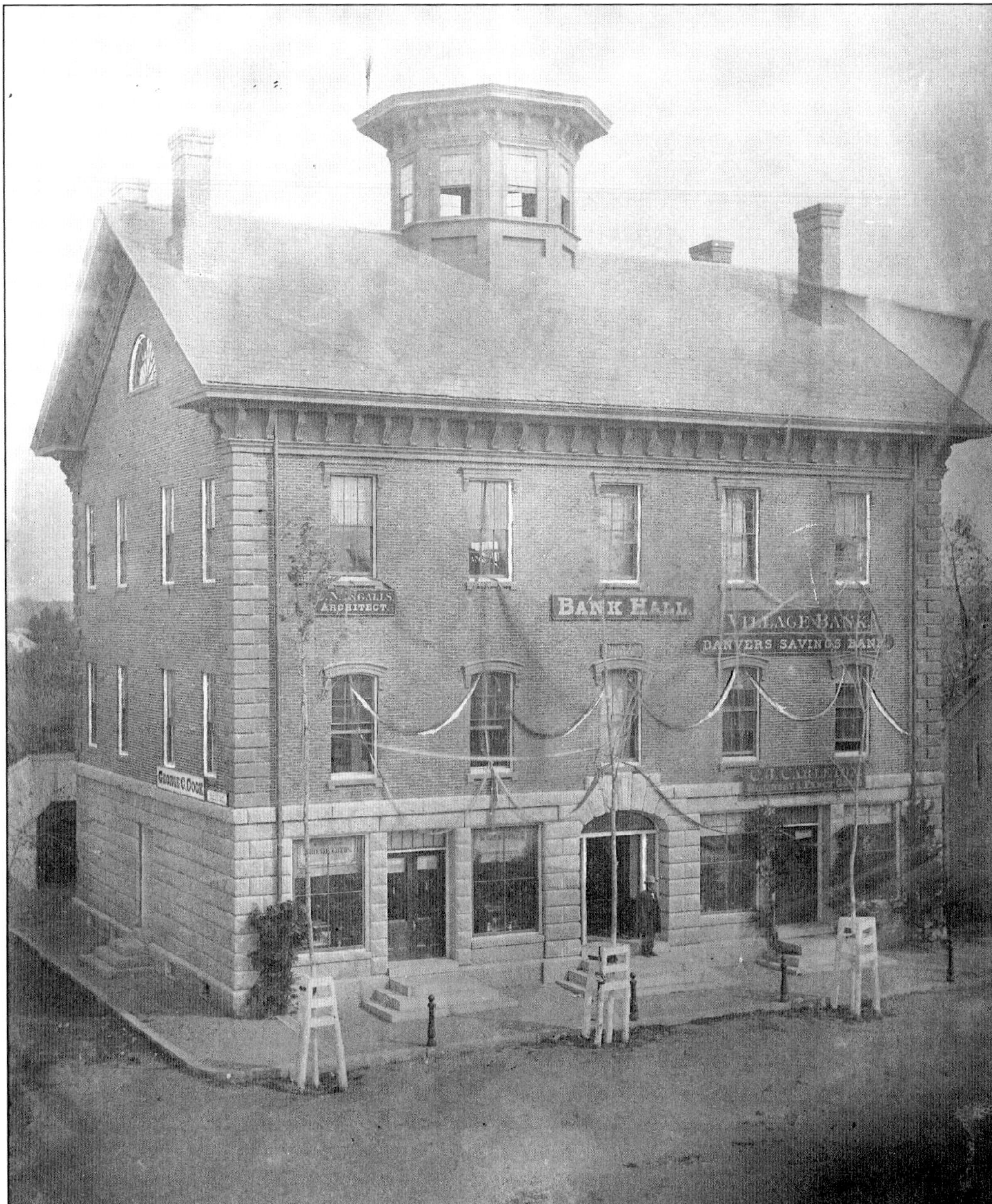

The Village Bank was a grand scale Italianate-style building of granite, brick, and sandstone. Built in 1854, it featured a roof cupola. This 1860s photograph by D.A. Clifford shows that the building's architect, Charles N. Ingalls, had an office within the new building (see also p. 14).

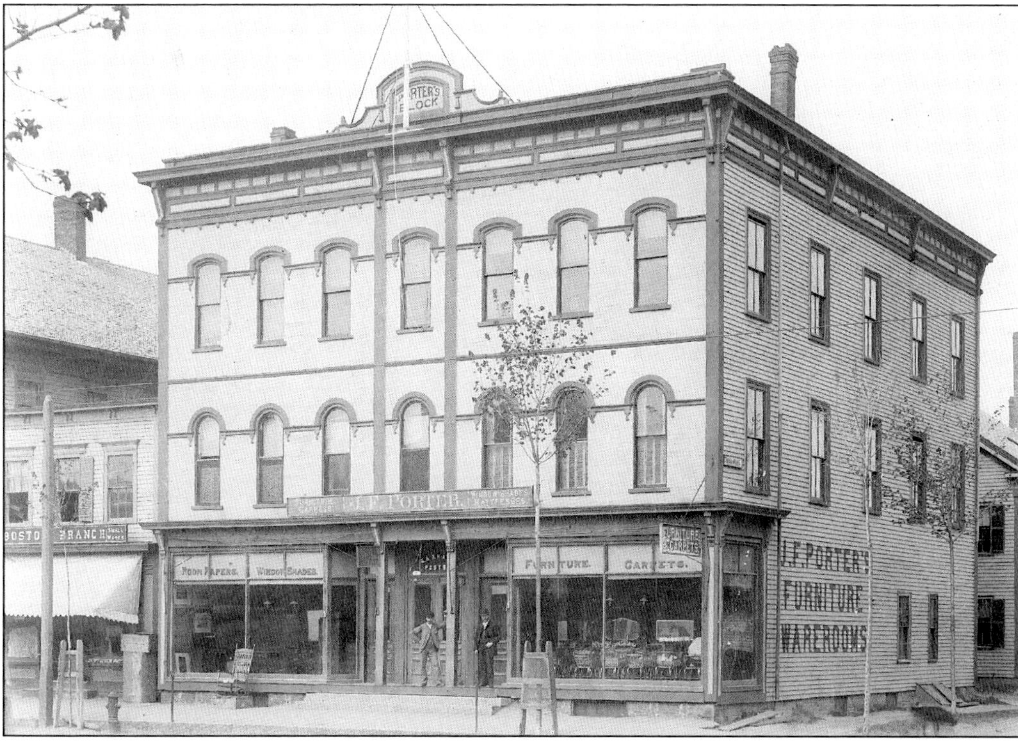

On the corner of Maple Street and Central Avenue stood the 1878 Porter Block, owned by furniture dealer and town activist J. Frank Porter.

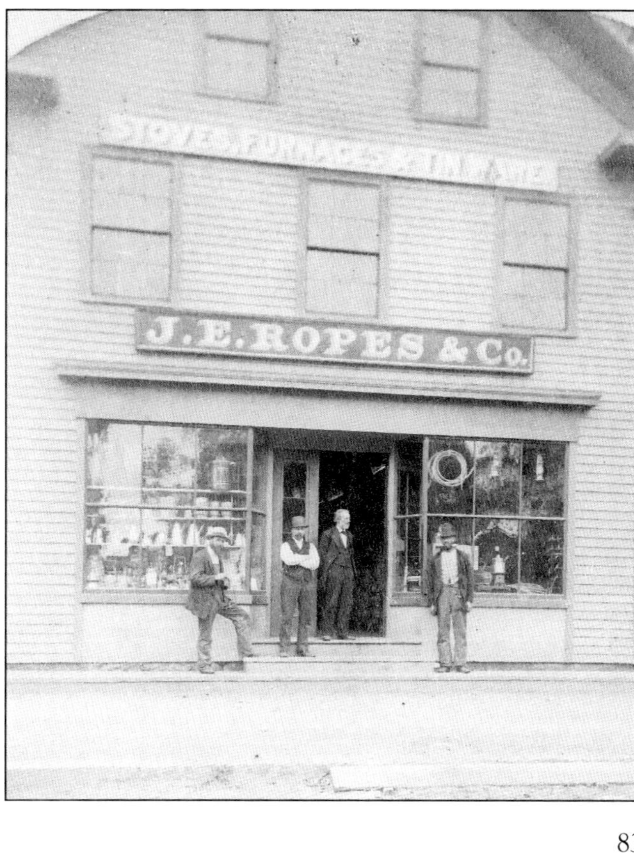

On the west side of Maple Street in this c. 1878 photograph is the Joseph E. Ropes & Co. stove and tinware company. The Greek Revival structure was built in 1848 at what is now 24 Maple Street. In April 1996 a fire severely damaged this and an adjoining building.

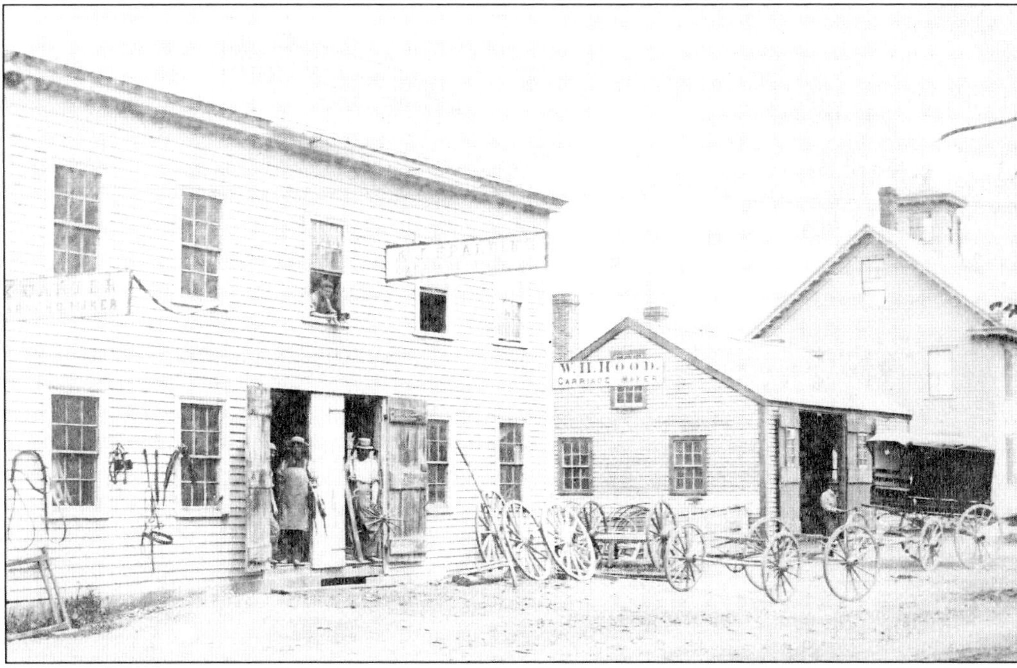

Venturing down School Street in the 1860s one would have visited Kendall Carter's harness shop as well as the businesses of carriage makers W.H. Hood and A.J. Spalding.

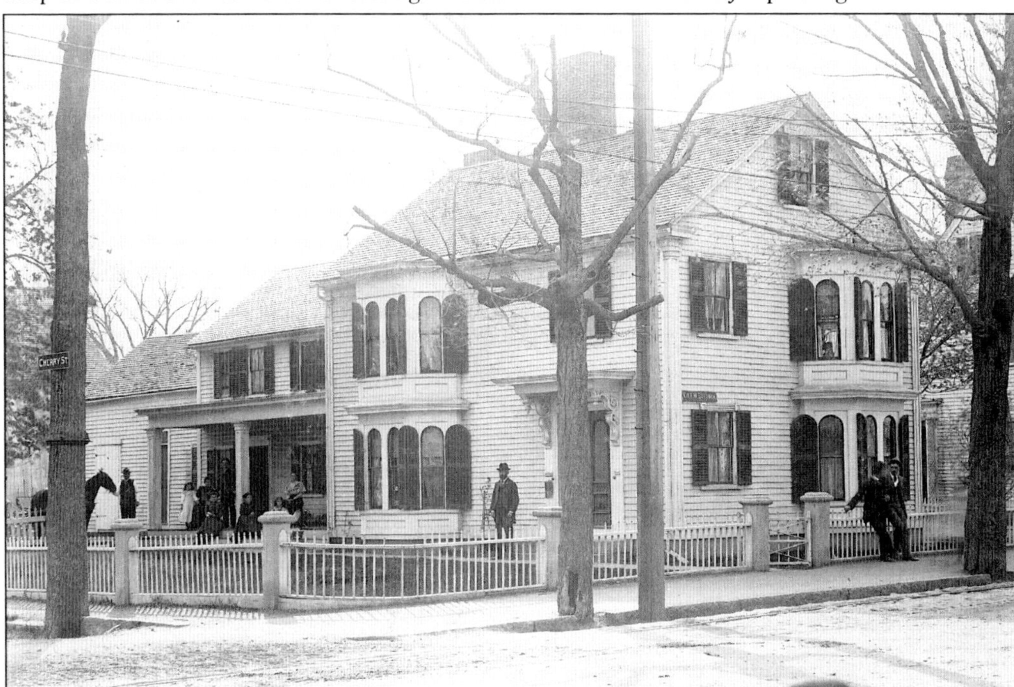

The 1835 Simeon Putnam Jr. house on the corner of Maple and Cherry Streets was photographed in the 1890s by A.O. Elwell. Dr. Frederick W. Baldwin, seen at the door, rented part of this building for his residence and office. In about 1910 the house was moved back to 5 Cherry Street.

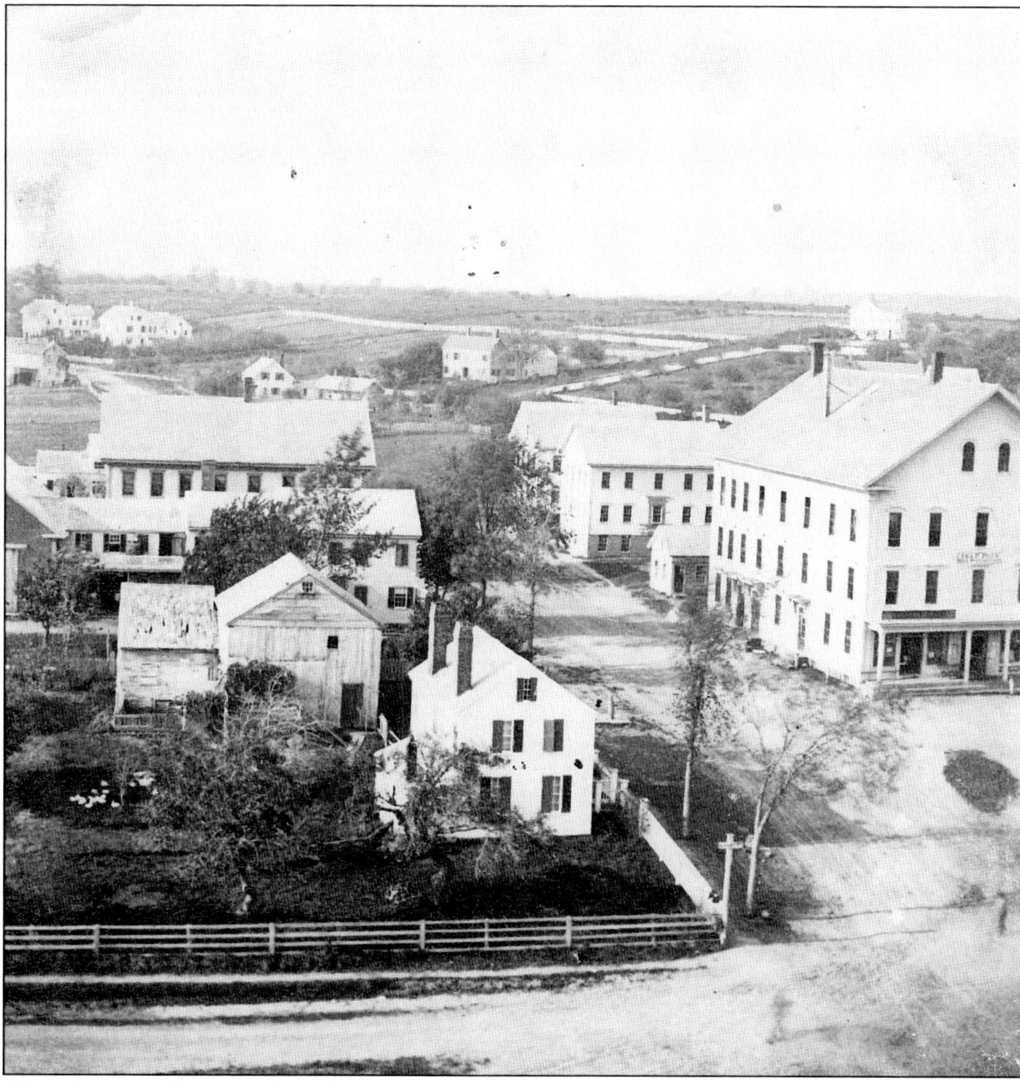

This photograph was taken about 1870 from the spire of the Maple Street Congregational Church looking toward Lindall Hill. The large structure on the right is the 1859 Spaulding building. The top floors were used by Ira P. Pope as a shoe manufactory. In the 1920s the building was converted into the town's central fire station, and was used for that purpose until 1995. Hobart Street is at the bottom of the photograph.

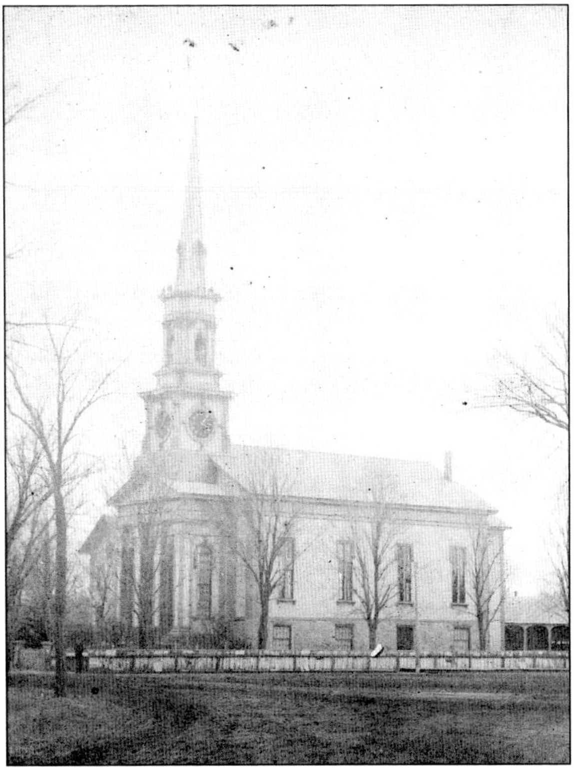

The Third Orthodox Congregational Church was established on Maple Street in Danvers Plains in 1844. The building was constructed to replace one that burned in 1850. In 1944 this edifice also fell to fire and was replaced by the current Maple Street Church.

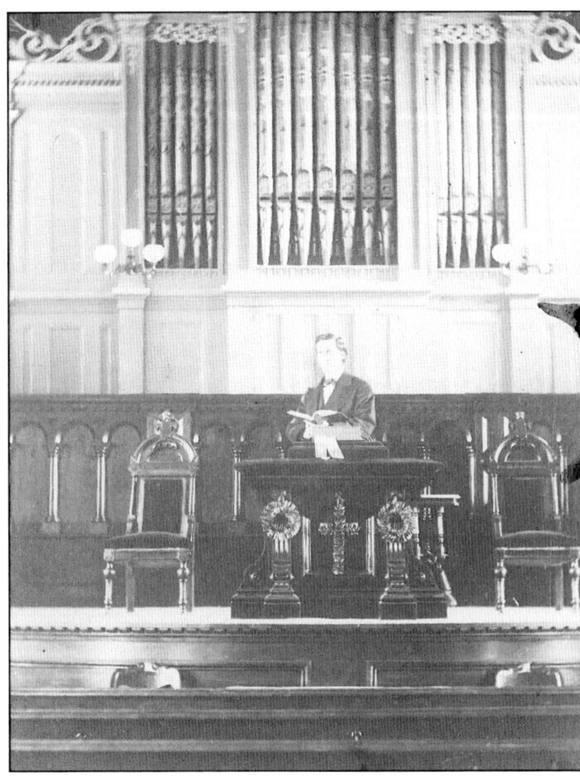

Reverend Walter Wright was minister at the Maple Street Church from 1875 to 1882. Here, amid a Gothic-style pulpit and side chairs, he presents a sermon.

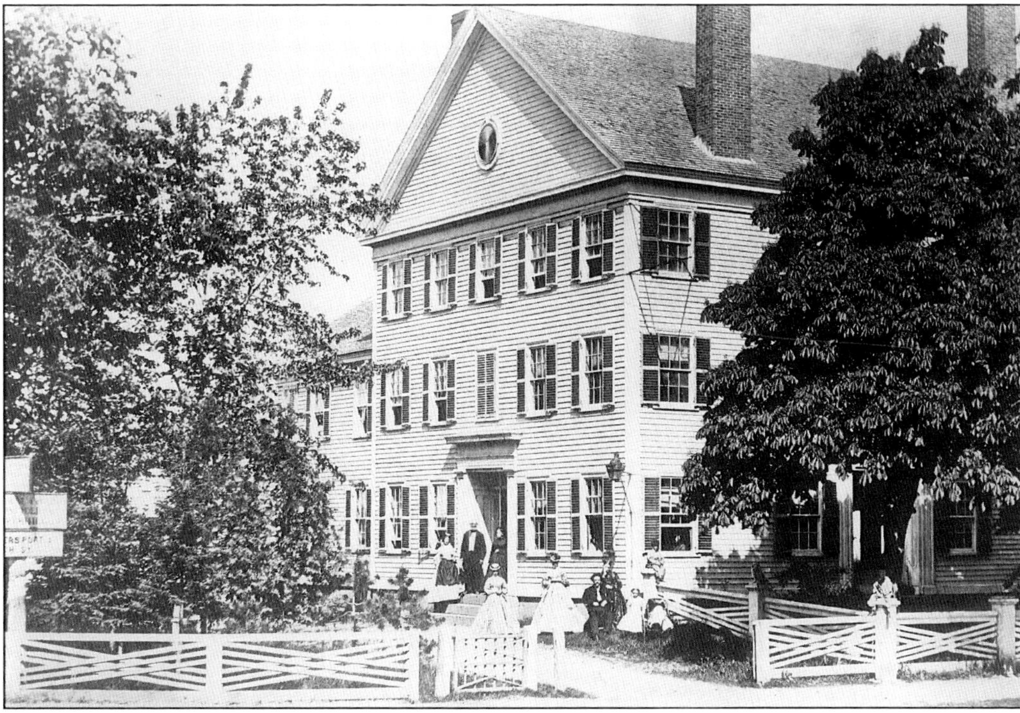

Eben G. Berry built this grand Greek Revival tavern in 1838 to replace the eighteenth-century one (see p. 77). In this 1840s Daguerreotype the Berry family, including Eben at the doorway and grandsons Charles and John Learoyd sitting on the fence posts, gaze out toward High Street.

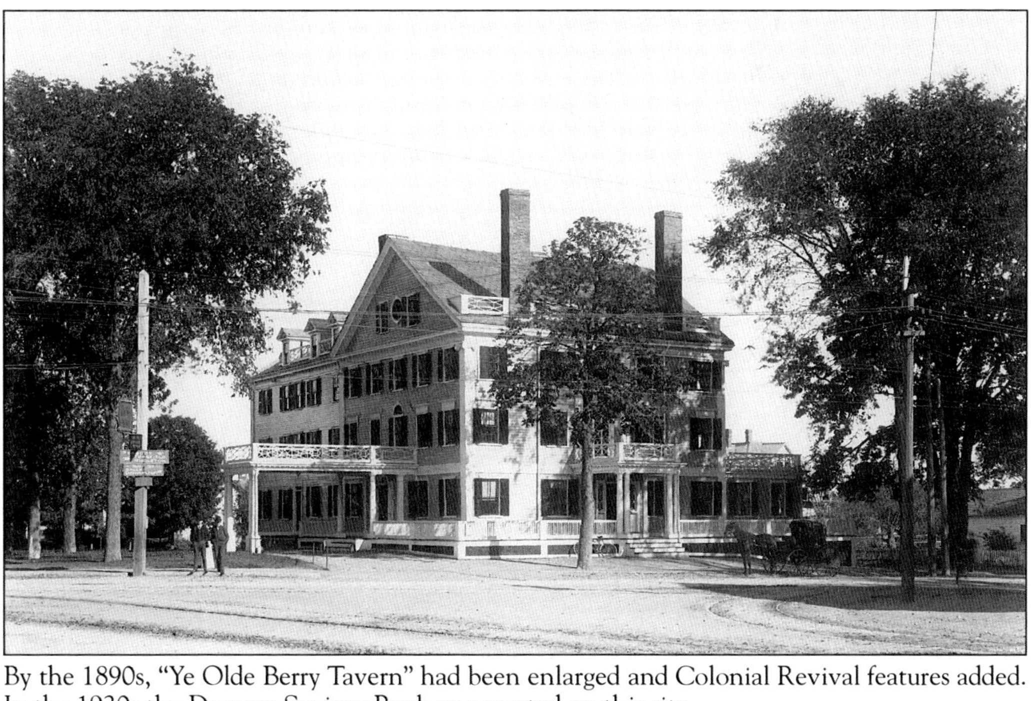

By the 1890s, "Ye Olde Berry Tavern" had been enlarged and Colonial Revival features added. In the 1920s the Danvers Savings Bank was erected on this site.

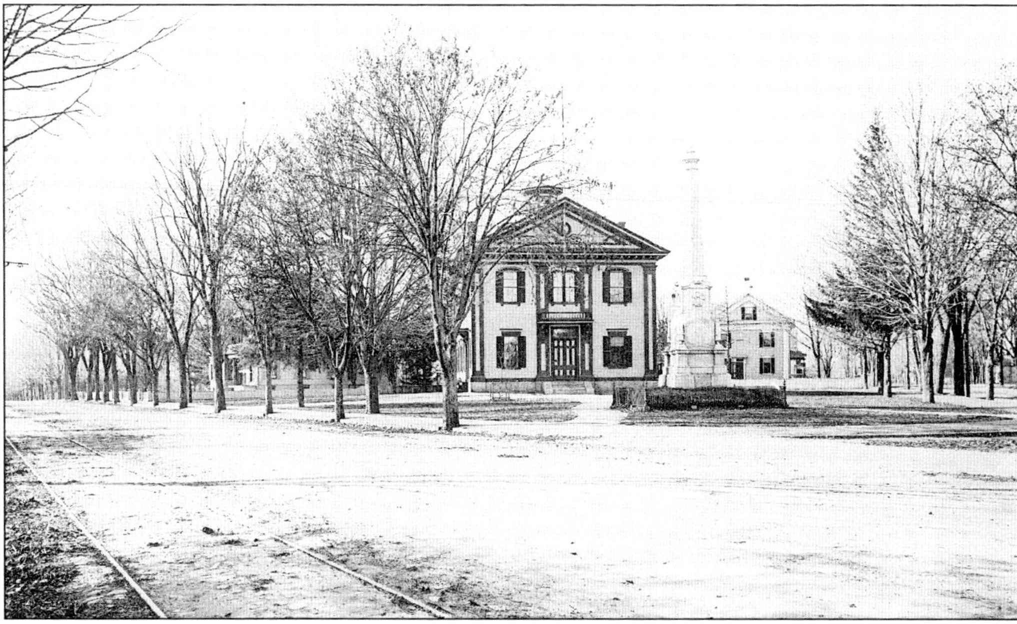

A *c.* 1890 photograph depicting the Danvers Town House and High School at the point of Sylvan and Holten Streets. Built in 1854 as the center of local government, the building was expanded in 1888 and had wings with towers added in 1897. In 1949 the towers were removed.

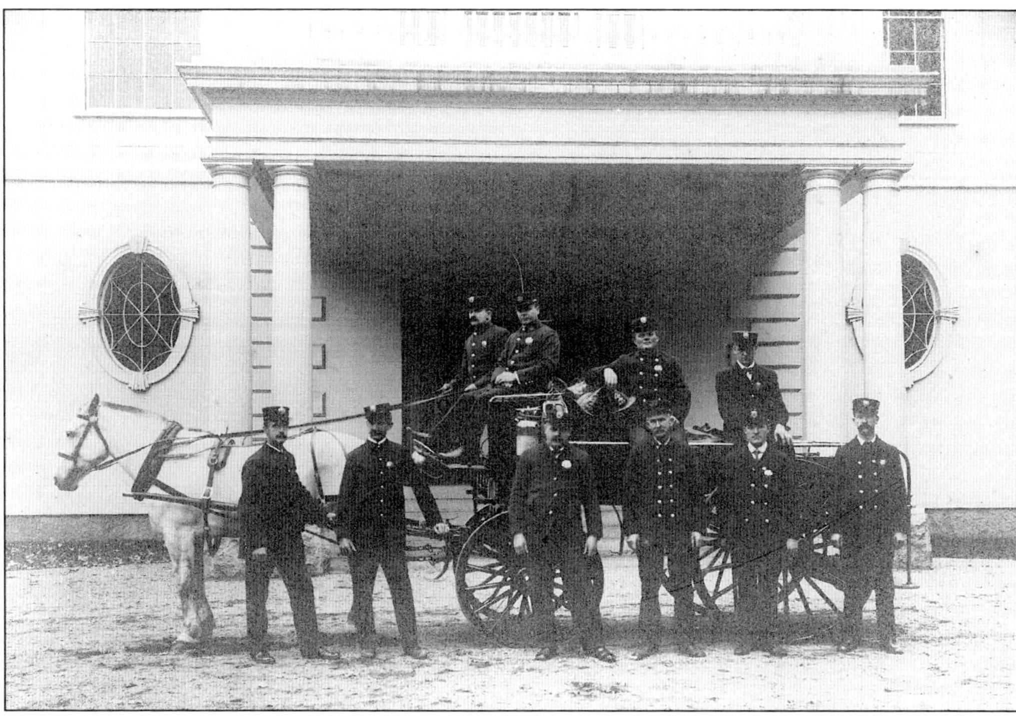

Members of the Danvers Fire Department's Major Chase Hose Company Number 4, shown here posing in front of the balconial-entry portico of the Peabody Institute Library. In the 1890s, when this photograph was taken, the hose wagon was stationed with Hose Company Number 1 on School Street .

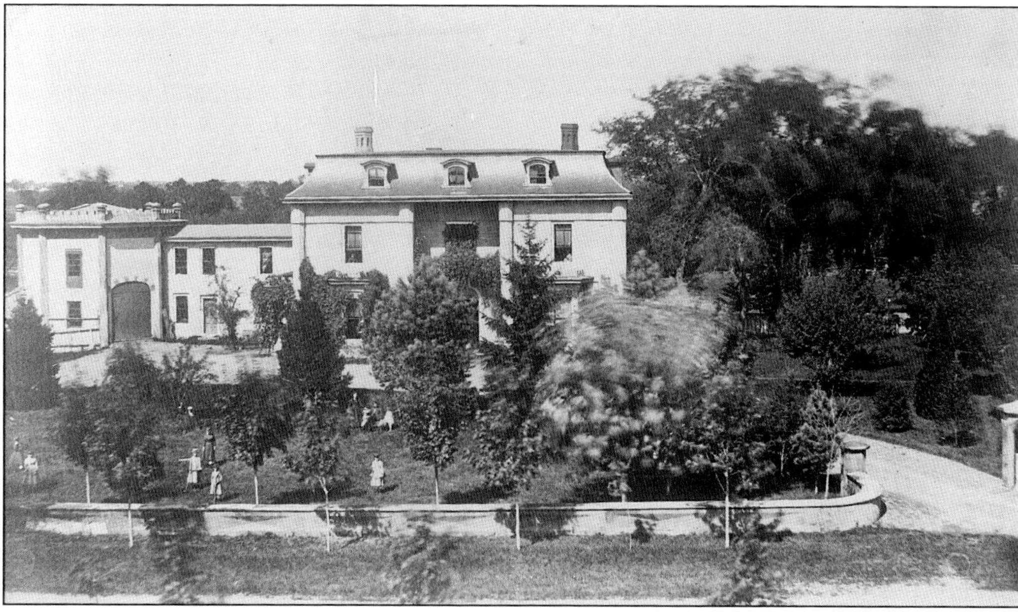

This stately mansard-roofed house was the first in the United States to be constructed with a Portland cement exterior. Containing an octagon-shaped stable and many other modernizations, the house at 11 Peabody Avenue was built 1857–58 for shoe manufacturer and library trustee Joshua Silvester.

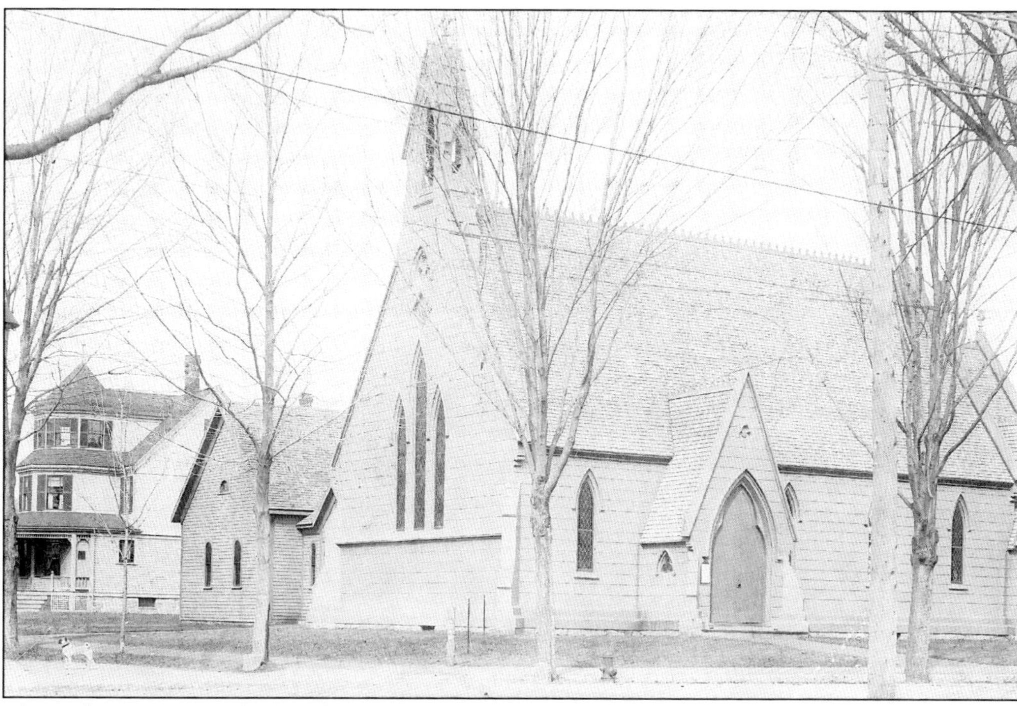

The Calvary Episcopal Church at 13 Holten Street was designed in 1859 in the Gothic Revival style by Enoch P. Fuller. By the time this photograph was made at the turn of the century, a parish hall and office facing Cherry Street had been added. The Queen Anne-style rectory on the left was built in 1890.

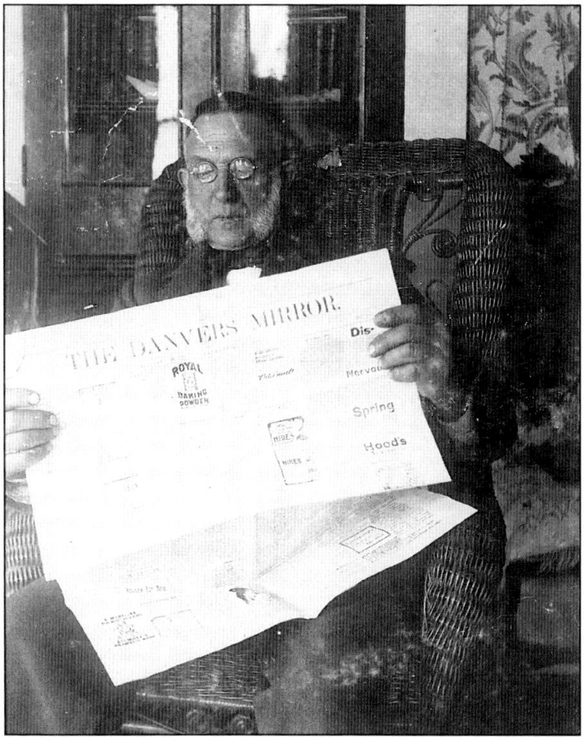

In this unusually candid snapshot photograph, Dean A. Perley, who owned a blacksmith shop, is seen reading the April 17, 1897 edition of *The Danvers Mirror* at his Poplar Street residence.

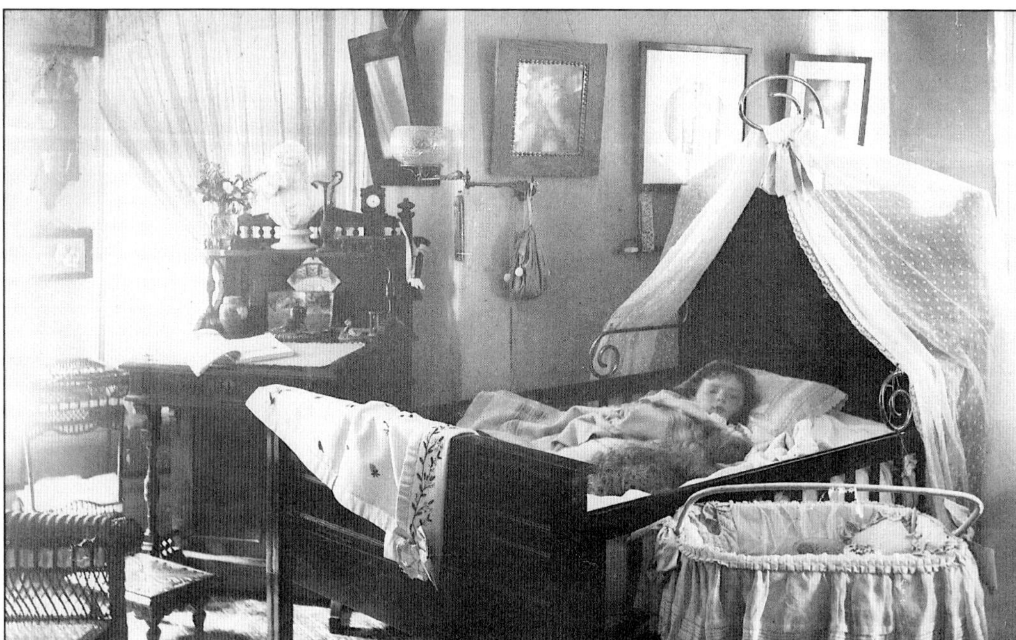

Four-year-old Alfred Fellows Masury in his room at 48 Elm Street in 1887. His house was visited during the anti-slavery days by such notables as William Lloyd Garrison, Harriet Beecher Stowe, and Frederick Douglass. Alfred's politically active mother, Evelyn Masury, later entertained Presidents Taft and Coolidge here. Alfred died in 1933 in the crash of the dirigible *Akron*. The house is now the George Peabody Cooperative Bank.

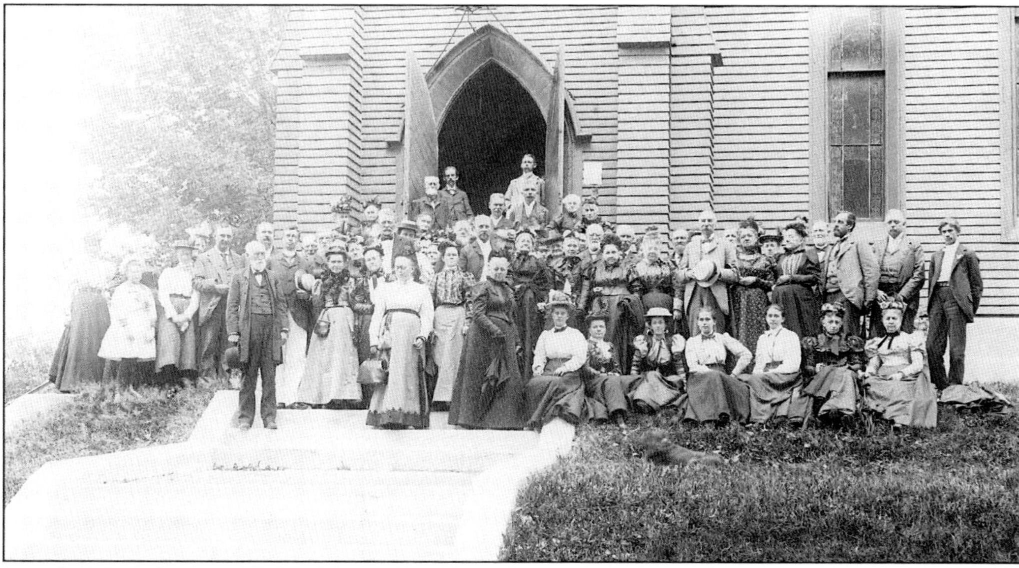

Members of the Porter family reunion gather together for a group portrait in front of the Universalist church on High Street on July 20, 1898.

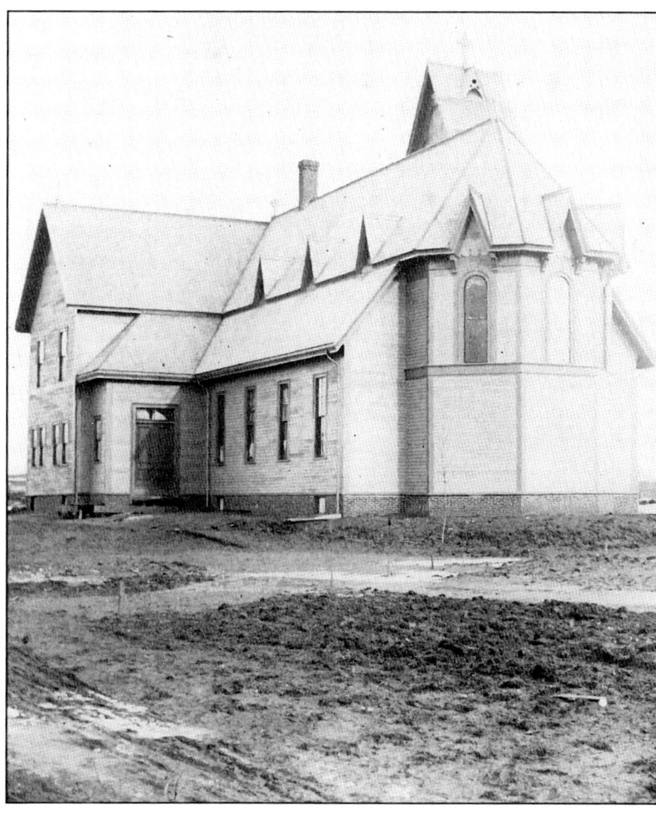

The Unitarian Congregational Society of Danvers built this chapel off High Street at the corner of Porter Street from the design of Andrew Nichols and Samuel F. Eveleth. In this 1871 stereograph view, the chapel has been completed but is without landscaping.

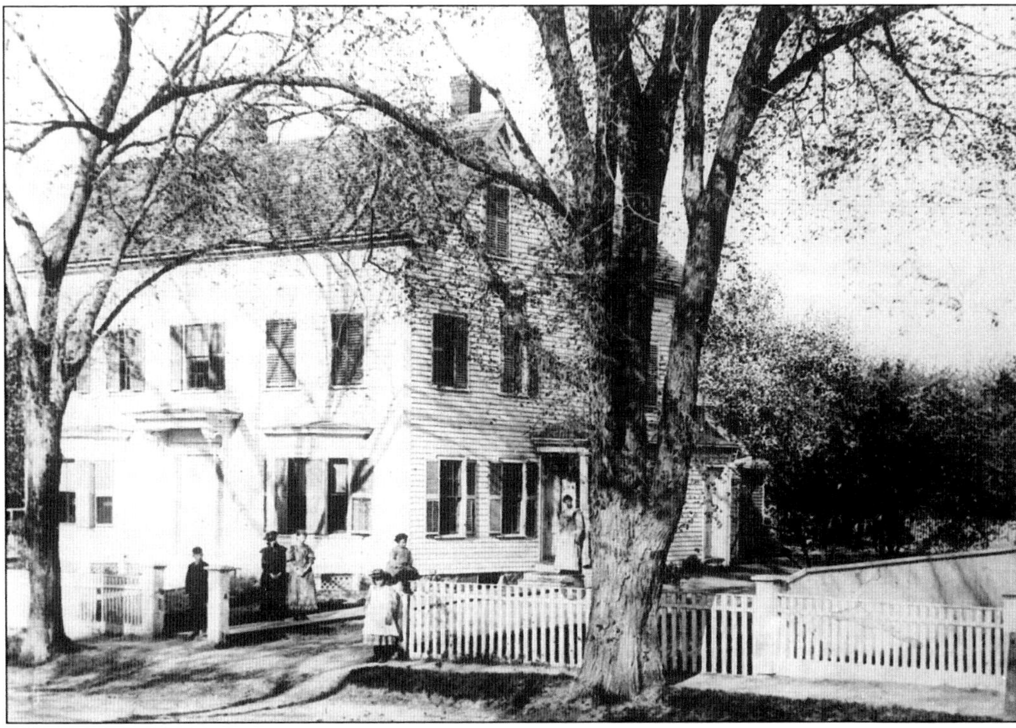

Begun as a modest one-story Greek Revival cottage in 1844 for harness maker John S. Barr, this structure at 51 Locust Street was enlarged in 1874 by jacking up the house and adding a new first floor and ell.

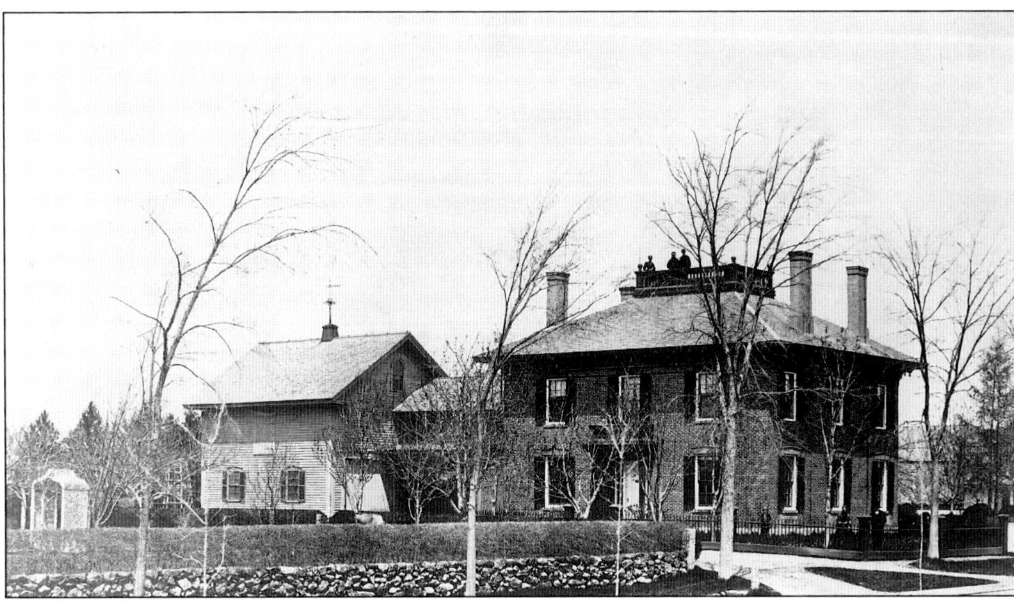

Nathan Tapley, brick manufacturer, used some of his locally made bricks to erect his residence at 127 Sylvan Street in 1852. At a later time the roof line was changed to accommodate a third story.

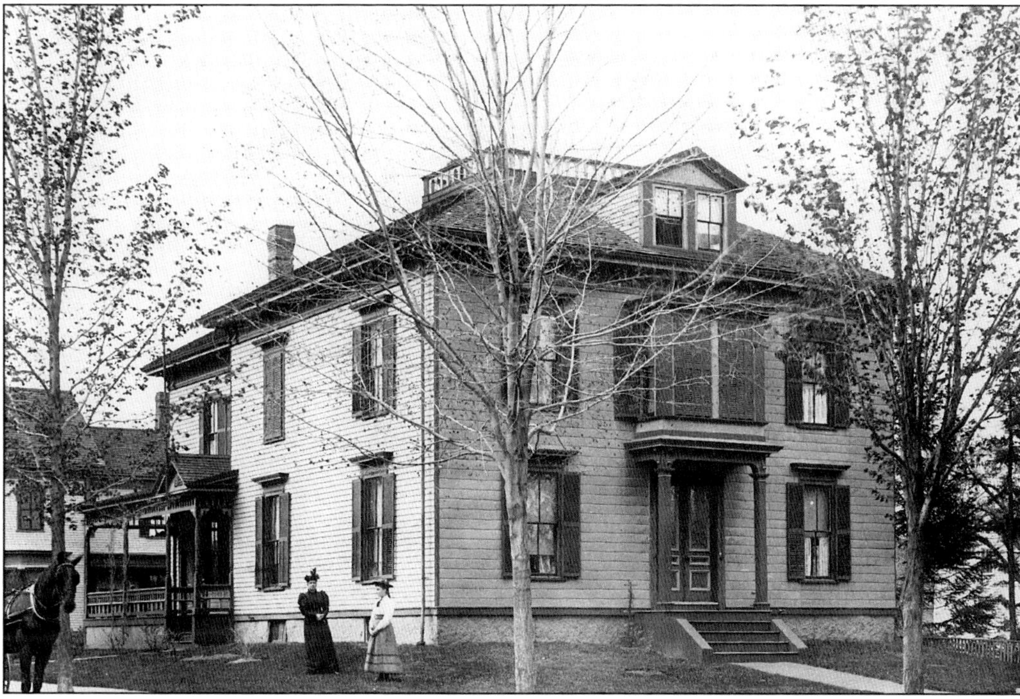

Yet another square, hip-roofed house in Danvers Plains was this dwelling at 19 Cherry Street. It was built in 1877 by Francis A. Couch for J. Frank Porter (see p. 83).

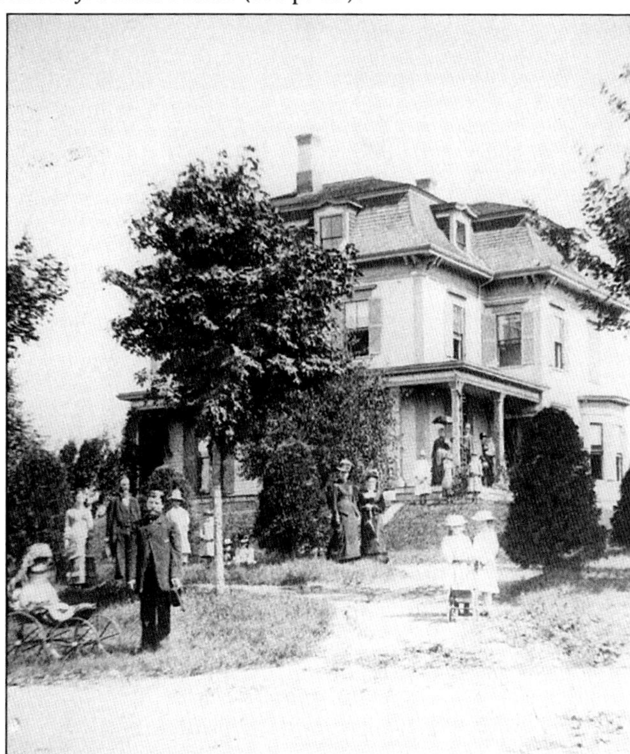

Lindall Hill is a glacial drumlin adjacent to Locust and Maple Streets. Beginning in the 1870s this hill became a choice new residential neighborhood. This mansard-roofed house was built on the corner of Lindall and Winthrop Streets and is shown here in 1878 with Attorney Edward L. Hill and his family out front.

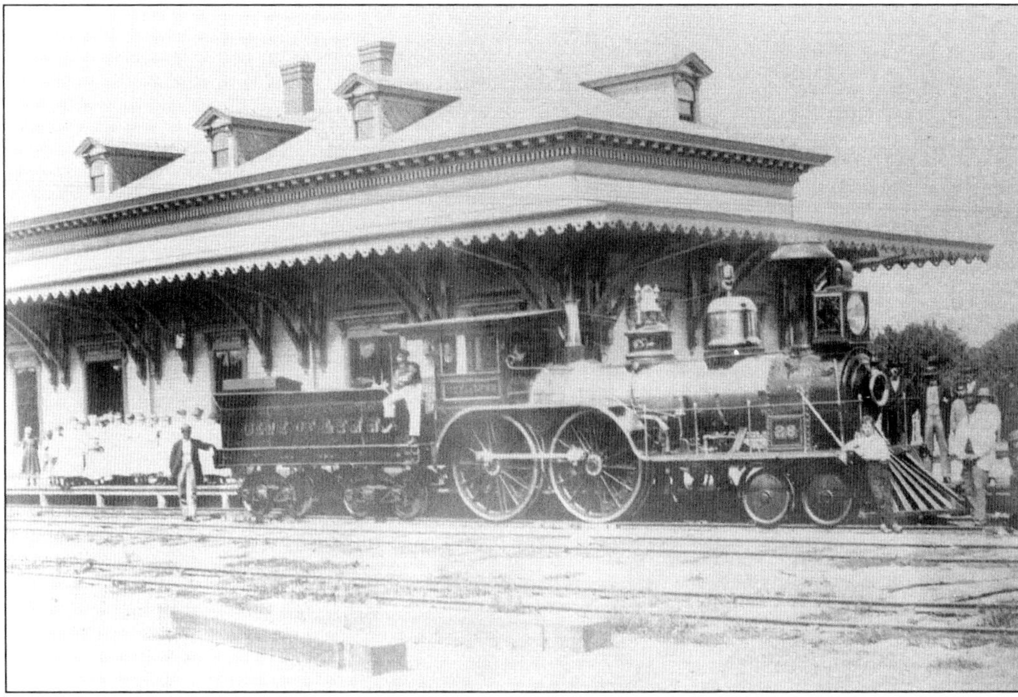

The locomotive City of Lynn, which was built in 1854, sits beside the Danvers Plains railroad station. In its heyday Danvers boasted nine separate stations serving the various villages and neighborhoods.

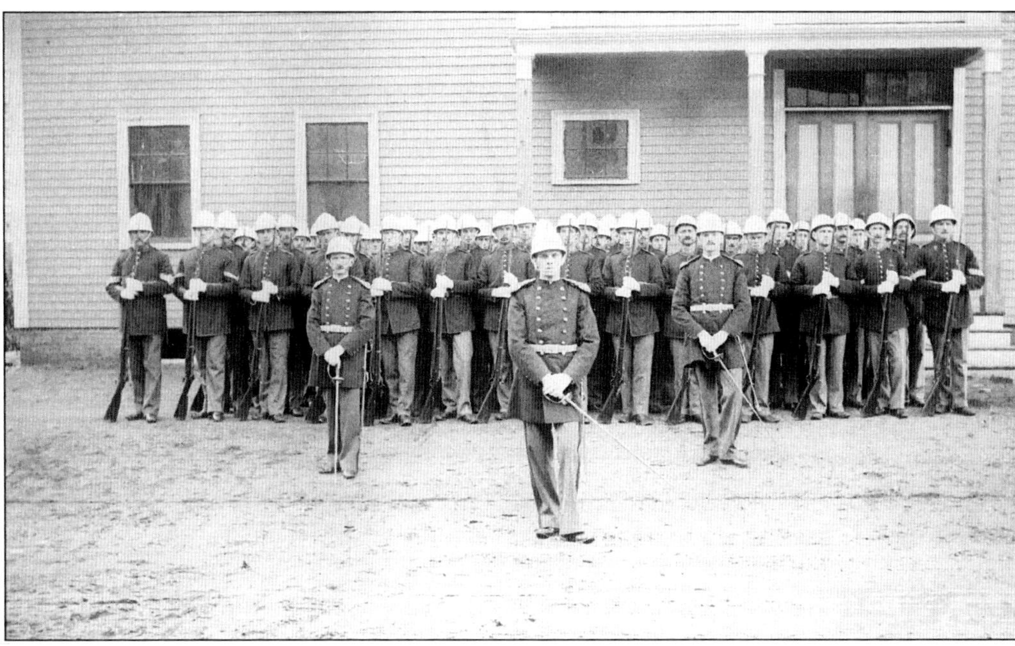

Captain Frank C. Damon stands before his men of the Danvers Light Infantry which are mustered in cork hats and tunics in front of their armory on Maple Street. This unit was founded in 1891 and soon became Company K of the 8th Regiment Massachusetts Volunteer Militia.

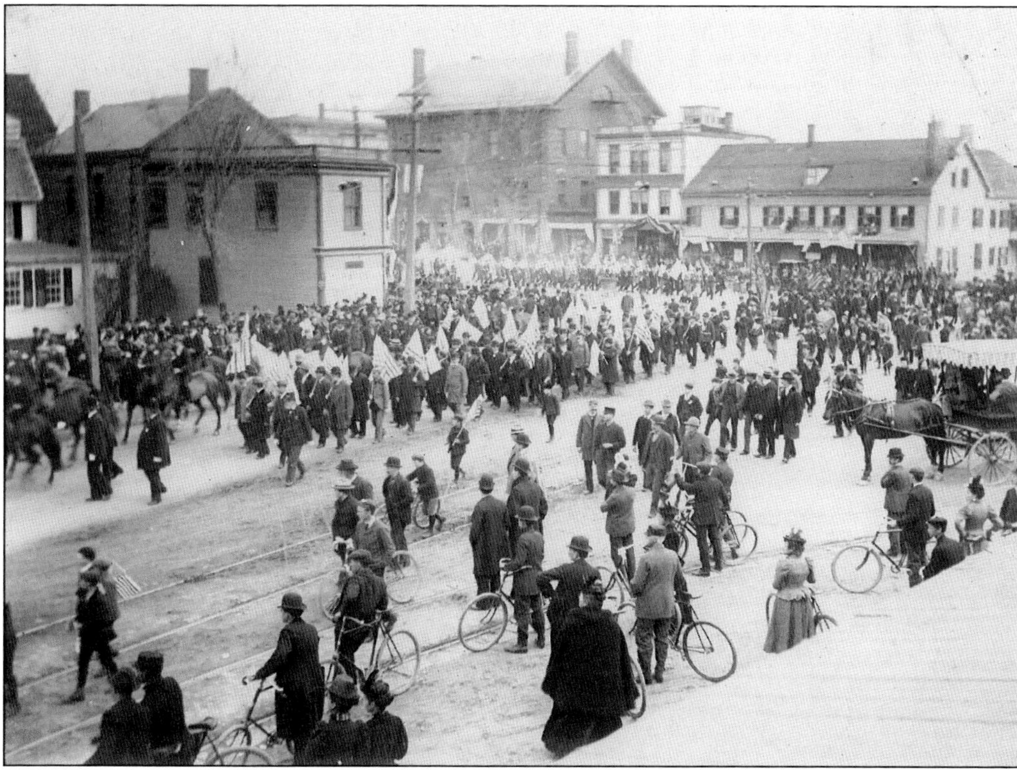

Company K was activated following the declaration of war with Spain in April 1898. On the morning of May 5, 1898, the citizens of Danvers turned out to watch the local parade of the company marching off to war. Civil War veterans are shown here on Elm Street, many carrying flags, as they march in the escort parade.

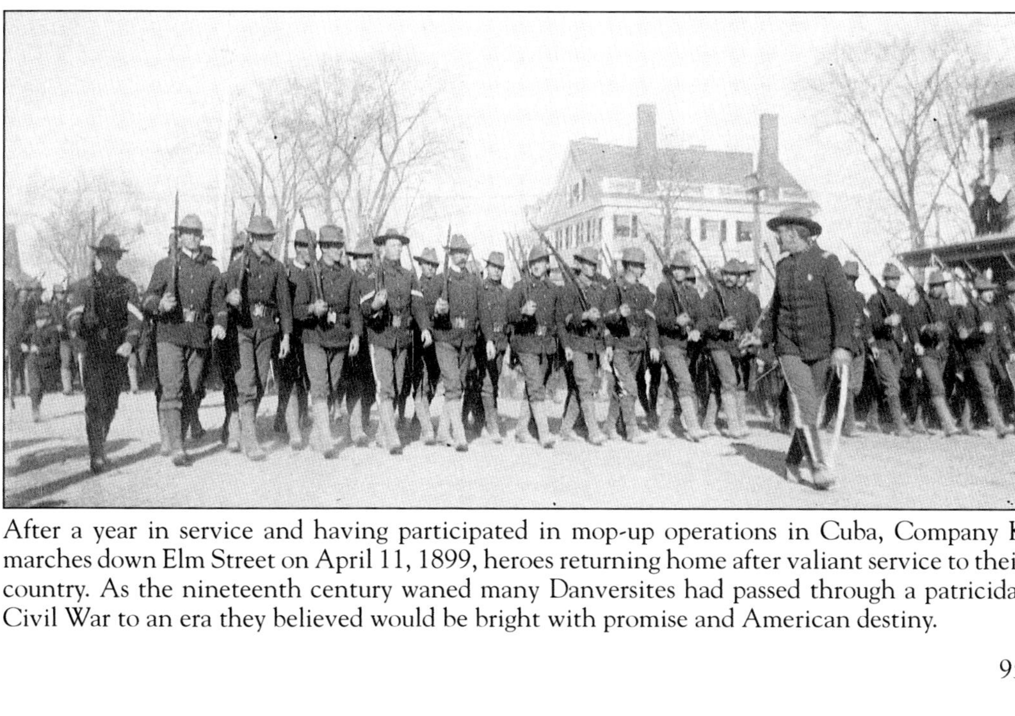

After a year in service and having participated in mop-up operations in Cuba, Company K marches down Elm Street on April 11, 1899, heroes returning home after valiant service to their country. As the nineteenth century waned many Danversites had passed through a patricidal Civil War to an era they believed would be bright with promise and American destiny.

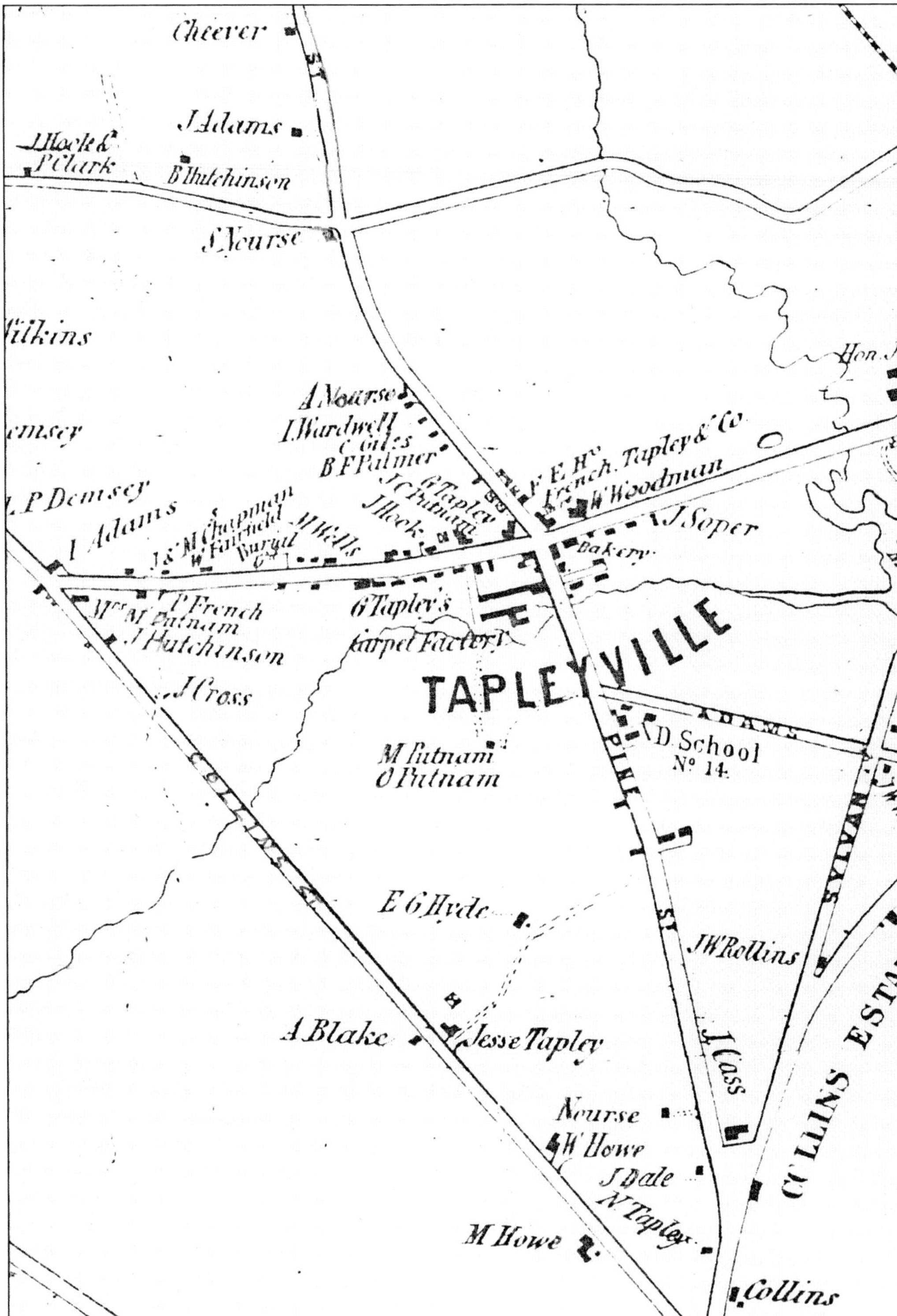

A map of 1852 Tapleyville.

Seven

Tapley Village

Radiating primarily from Holten and Pine Streets, this area of Danvers was chiefly farmland up through the 1830s. In 1843 Perley Tapley, an experienced mover of buildings, joined with his brother Gilbert to establish a carpet manufactory. Skilled weavers were sought from England and Scotland and numerous old buildings were moved to this area to be converted into worker housing and other necessary buildings.

By 1847, 60 employees, 30 looms, and a 25-horsepower engine were producing 60,000 yards of carpeting per year; by 1860, this would rise to 100 men and 50 women employees producing 100,000 yards of carpet. Though the business was discontinued in about 1880, the village, now known as "Tapleyville," was firmly established. A residential and commercial neighborhood with a population in 1895 of 1,300, Tapleyville was the third most populated section of Danvers.

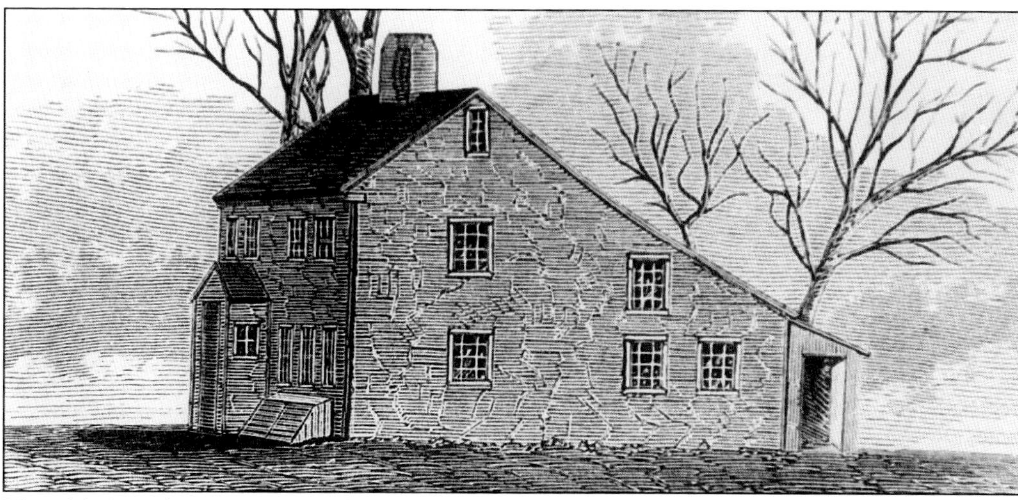

The old Nurse house as pictured in an 1866 engraving.

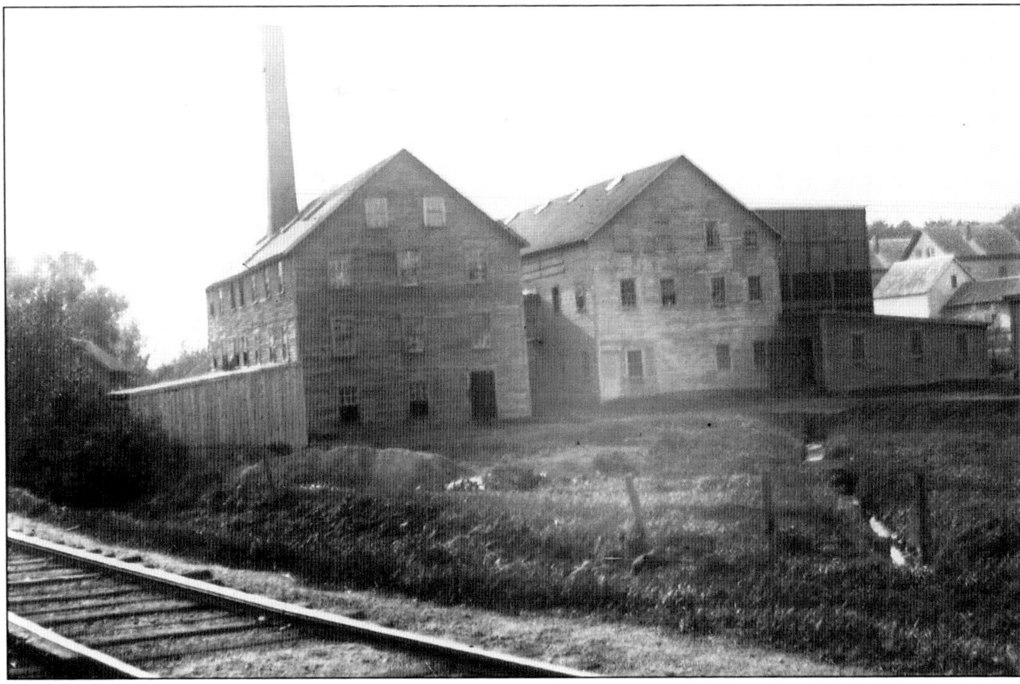

The Tapley Carpet Factory off Holten Street was the driving force for the creation of the Tapley village area. This late-nineteenth-century photograph shows part of the old factory complex. The now shabby buildings were still functioning, though for leather processing rather than carpet weaving.

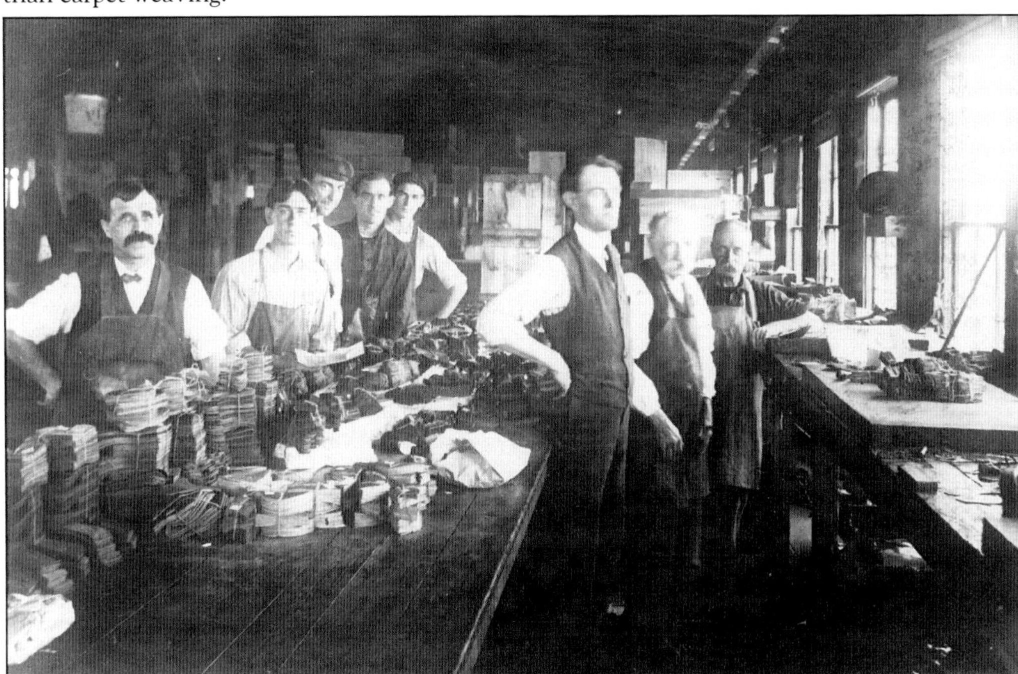

A glimpse into the shoe cutting room of the Martin Kelley Shoe Company at Holten and Pine Streets.

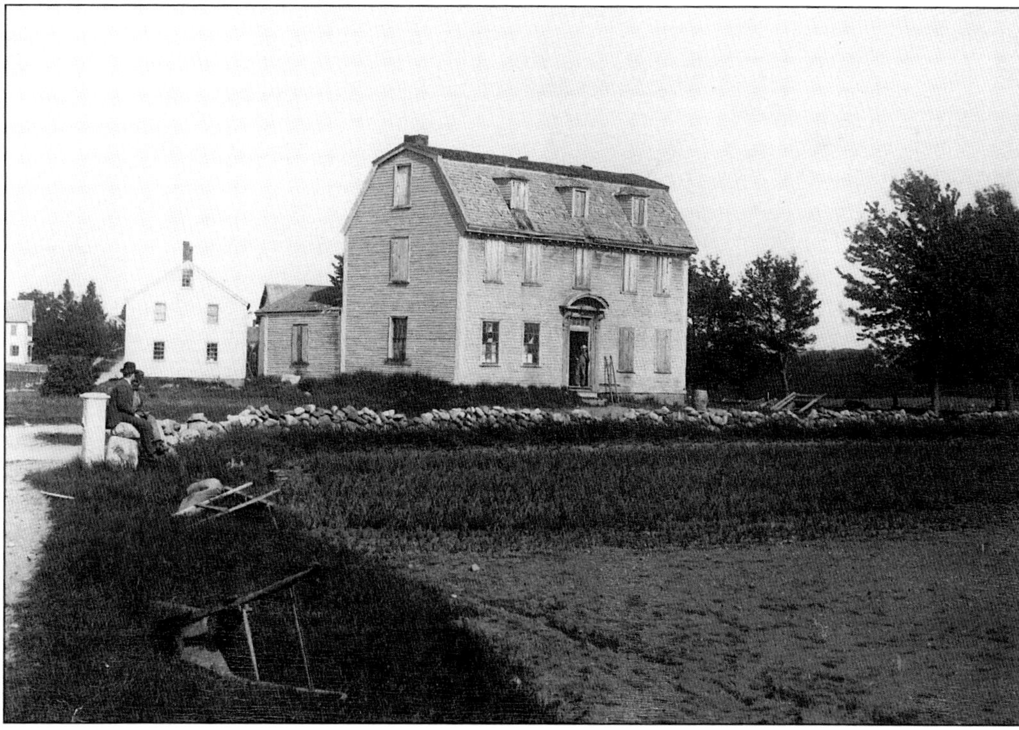

Many of the residential buildings in Tapleyville were moved into the village as an inexpensive alternative to new construction. Here, at the corner of Pine and Adams Streets, is a lovely gambrel-roofed house moved to this site from Salem and owned by Gilbert A. Tapley.

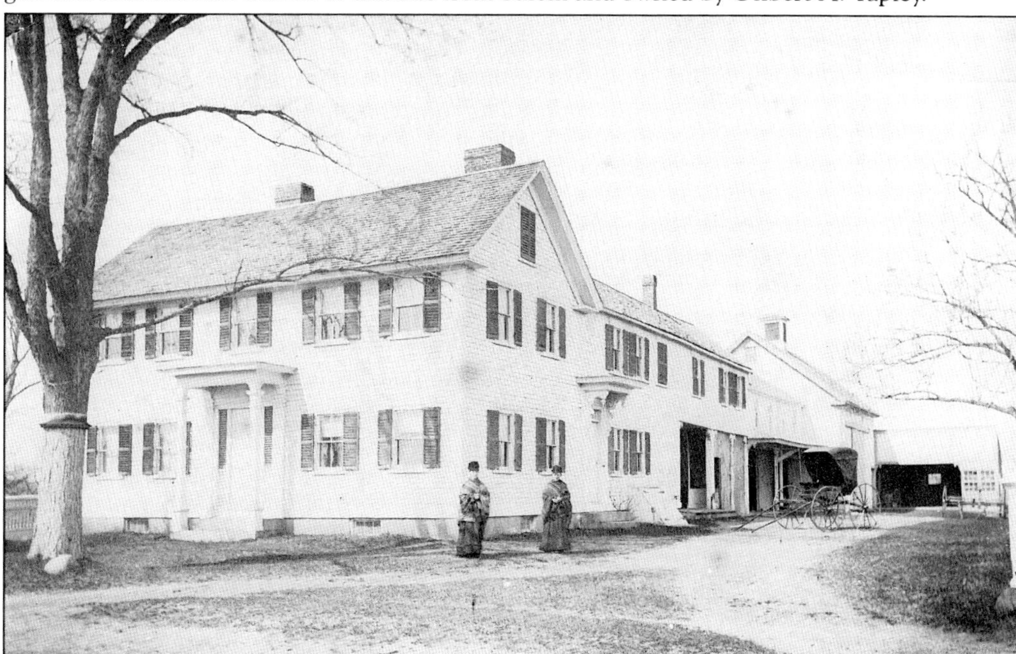

The *c.* 1828 Jesse Tapley house at 86 Collins Street included numerous attachments strung out to the rear of the dwelling, including carriage sheds and a barn.

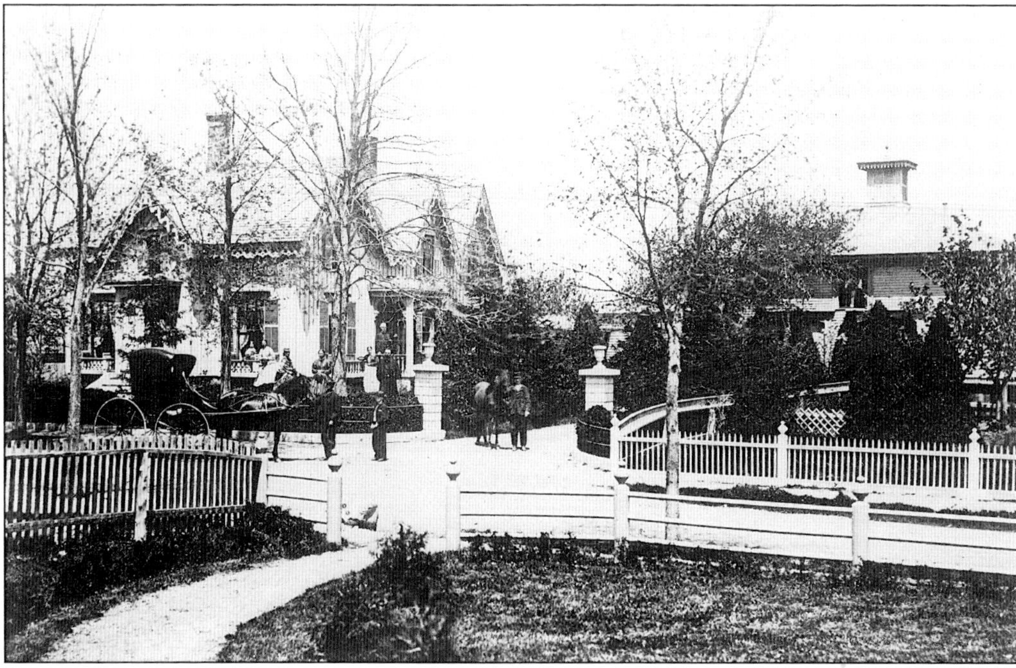

With its board and batten siding and vergeboards under its slate roof, the 1855 Dr. Jesse W. Snow house at 141 Holten Street was one of the few Danvers examples of Gothic Revival-style dwellings.

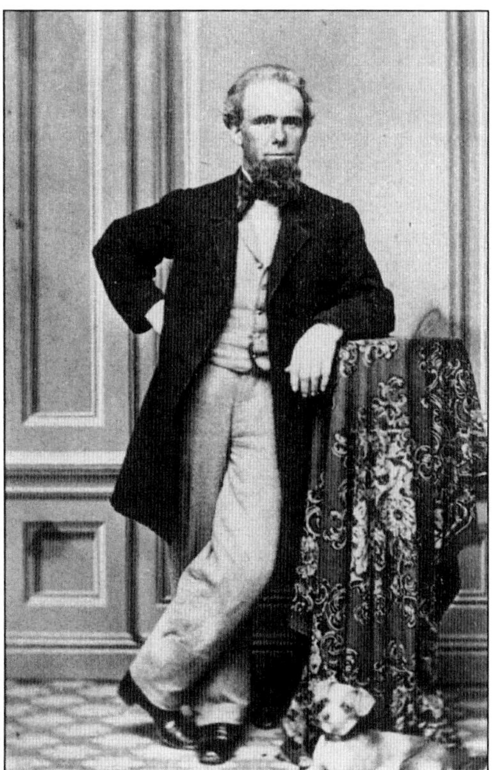

Born in 1820 and a graduate of Harvard Medical School, Dr. Snow came to Tapleyville in 1850 and practiced here for seventeen years. He is shown here posing with his dog in an 1860s carte-de-visite photograph.

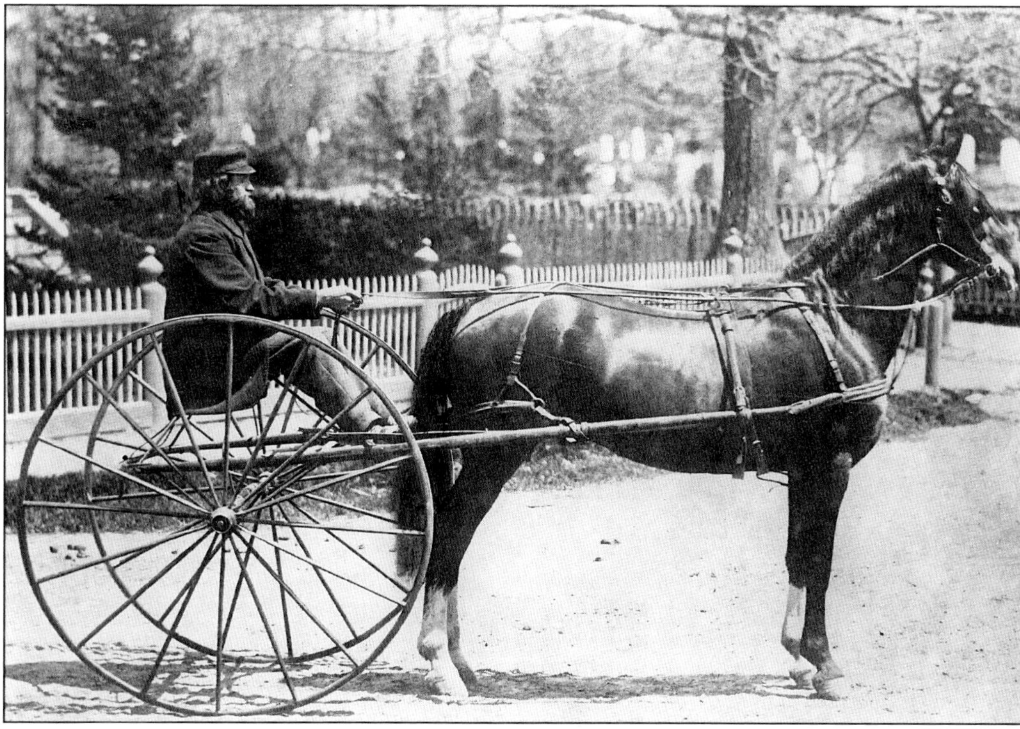

"Danvers Boy," a bay stallion owned by shoe manufacturer George B. Martin, was believed to be the fastest stallion in the world in the 1870s. In this 1869 photograph, handler Charles Rundlett steadies the horse on Holten Street by the front fence of the Dr. Snow residence.

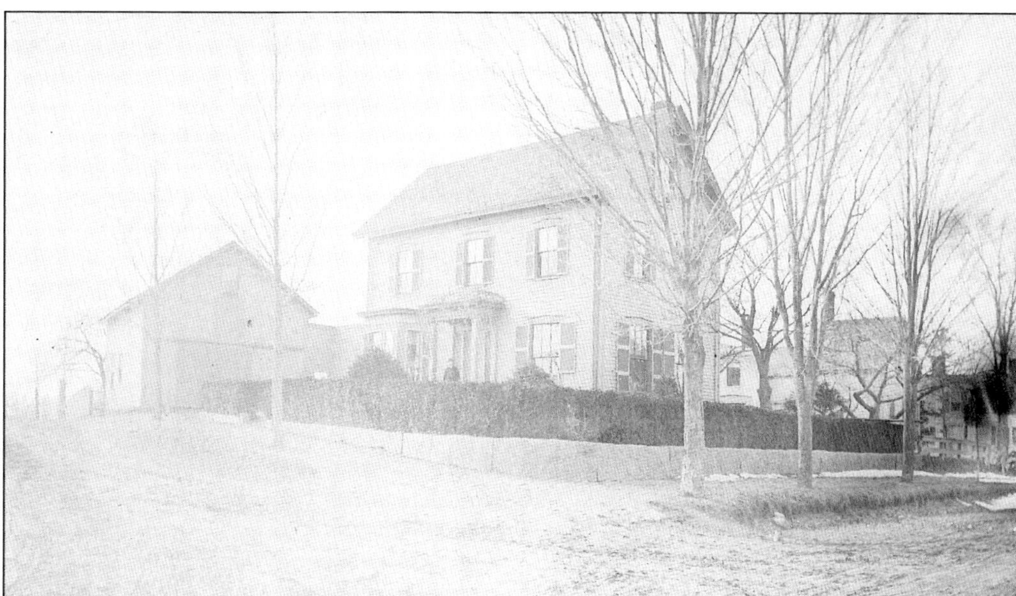

Built about 1851 at the corner of Washington and Pine Streets for shoemaker Benjamin H. Palmer, this house was acquired in 1869 by Charles Tapley. Noted twentieth-century local historian Charles S. Tapley was a member of the third Tapley generation to inhabit the dwelling.

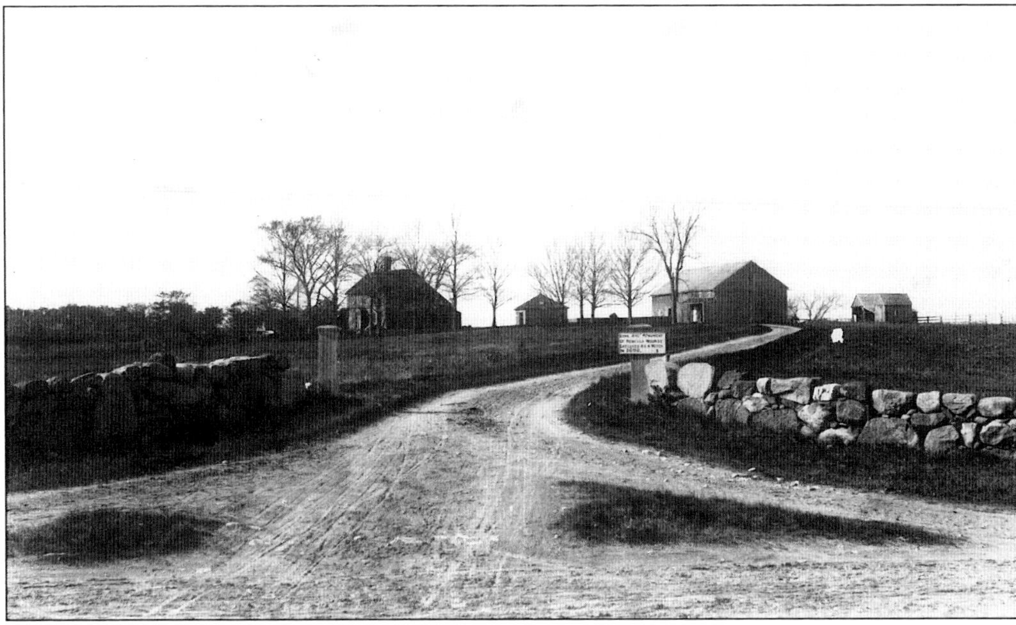

Shown here in a view from Pine Street, the historic Rebecca Nurse homestead has been occupied as a farm from about 1636. In this glass-plate image from the 1890s, one can pick out the "saltbox"-style First Period house which traditionally dates from 1678, as well as numerous other agricultural outbuildings.

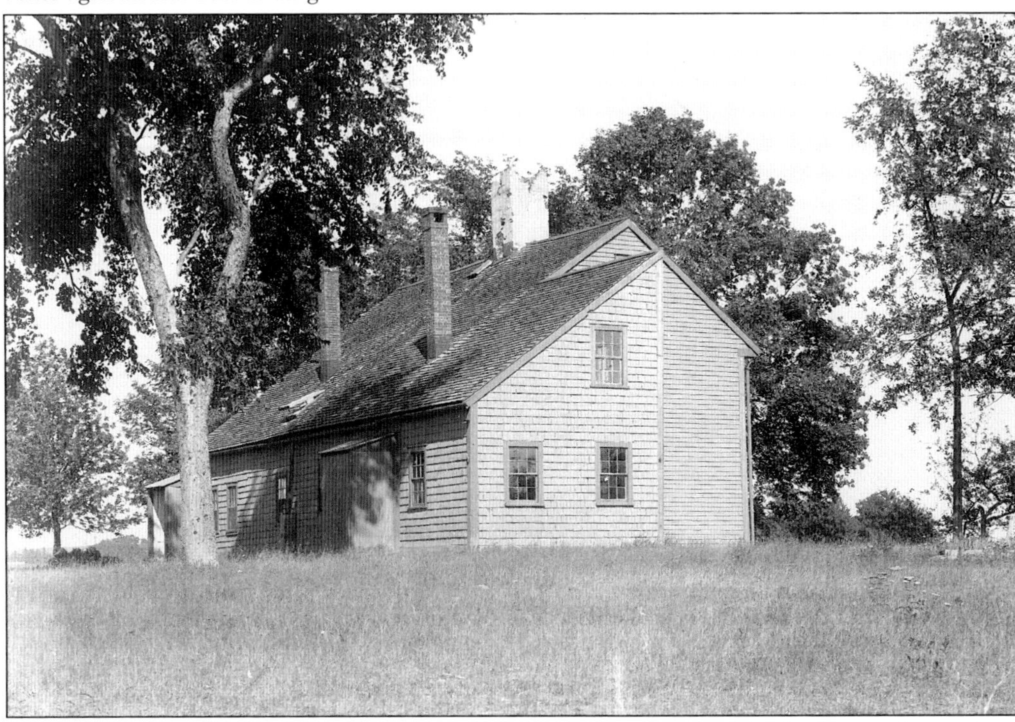

This is the west side of the Nurse house showing its sloping rear roof. The house also includes a wide nineteenth-century "Beverly Projection," having only a rear roof and built onto the side of the house.

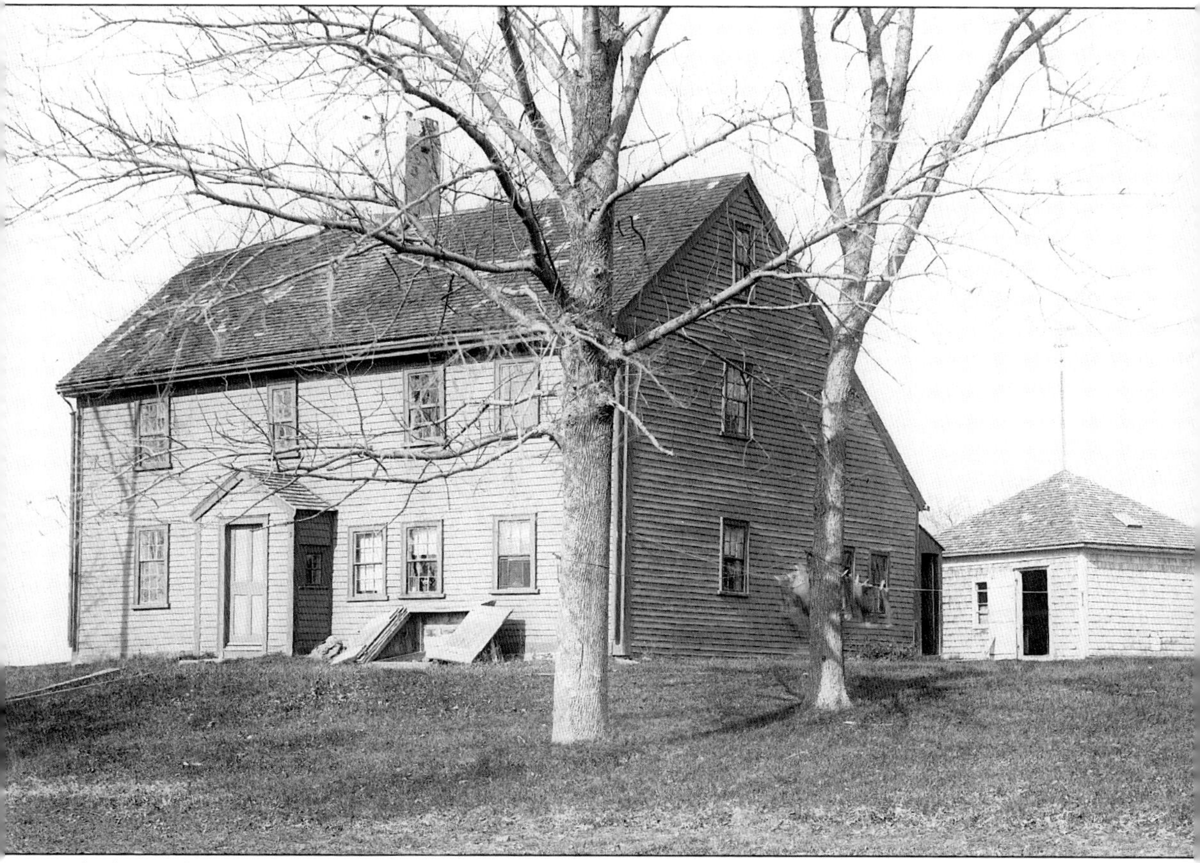

The house faces south to take best advantage of the winter sun, and included a "sentry box" front entry. Behind the house is a square well house. In 1692 the family of Francis and Rebecca Nurse lived on the 300-acre property. On March 23, 1692, the seventy-one-year-old Rebecca was arrested, having been accused by neighborhood girls of afflicting them by means of witchcraft. Declaring, "I can say before my Eternal father I am innocent, & God will clear my innocency," Nurse was subsequently tried and executed on July 19, 1692. She and eighteen other hanging victims chose truth over life, refusing to confess to something they did not do.

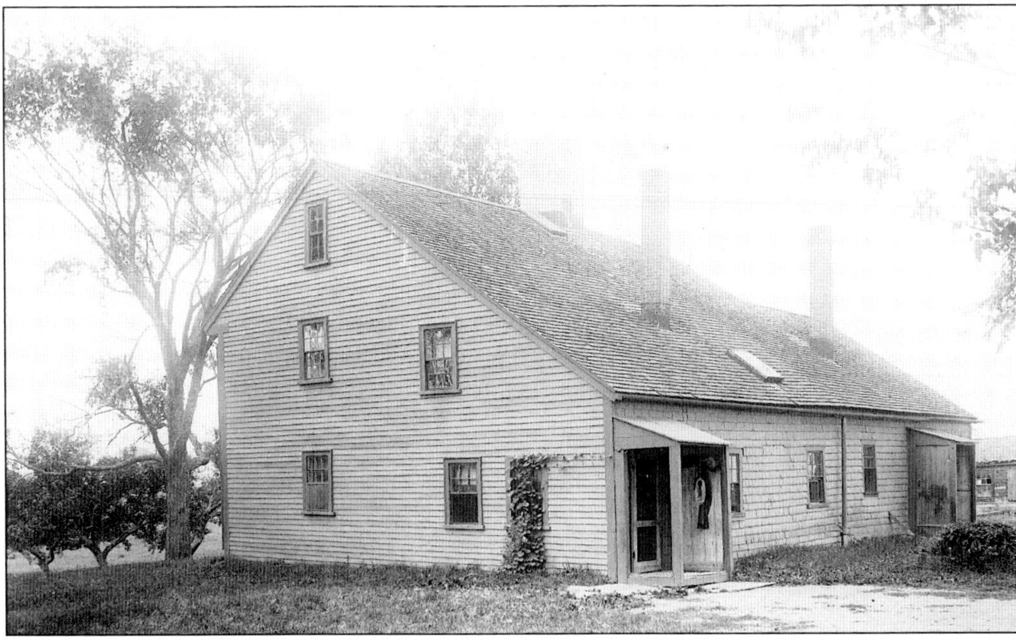

A c. 1880s view of the east side of the Nurse house. In 1907 the Rebecca Nurse Memorial Association purchased the house and 30 acres to preserve it as a house-museum. Since 1981 the property has been owned by the Danvers Alarm List Company, which continues to interpret, preserve, and keep the property open to visitors.

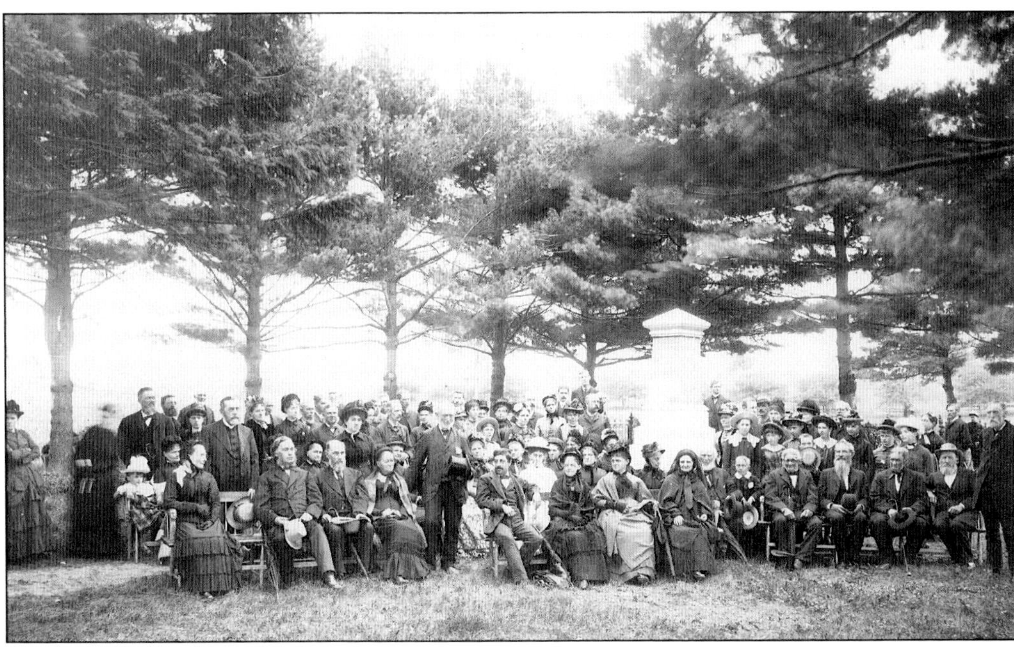

On July 30, 1885, a large number of Nurse descendants and others gathered at the homestead graveyard to dedicate a monument to Rebecca's memory. The dedication ceremony was described as "quiet, modest and deeply impressive." This photograph was taken at the conclusion of the ceremony at 4 pm. Reverend Charles B. Rice of the First Church sits second from the left.

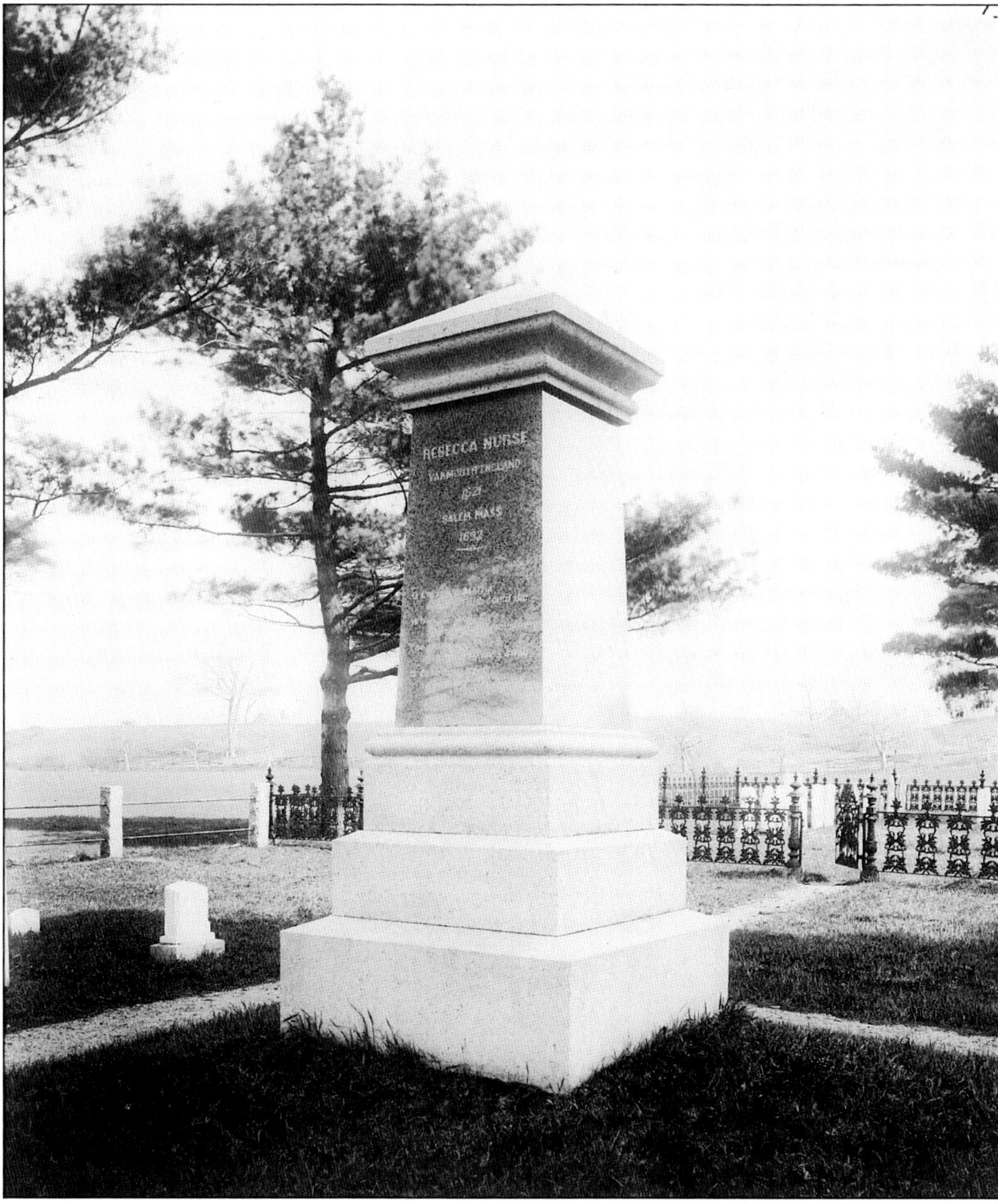

Following Nurse's execution, her body was brought back to her homestead for secret burial. According to tradition she was buried on the south side of the graveyard. This memorial, made of a Quincy granite shaft with a base and cap of Rockport granite, cost $400 in 1885, and is shown here in an 1890s view was made by Frank Cousins. Famed poet John Greenleaf Whittier wrote a poetic inscription for the memorial.

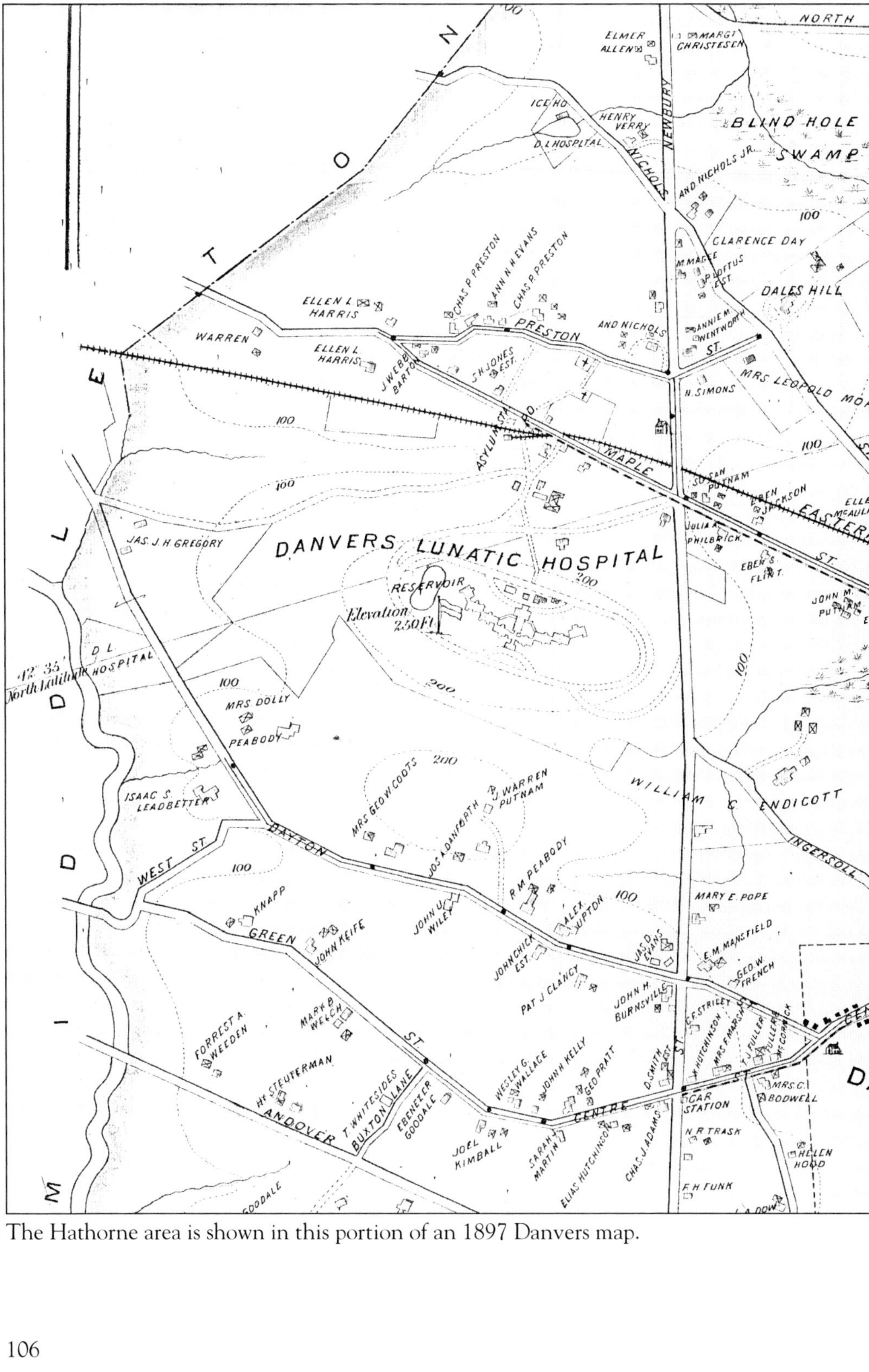

The Hathorne area is shown in this portion of an 1897 Danvers map.

Eight

Hathorne

The territory in west Danvers was always more sparsely settled than the other sections of town. A major feature of this area was a 257-foot-high glacial drumlin hill known from the seventeenth century as "Hathorne Hill" for its original owner, William Hathorne of Salem. Beginning in the nineteenth century, Danvers' cultivation of several vegetables became well known throughout the country. In west Danvers and elsewhere the "Danvers" onion, a hearty, heavy-skinned yellow onion, was cultivated on every farm. In good years over 200,000 bushels were produced in town and traded extensively. Another vegetable, the Danvers half-long carrot, also attained notoriety and became a popularly traded and cultivated vegetable.

Hathorne attained the designation of a village much later than the other sections of Danvers, and not so much for its own homegrown development. In the early 1870s the Commonwealth of Massachusetts needed to establish an additional lunatic hospital for the care of the state's mentally ill population. The old Dodge farm located on and around Hathorne Hill seemed an ideal site, and with the state's eventual acquisition of over 500 acres of this property, in 1874 it began to build an immense and most modern brick facility. The Danvers Lunatic Hospital and the neighborhood surrounding it soon took on the characteristics of an additional Danvers village.

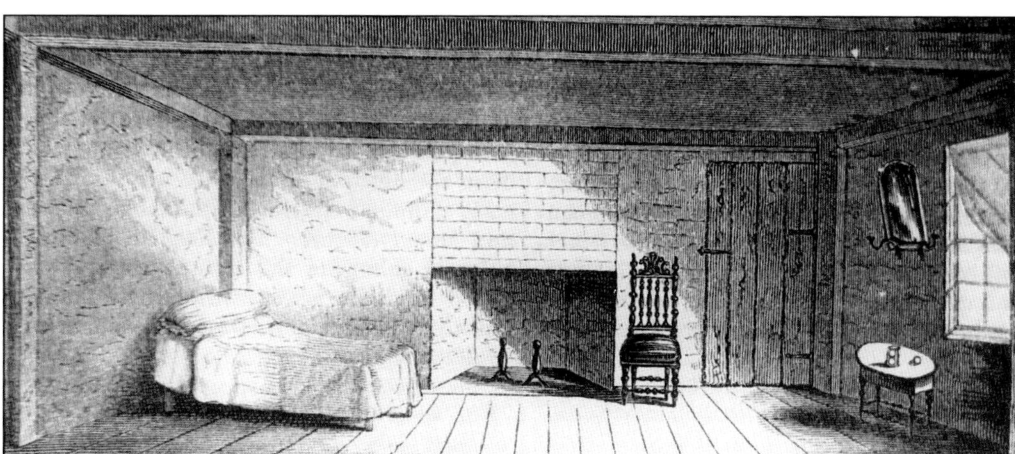

An 1856 illustration from a sketch of Maurice Oby of the room in which General Israel Putnam was born.

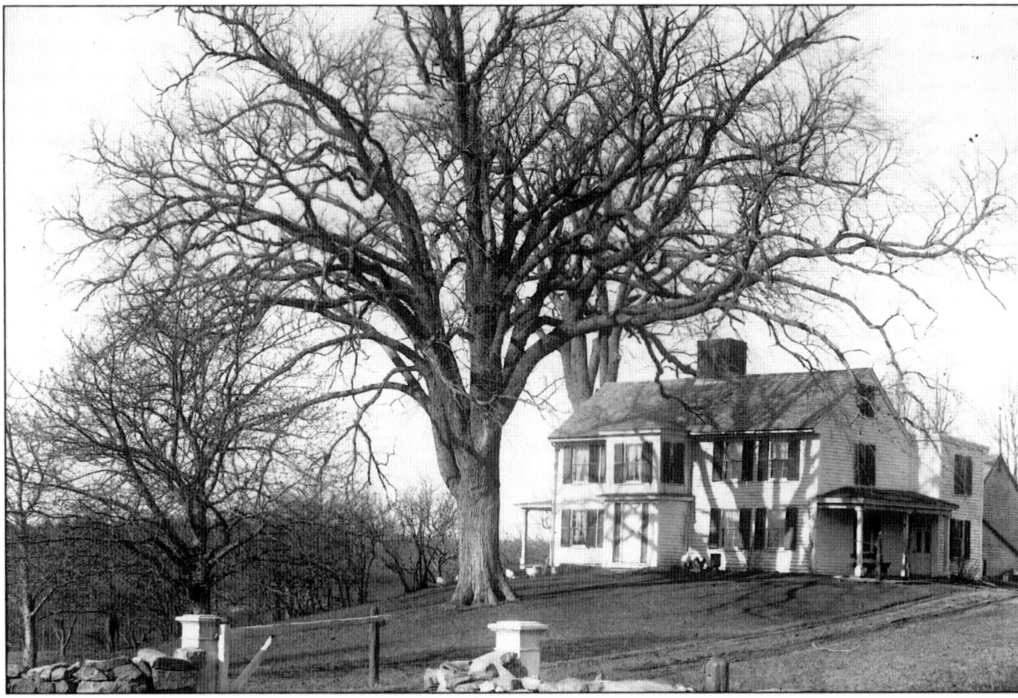

On the corner of Dayton and West Streets stood the house of "Carolina" John Putnam. In 1692, during the witchcraft episode, one of the afflicted children, Mercy Lewis, lived here. In 1698 a meeting of peace occurred here which brought together a number of church members who had left due to the witch persecutions. The house was destroyed by fire in 1904.

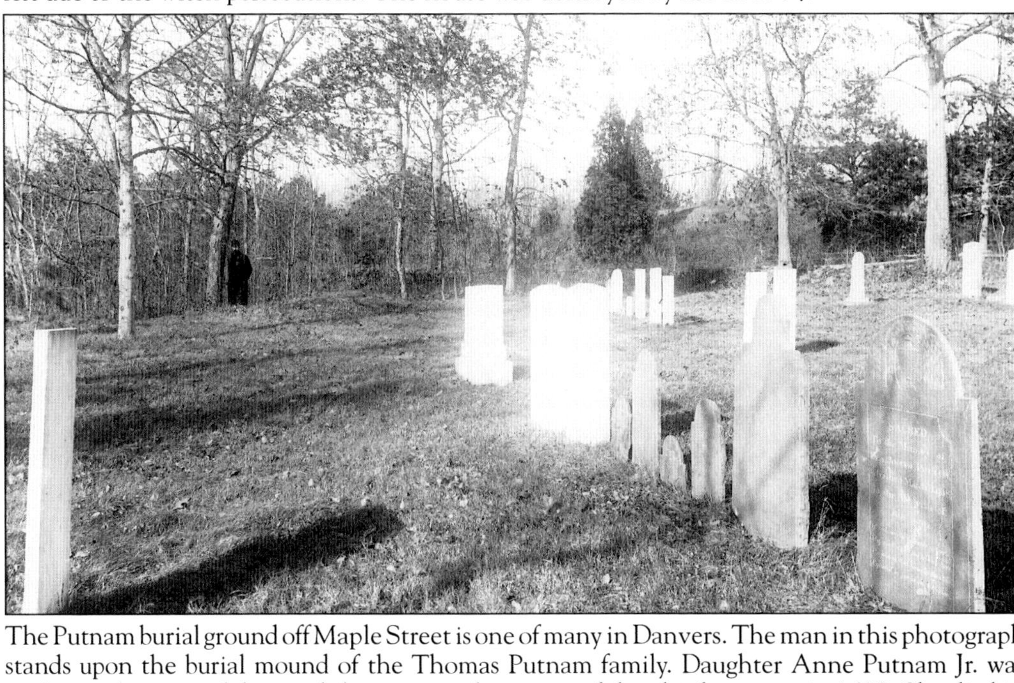

The Putnam burial ground off Maple Street is one of many in Danvers. The man in this photograph stands upon the burial mound of the Thomas Putnam family. Daughter Anne Putnam Jr. was twelve at the time of the witch hysteria, and was one of the chief accusers in 1692. She died in 1716 and is buried here with her family.

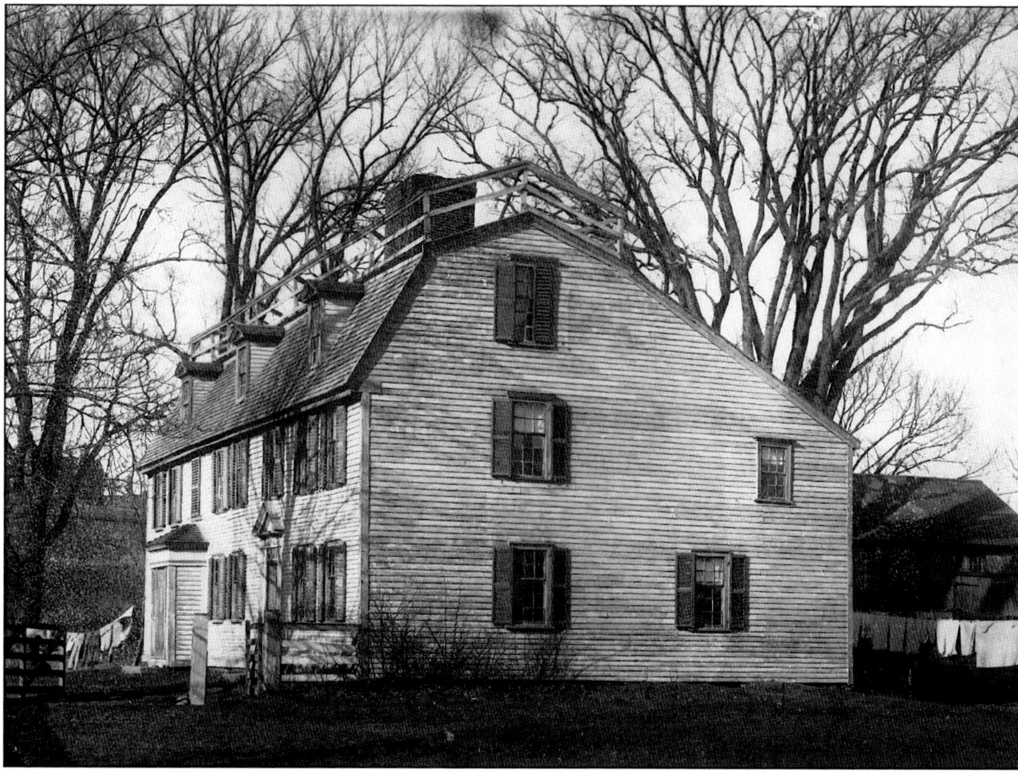

Clothes dry in the sunlight at the Colonel Jesse Putnam farm in this glass-plate print. Built about 1750 for Joseph Putnam, the house exhibited a combination of a gambrel front and lean-to rear roof. It was located off old Maple Street.

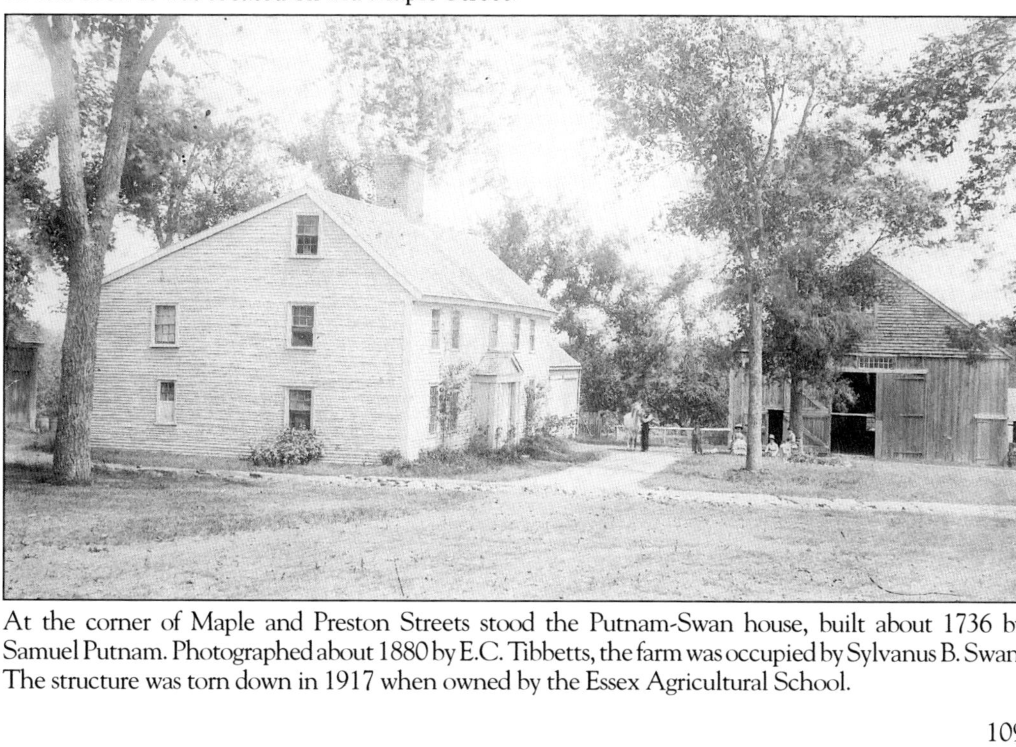

At the corner of Maple and Preston Streets stood the Putnam-Swan house, built about 1736 by Samuel Putnam. Photographed about 1880 by E.C. Tibbetts, the farm was occupied by Sylvanus B. Swan. The structure was torn down in 1917 when owned by the Essex Agricultural School.

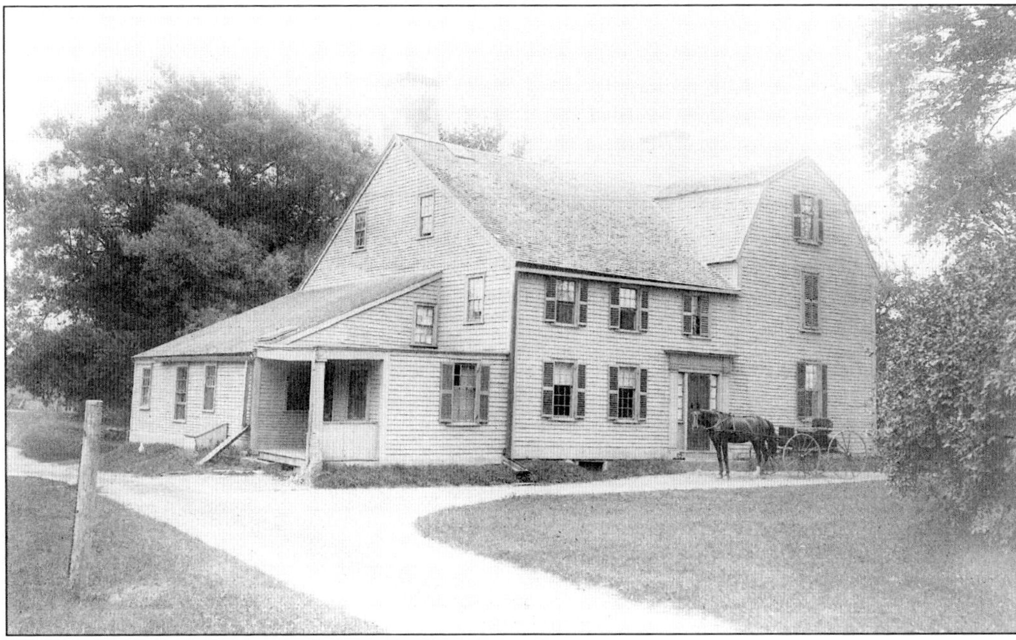

The Putnam house at 431 Maple Street is now owned and preserved by the Danvers Historical Society. Traditionally the central part of the house was built *c.* 1648 for Thomas Putnam, while the Georgian, gambrel-roof addition was built by David Putnam in the mid-eighteenth century. Israel Putnam and Robert Winthrop Putnam were born here (see pp. 27 and 107).

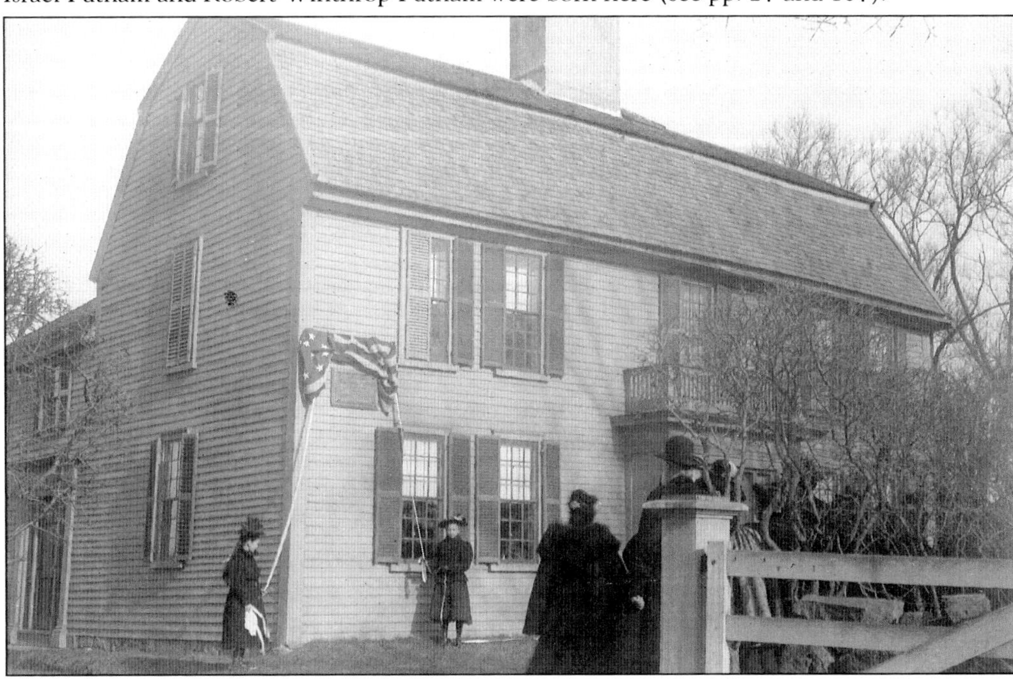

Two young girls unveil the metal plaque commemorating the birthplace of General Israel Putnam in this 1897 photograph. Israel, born in 1718, was an officer in the French and Indian War and in the American Revolution. During the nineteenth century Putnam's published exploits made him a genuine folk hero.

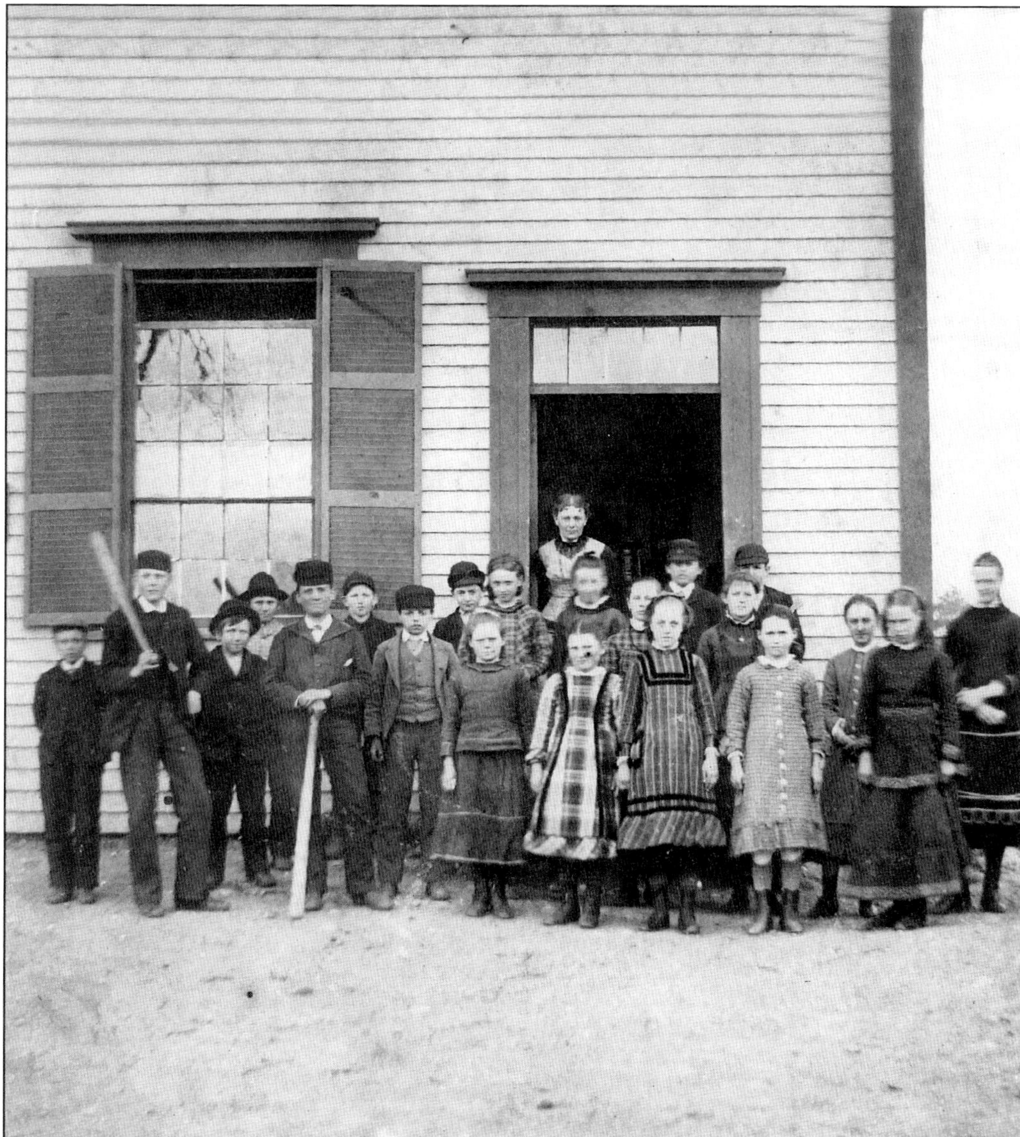

In the nineteenth century each section of the town had a separate school district committee and schoolhouse. The schoolhouse for District Number 4 was a typical one-room structure located on Newbury Street. This photograph, taken as a stereograph view in the 1870s, shows the 1852 building with local scholars, including two boys with baseball bats, posing near one of the two front doorways.

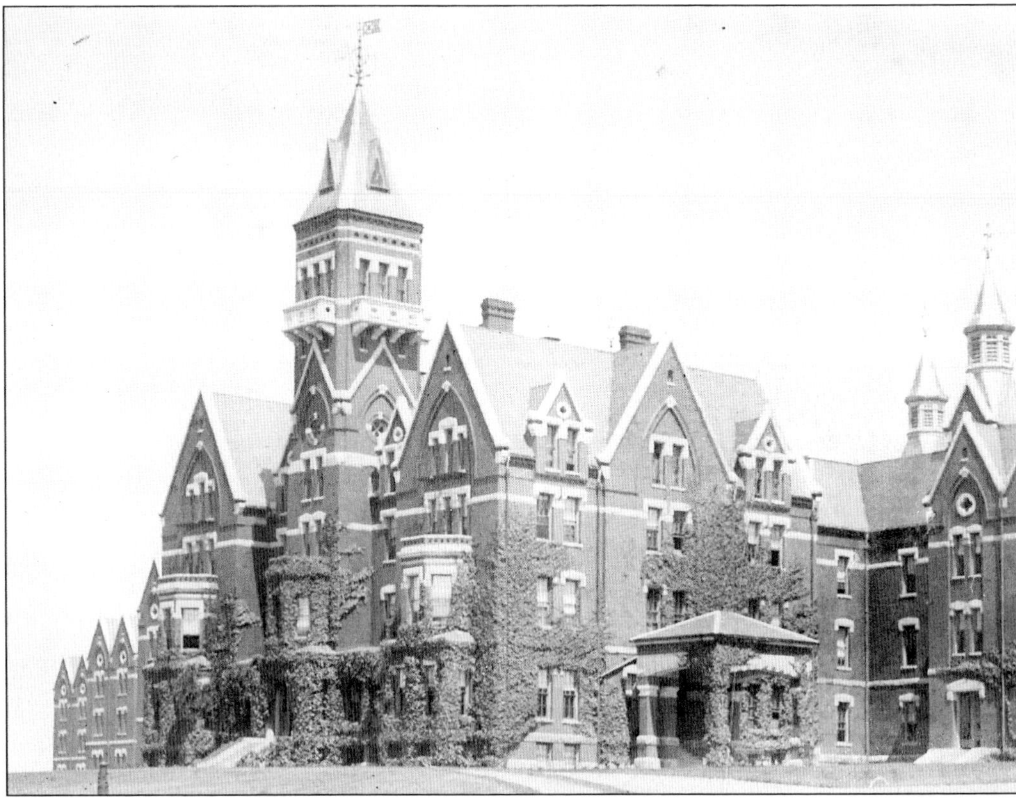

The Danvers State Lunatic Hospital was built between 1874 and 1877 from the Victorian Gothic design of architect Nathaniel J. Bradlee. Utilizing local bricks, granite, and polychromatic exterior finish, the double-winged structure functioned to assist in curing rather than warehousing patients. The facility was built at a cost of $1.4 million to accommodate 450 patients.

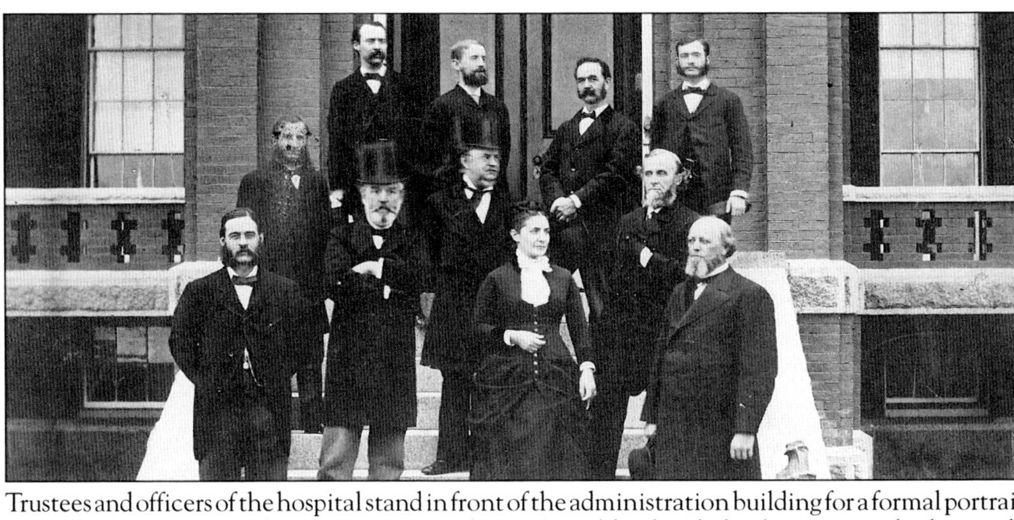

Trustees and officers of the hospital stand in front of the administration building for a formal portrait in about 1880. Among the group are Dr. Julia K. Cary (the first lady physician at the hospital) and, in the front right, Danvers resident and trustee Charles Putnam Preston (1820–1887).

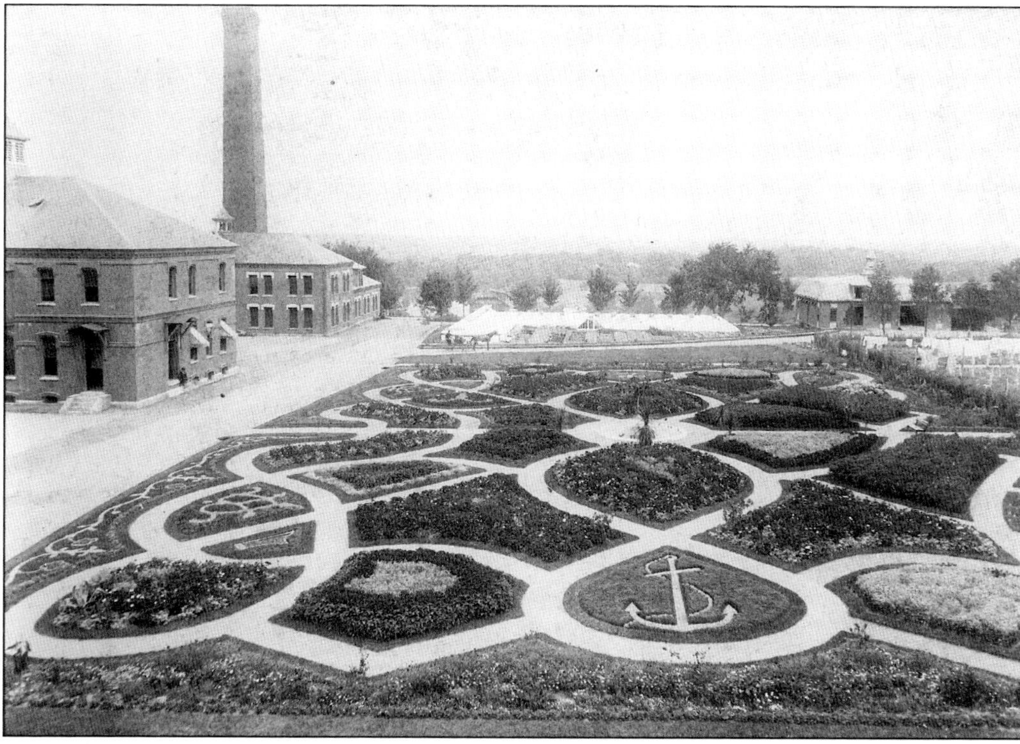

An outline of an anchor of hope graces the extensive and beautiful garden on the grounds of the hospital adjacent to the rear mechanical buildings. Townsfolk delighted in visiting the massive and well-regulated hospital grounds.

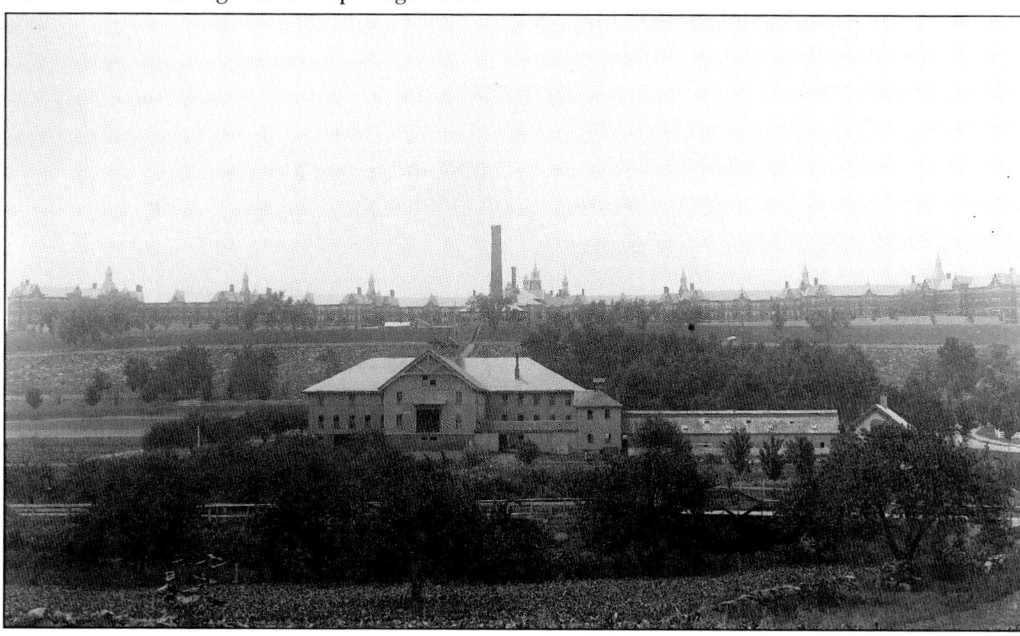

This 1884 rear view reveals the brick hospital complex on Hathorne Hill, and the extensive farm on the area below the hill where patients cultivated crops and raised animals as a supplementary fresh food source.

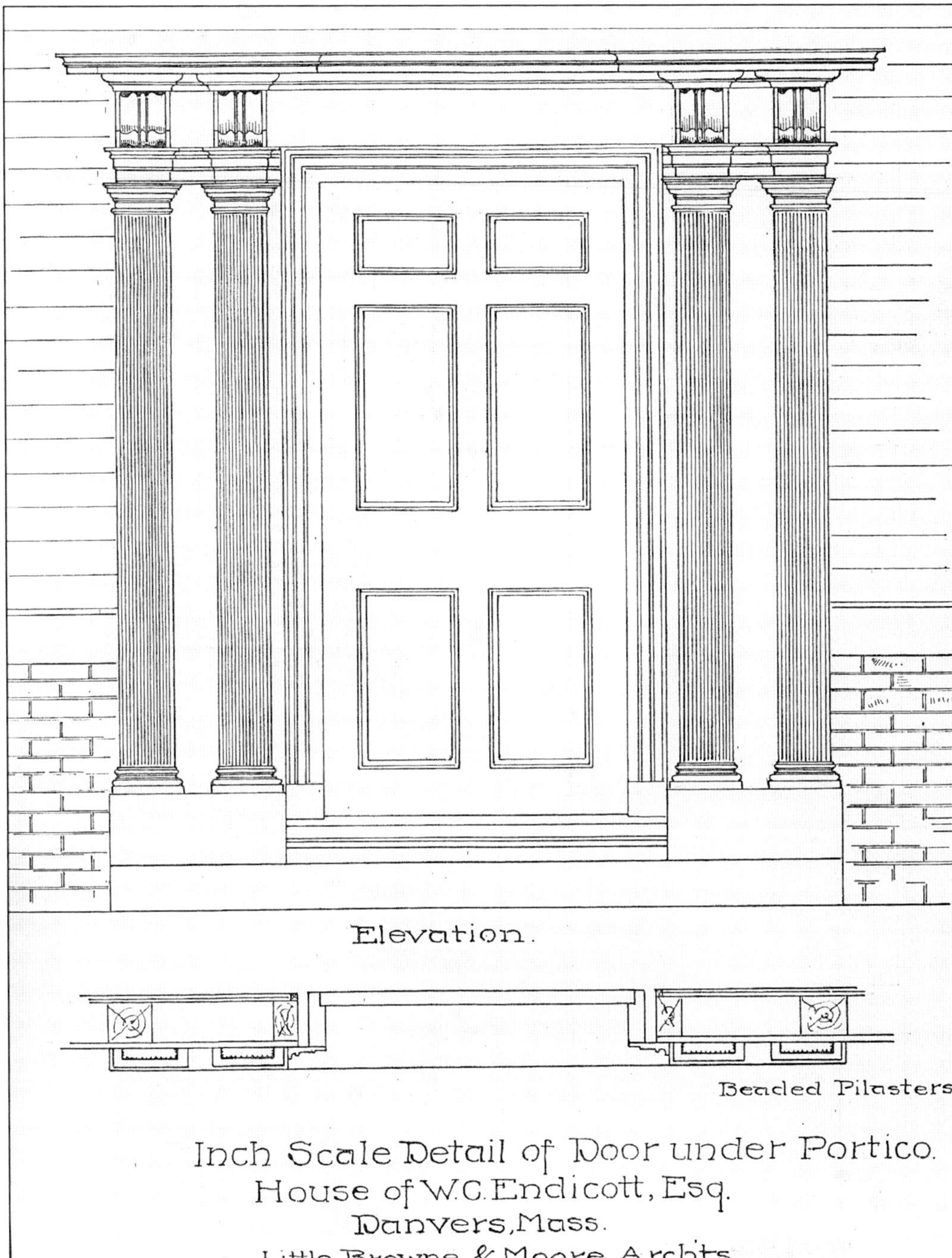

An 1893 drawing for the new front entrance at Glen Magna Farm.

Nine

Country Houses

From the eighteenth century, Danvers, with its broad expanses of woods, meadows, and uplands, was regarded by residents of larger towns such as Salem and Marblehead as an attractive location for country estates. Escaping the bustle of business and people, these part-time residents of Danvers built all styles of country houses from grand architectural gems to simple but ample country residences. Names given to these country estates reflected their owners' regard for rural bliss: "The Lindens," "Overlook," "Maplebank," "Riverbank," "Oak Knoll," "Pine Knoll," "Porphyry Hall," "Robin's Hill Farm," "Maplewood," "Locust Lawn," and "Arch Meadow." Many of these properties were only inhabited for small portions of the year, and most were owned by families that kept the shallowest of roots within the community, regarding Danvers as a frame of mind rather than a home town.

Virtually all of these country homes have now disappeared or been redesigned for other functions. Only old photographs allow us a fragmented glimpse of a local era never to be seen again.

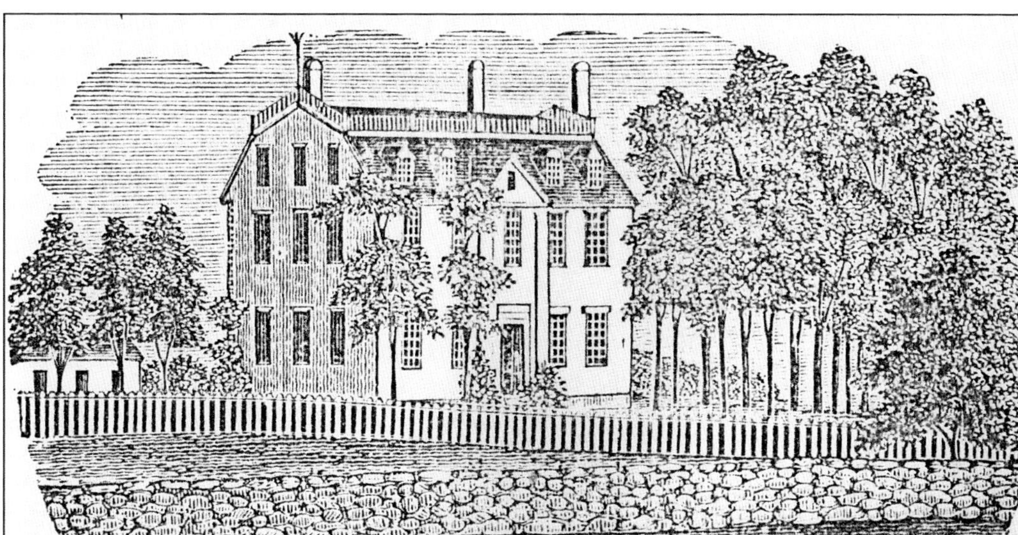

An 1840s woodcut engraving of the eighteenth-century summerhouse of Robert Hooper.

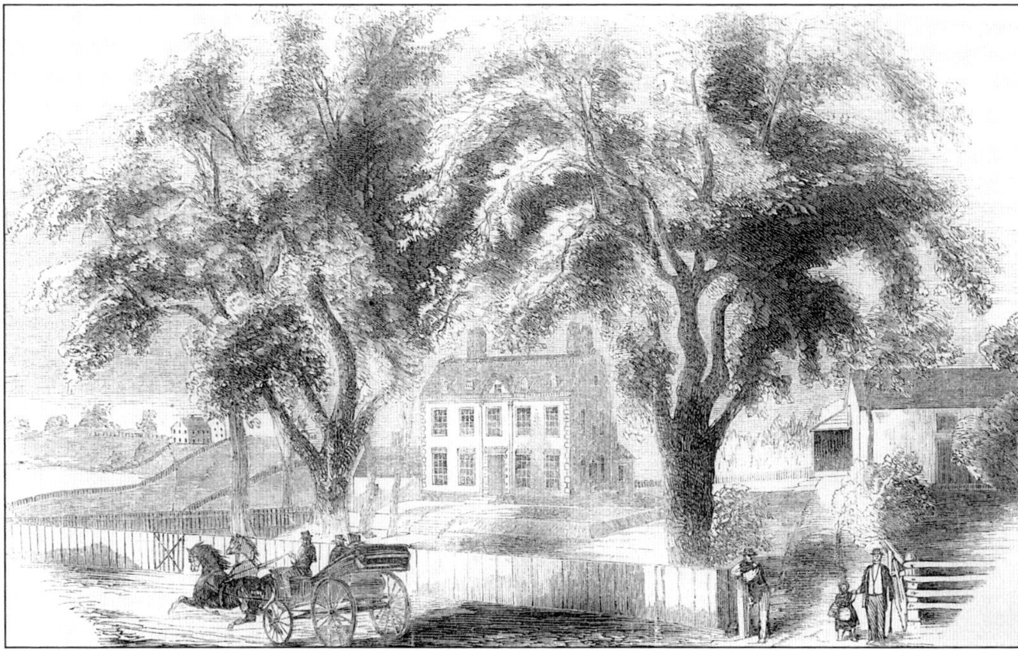

Marblehead merchant Robert Hooper had this grand Georgian house built as a summer residence prior to the Revolution. In the summer of 1774 it was used as headquarters by Governor Thomas Gage when the capital was moved from Boston to Salem. British troops guarded the governor, whose presence was not welcomed by the locals. During the Revolution Hooper fled the country.

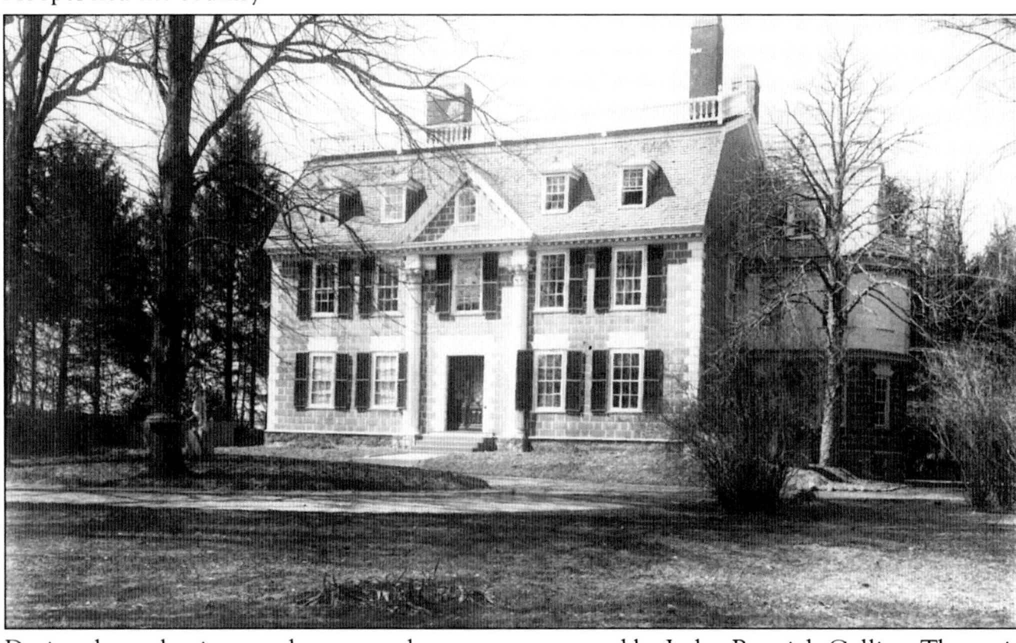

During the early nineteenth century the estate was owned by Judge Benajah Collins. The main house exhibited a gambrel roof with balustrade, a simulated ashlar finish with corner quoins, and monumental front columns. In 1860 Francis Peabody of Salem acquired the house and named the estate "The Lindens."

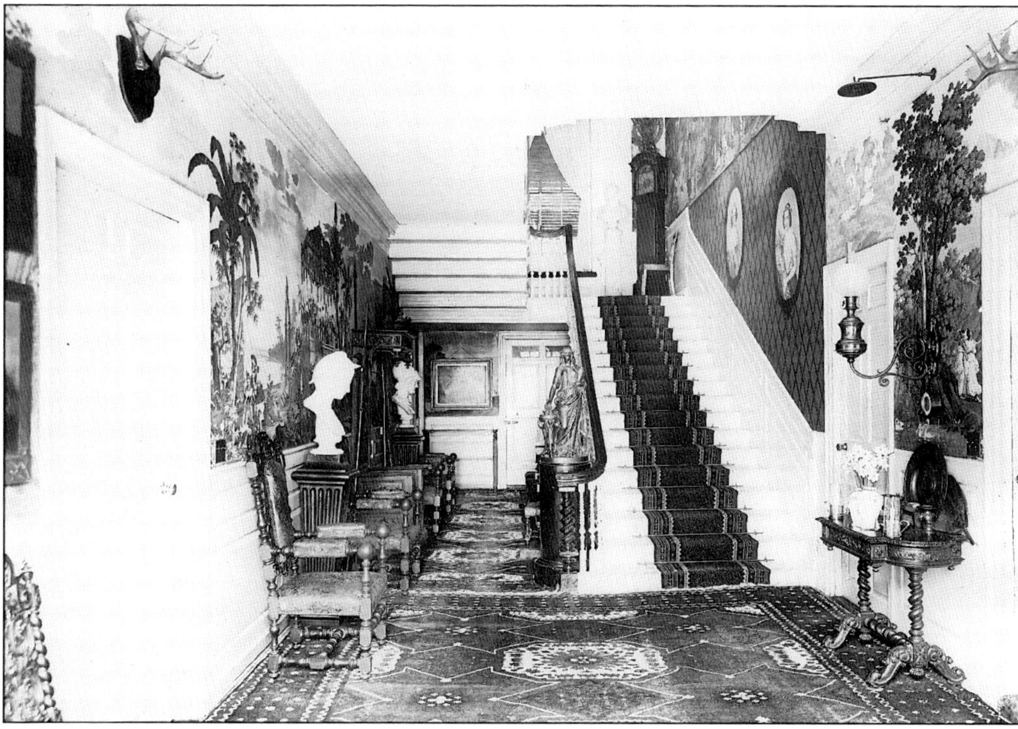

Francis Peabody made extensive improvements to the property and filled the house with family possessions. Guests entertained here included George Peabody and J.P. Morgan. Located off Sylvan Street, the house was dismantled in the 1930s without much local warning, and moved to Washington, D.C., for use as a private residence.

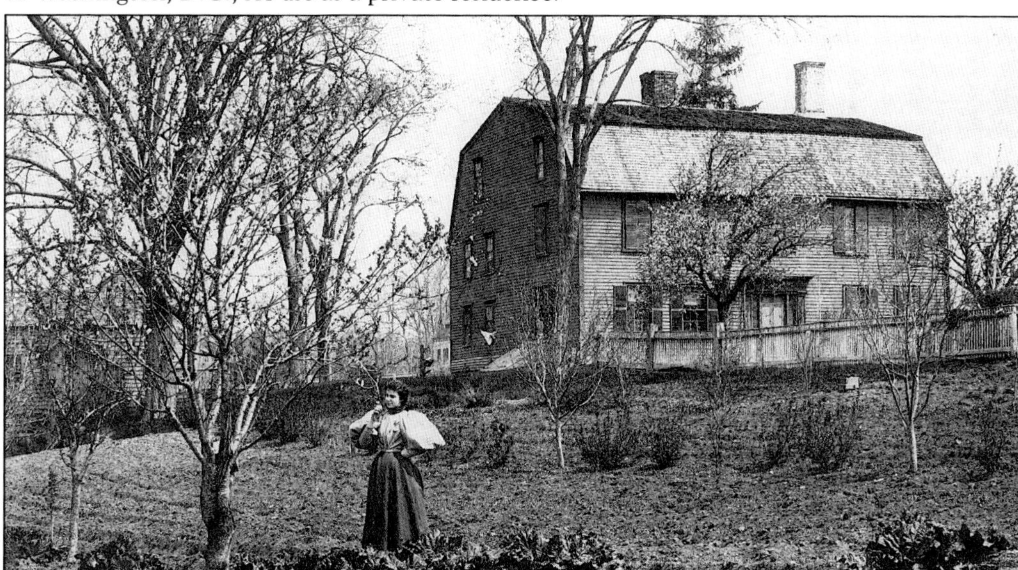

Built about 1715, this house at 42 Summer Street was expanded in the mid-eighteenth century into a two-room deep, gambrel-roofed structure. The birthplace of James Putnam, a tory lawyer who became justice of the New Brunswick Supreme Court, the house was rented from 1802 to 1804 by Timothy Pickering, secretary of state under Presidents Washington and Adams.

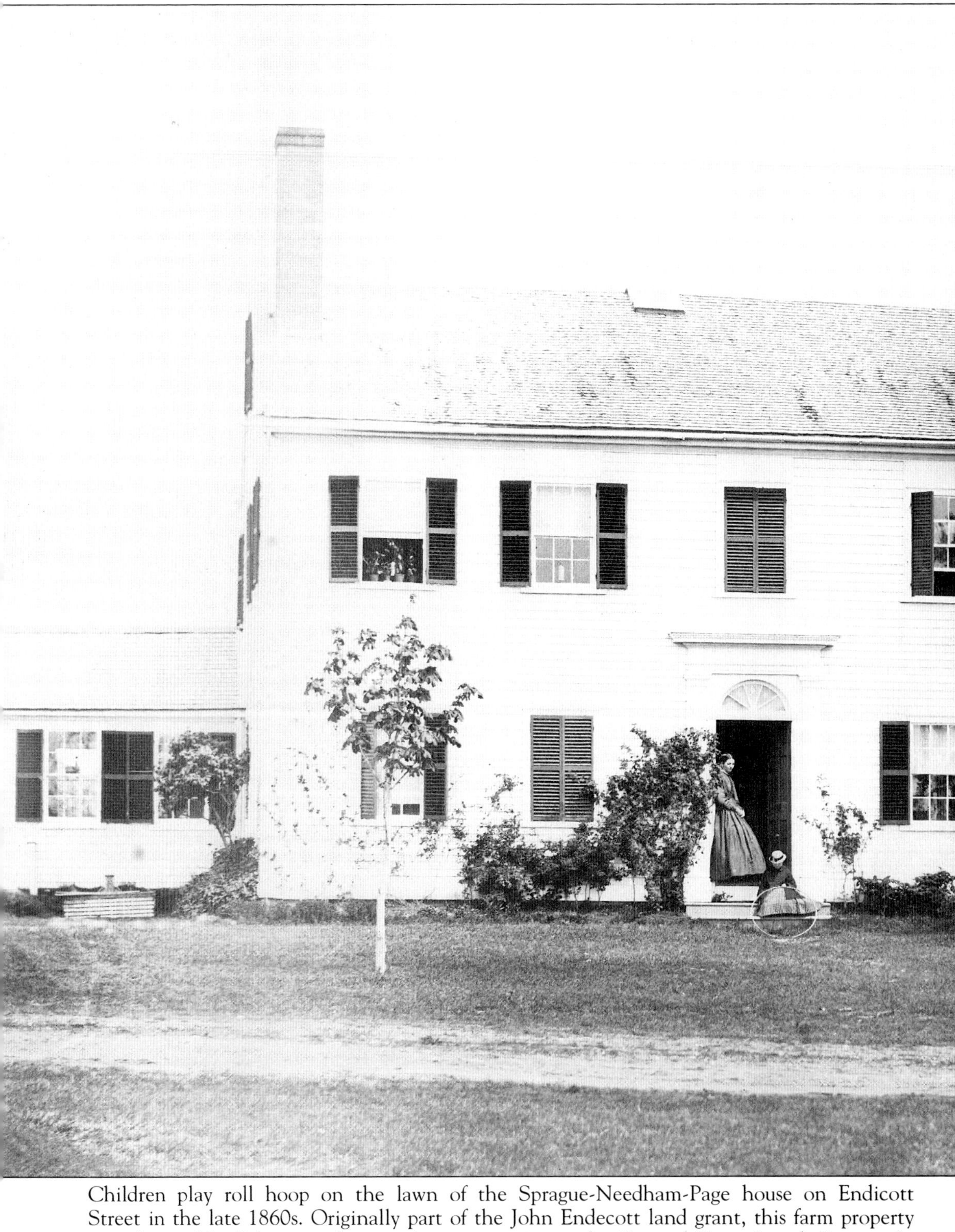

Children play roll hoop on the lawn of the Sprague-Needham-Page house on Endicott Street in the late 1860s. Originally part of the John Endecott land grant, this farm property was obtained by Salem merchant and representative to the General Court Joseph Sprague Jr.

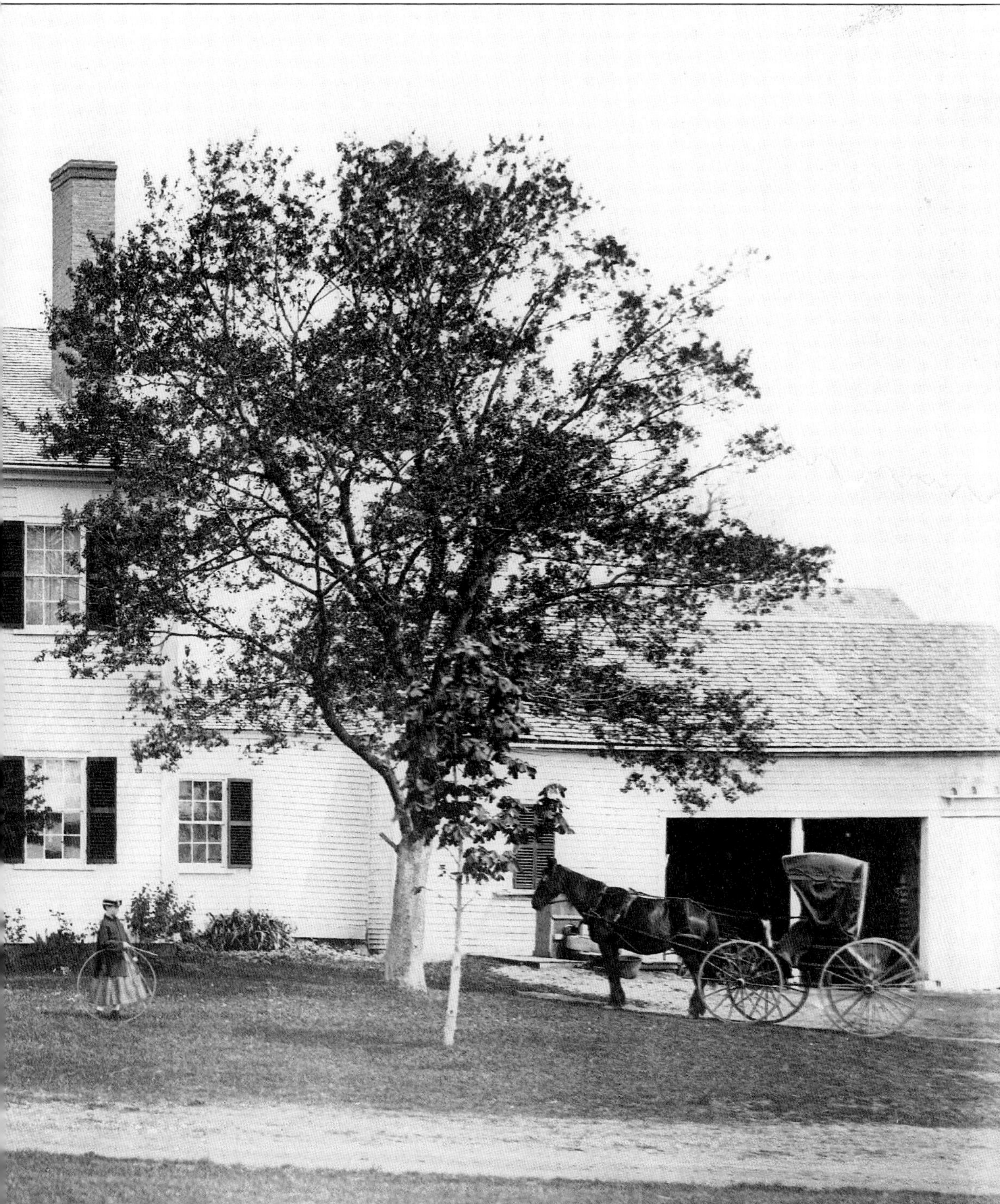

Sprague built this country Federal house for use as a summer residence in 1810. The house is now 59 Endicott Street.

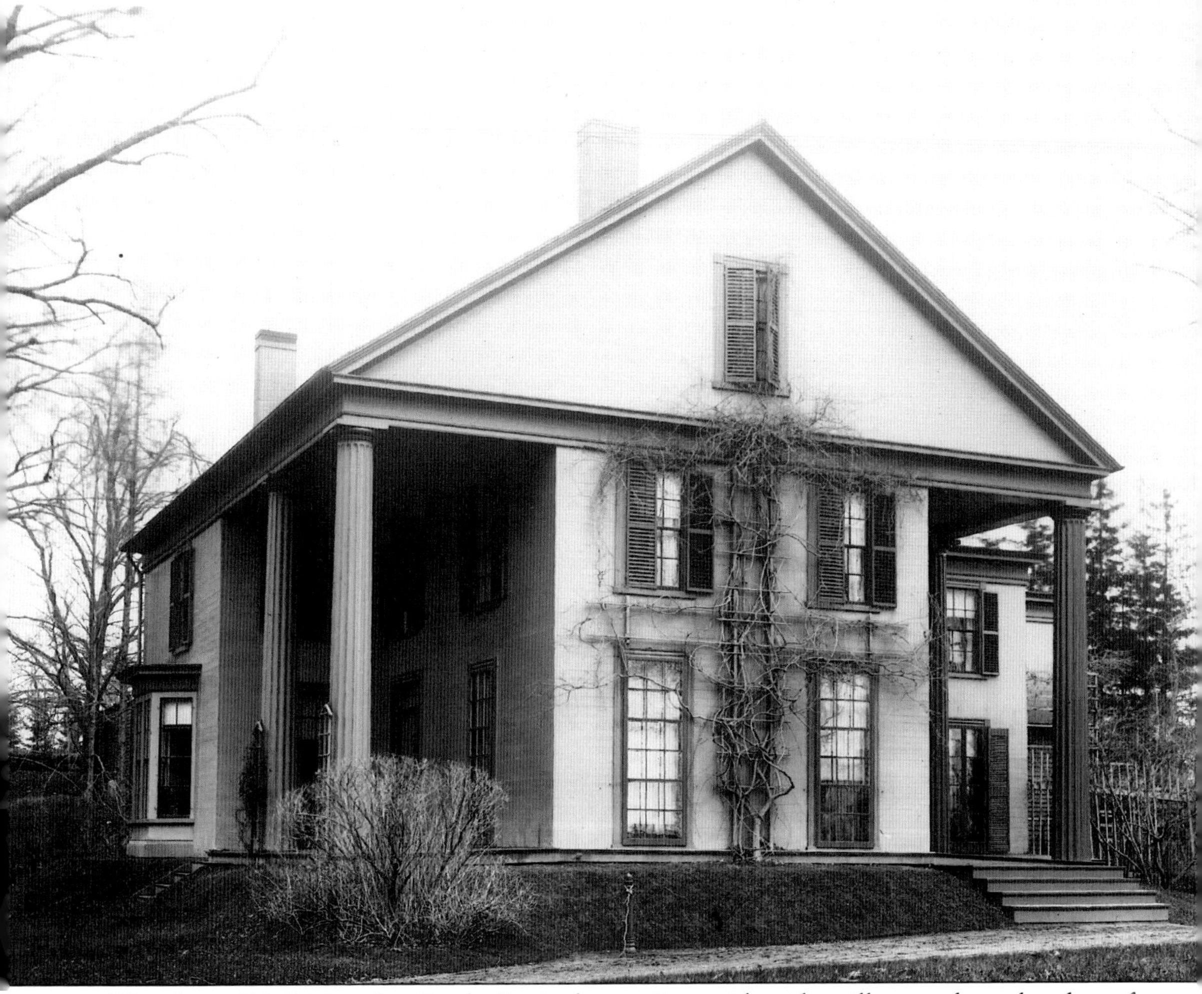

This beautiful high-style Greek Revival mansion with side pillars and enclosed roof pediment was built in 1842 as a summerhouse for William A. Lander of Salem. In 1875 Colonel Edmund Johnson purchased the property, which was located on Summer Street.

John Greenleaf Whittier (1807–1892) was a powerful spokesman for the abolition of slavery. Of Quaker upbringing, Whittier gained international fame for his poetry. His most famous work, *Snow-Bound*, won him the long-lasting affection of late nineteenth-century America. In 1876 Whittier moved to the home of his cousins, the Johnsons, and lived there for the next sixteen years.

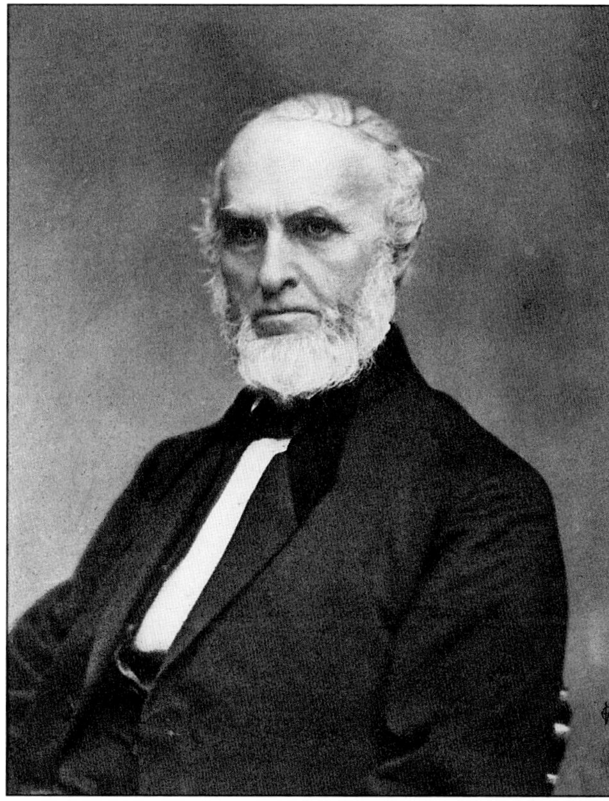

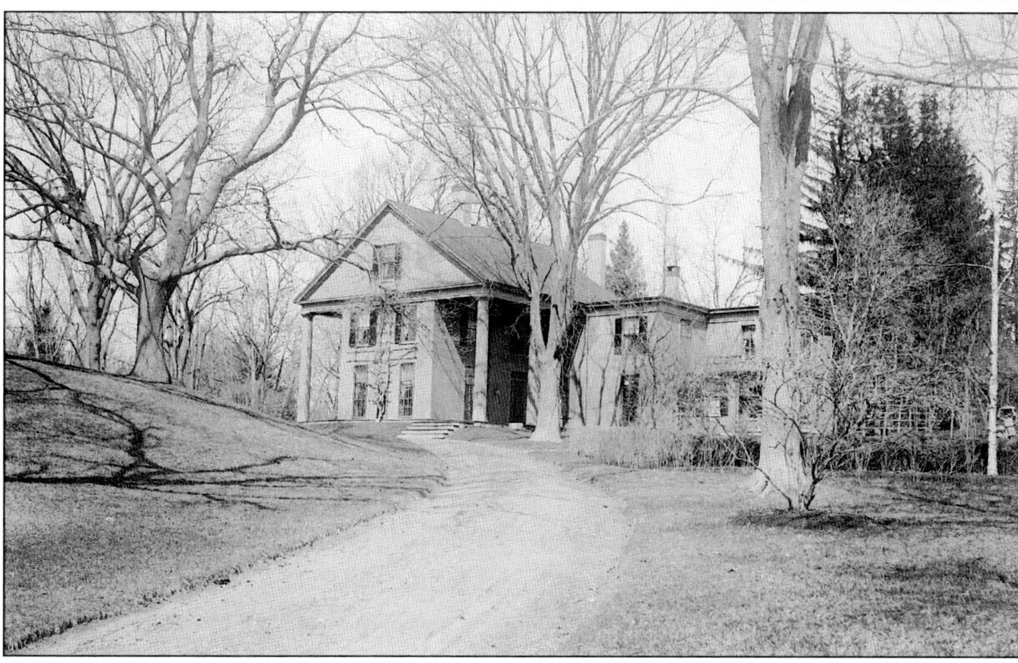

A dirt driveway circled around the front entrance of the Johnson's estate. The property was named "Oak Knoll" by the poet for the stately tree at the left in front of the house. In 1958 the house was demolished to make way for a housing development.

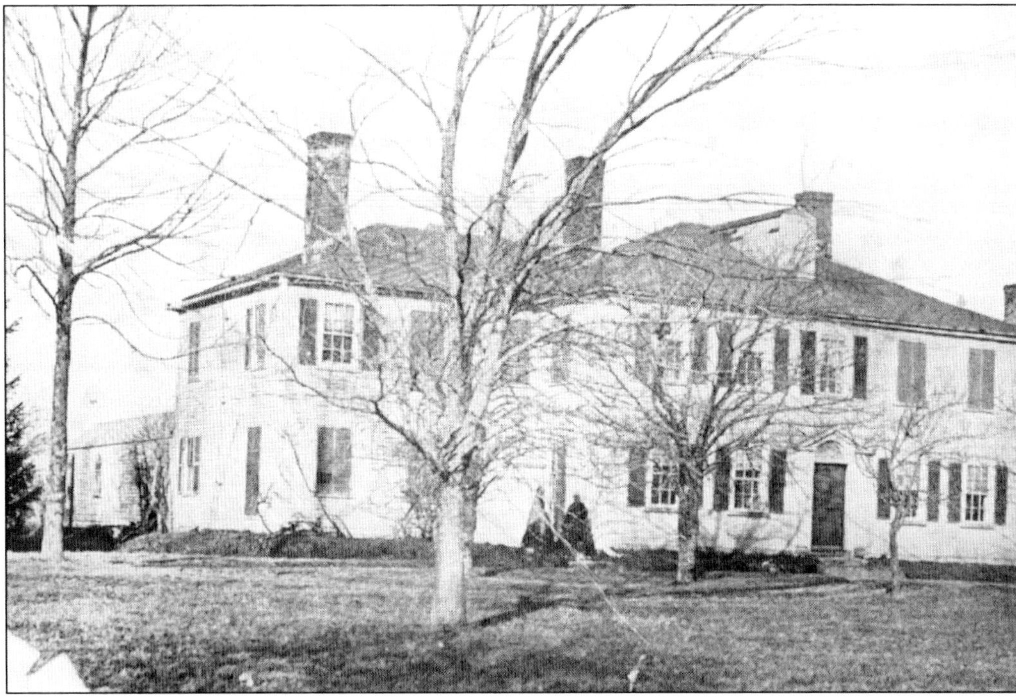

This 1860s photograph shows the country residence of Salem merchant Nathan Peirce at 36 Spring Street. It was built about 1800 in the Federal style. The house and 140-acre estate were bought by Captain Stephen Phillips in 1826, and by Charles Lawrence in 1836. Both men made additions to the house.

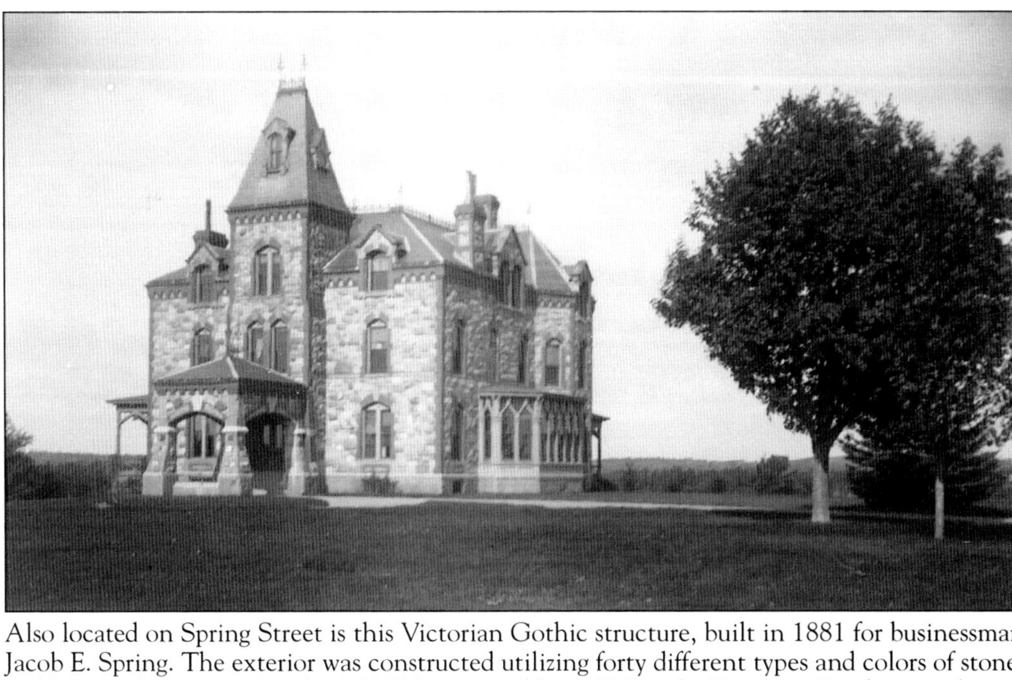

Also located on Spring Street is this Victorian Gothic structure, built in 1881 for businessman Jacob E. Spring. The exterior was constructed utilizing forty different types and colors of stone, and became known as "Porphyry Hall." It was sold in 1891 to the Xaverian Brothers, and since that time has been used as the administration building for Saint John's Preparatory School.

Off Nichols Street was the 100-acre estate known as "Locust Lawn." This 1880s glass-plate print was taken during the ownership of Boston businessman Philip H. Wentworth, who enjoyed improving the grounds and creating avenues through wooded areas.

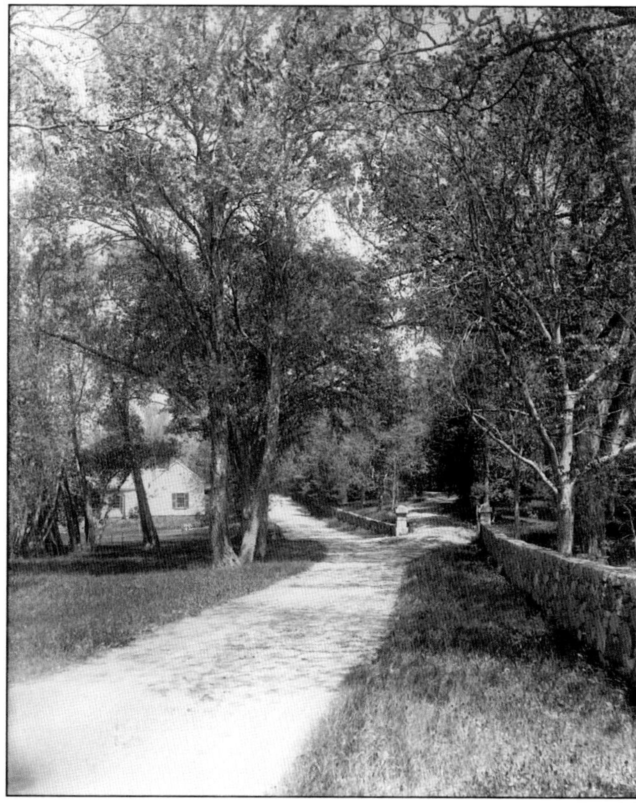

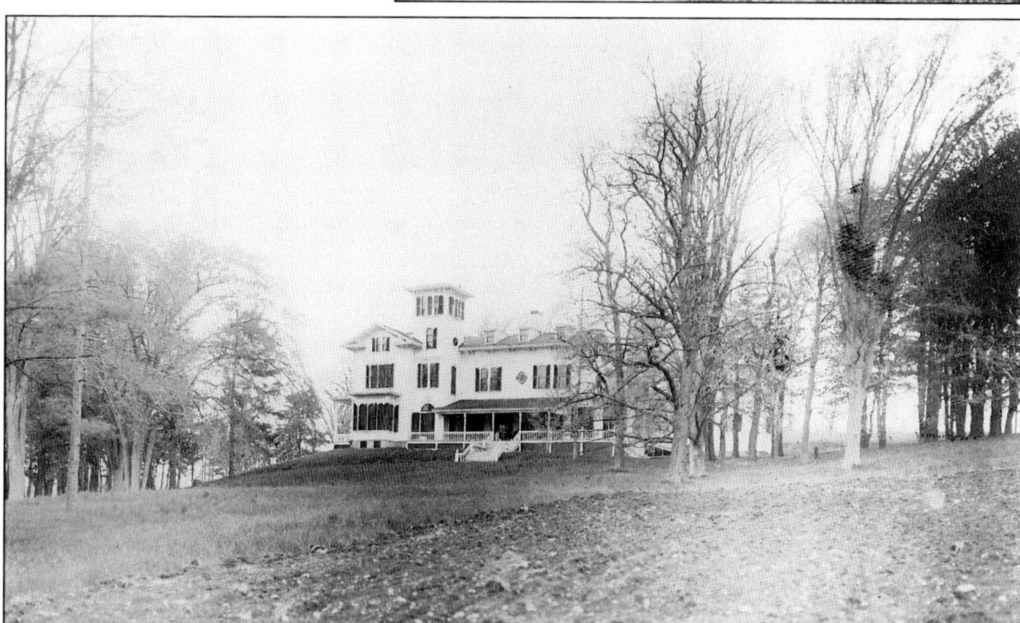

The main house at Locust Lawn was built in the Italianate style in 1856 by then-owner Edward D. Kimball of Salem. Erected on the side of Dale's Hill, the dwelling allowed a sweeping view of the surrounding area.

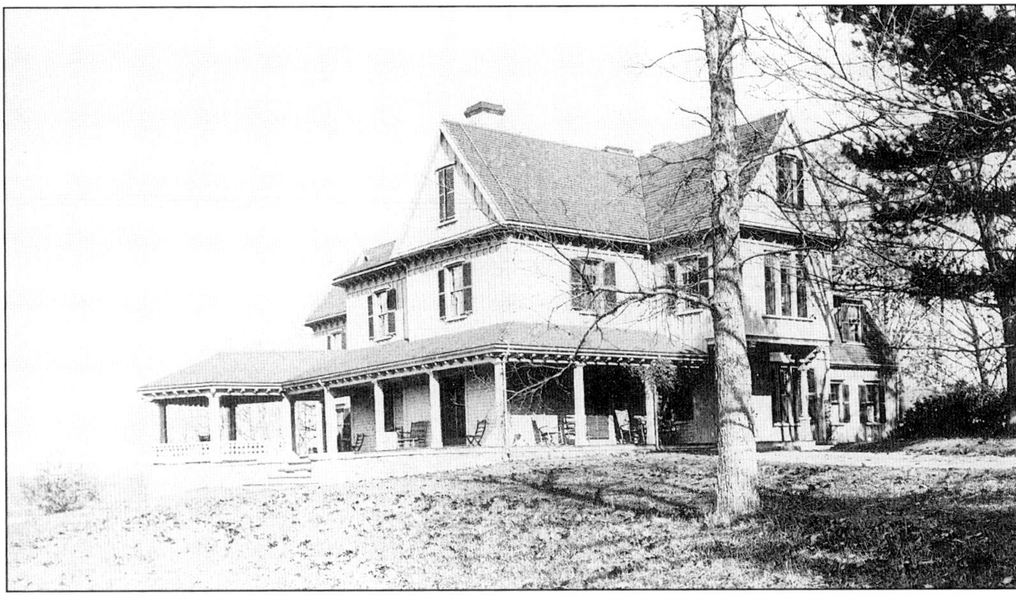

One of the earliest and most extensive nineteenth-century Danvers estates was "Burley Farms," named after Boston Captain William Burley. William Henry Moody, who served as attorney general and a justice of the Supreme Court, lived on the farm as a youth. In about 1850 the dwelling shown here was built for Frederick Howes.

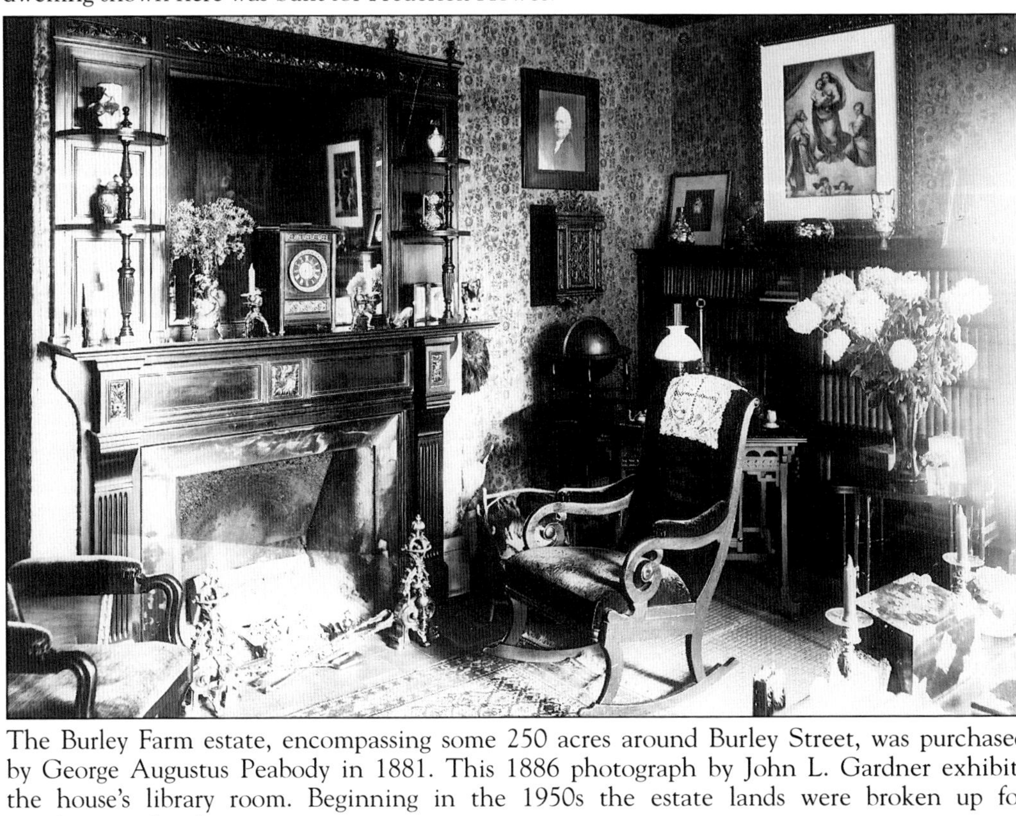

The Burley Farm estate, encompassing some 250 acres around Burley Street, was purchased by George Augustus Peabody in 1881. This 1886 photograph by John L. Gardner exhibits the house's library room. Beginning in the 1950s the estate lands were broken up for new housing developments.

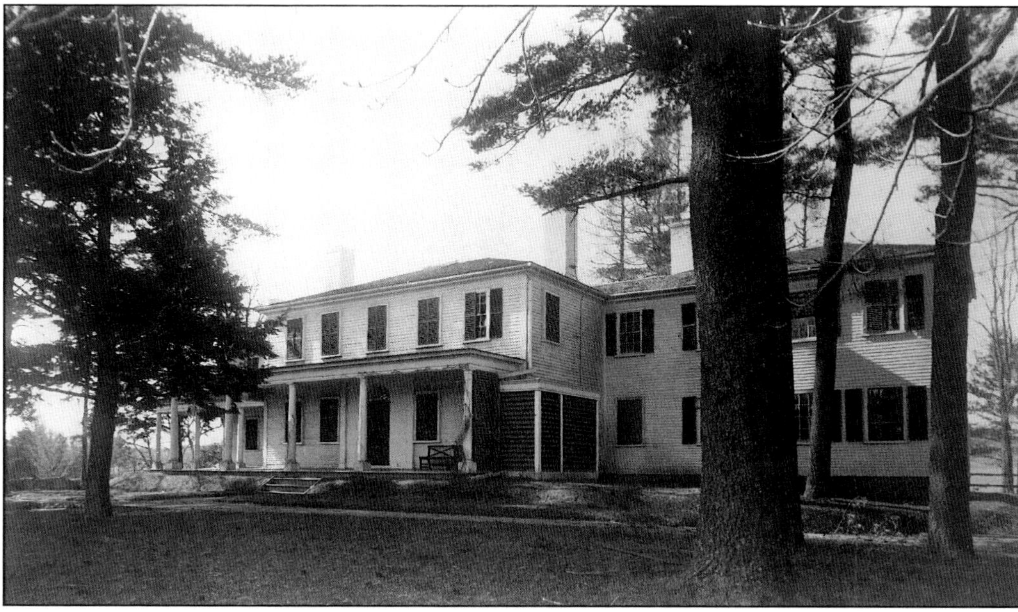

In about 1790 Captain Jonathan Ingersoll built a Federal country house off Ingersoll Street. The property was purchased by Captain Joseph Peabody of Salem during the War of 1812 as a safe-house. Over the decades the house and land were expanded. Through marriage, the property eventually came into the possession of William C. Endicott Sr. This photograph was taken in March 1892.

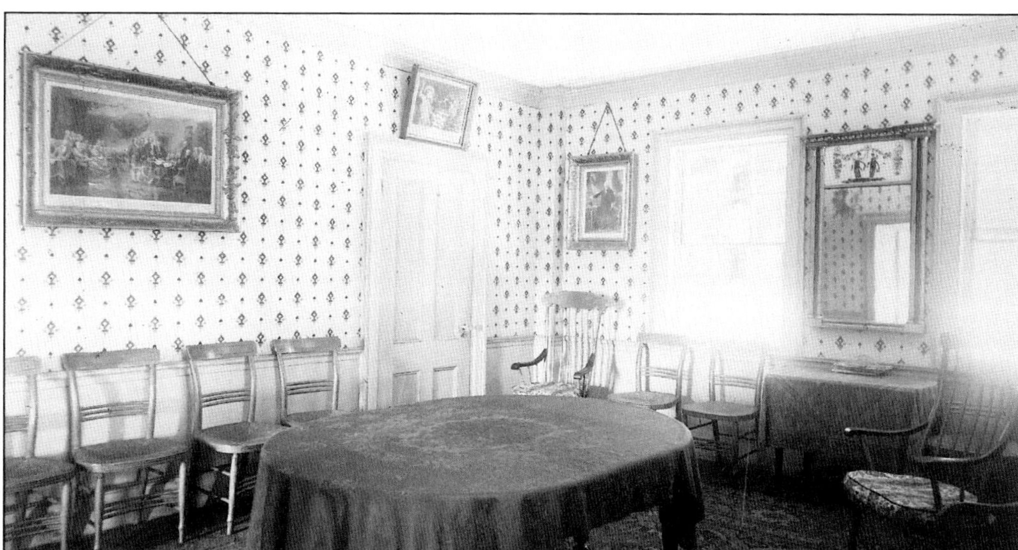

An 1892 view of the dining room displays a line of utilitarian chairs at the ready, while on the wall are several popular framed prints.

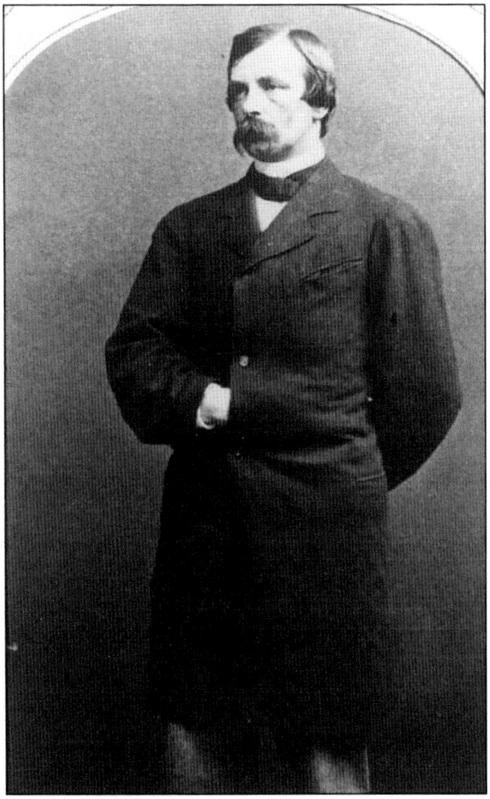

William Crowninshield Endicott Sr. (1826–1900) married Ellen Peabody in 1859. A lawyer and descendant of the first Massachusetts governor, Endicott was appointed associate justice of the Supreme Judicial Court of Massachusetts in 1873. He ran unsuccessfully for governor in 1884, and served as secretary of war in President Grover Cleveland's first administration.

Beginning in 1893 William C. Endicott Jr. (1860–1936) oversaw the enlarging and transforming of the house into a Colonial Revival mansion. Hiring the architectural firm of Little, Browne & Moore, a third floor was added, as were surrounding porches and a monumental front entrance. This photograph from 1898 is of what was by then being referred to as "Glen Magna Farm."

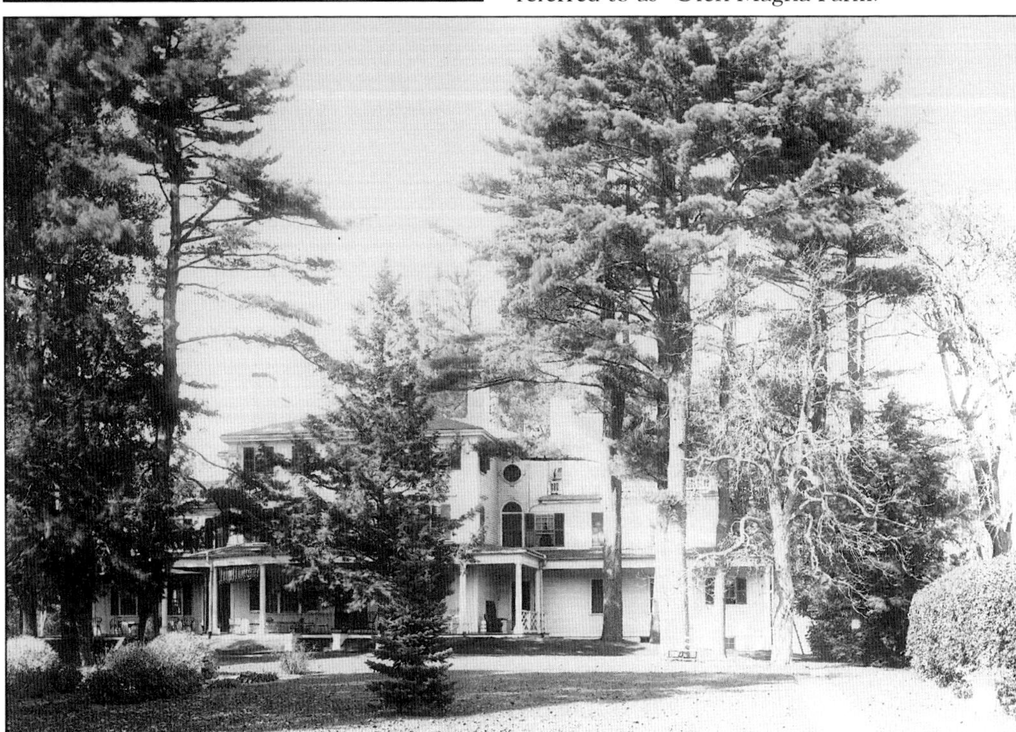

Mary C. Endicott (1864–1957) was the daughter of William Sr. In 1880 she posed as a milkmaid for this whimsical portrait. In 1888 Mary married the Rt. Honorable Joseph Chamberlain. Chamberlain, the British colonial secretary, visited Glen Magna several times and assisted in laying out new gardens. On one occasion there was an abortive assassination attempt while he was there.

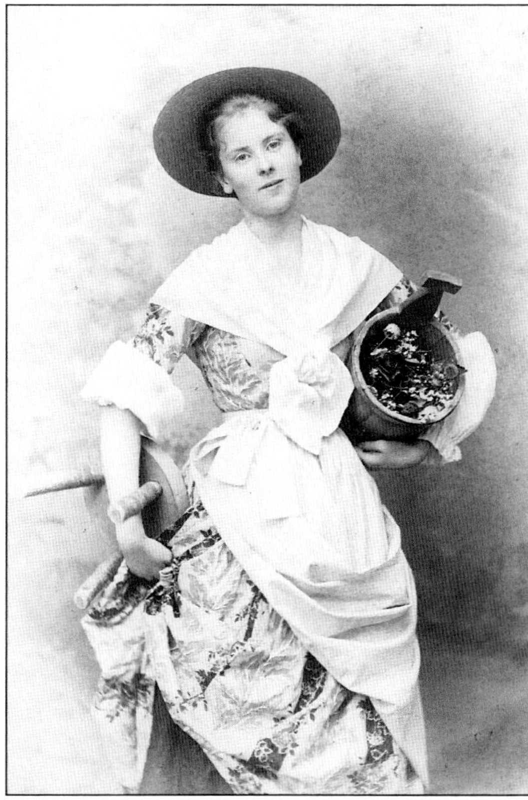

In the early 1890s famed landscape architect Frederick Law Olmstead designed the estate's tree-lined entryway. This property is one of the few estates in which buildings and open space survive, thanks to the central portion of the Endicott Estate being purchased and preserved by the Danvers Historical Society. The Town of Danvers acquired the surrounding acres of land now known as Endicott Park.

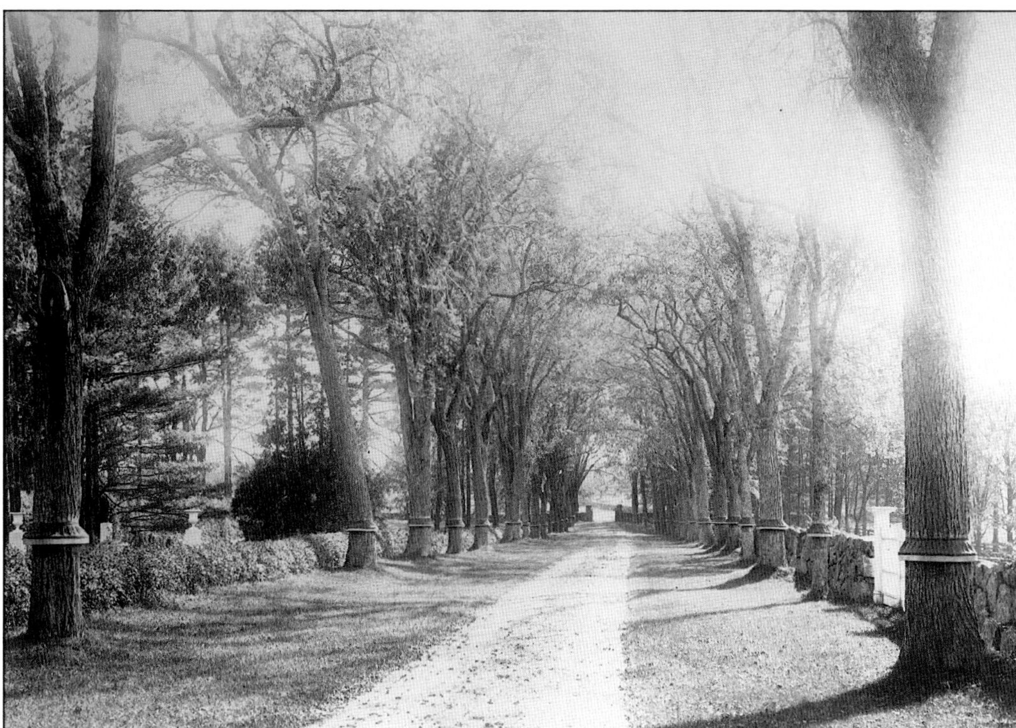

To Preserve the Future

What makes a village, town, or city unique? The most important contributing factors are the combination of geography, people, and the built environment. The growth and development of an area over time brings the mix of these three factors into an evolutionary uniqueness. Of the three factors, geography tends to remain the least susceptible to dramatic change, even though occasional development projects may fill in lowlands or remove hilltops. The changes in population through birthrate, migration, and immigration add to the rich history, diversity, and culture of an area. But by far the most visual determinant of the identity of an area rests in the progression of its built environment—the dwellings, ancillary buildings, commercial, and industrial structures which give an area its architectural uniqueness. Without the retaining, cherishing, and preserving of the best of the past, an area can easily change from being a place with a story, tradition, and culture of its own, into a mushy, culturally neutral, and uninspiring "anywhere, USA." Unfortunately, such is often the case in much of our country today, as precious regional architectural gems are demolished leaving in their wake an uninspired and uninspiring sameness. Each community must realize the danger of losing its cultural identity and quality of life by retaining through planning, preserving, or adaptively reusing its historical and architectural properties and neighborhoods.

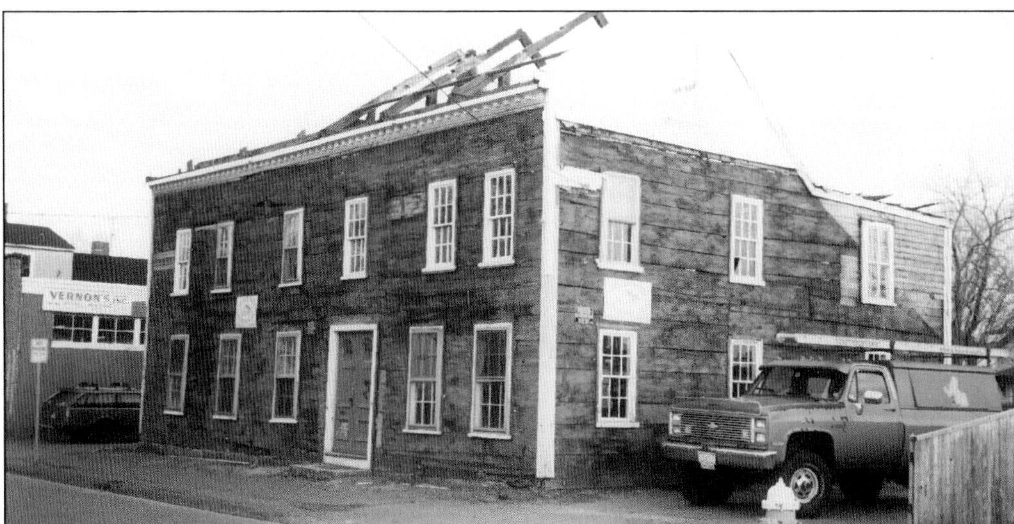

This rare seventeenth-century dwelling at 11 School Street was dismantled in 1994 to be removed out-of-state and replaced by a parking lot. Proposals to keep the frame in Danvers were rejected. Losses such as this diminish a community's uniqueness.